Žižek and Politics

D1344498

ŽIŽEK AND POLITICS
A CRITICAL INTRODUCTION

Matthew Sharpe and Geoff Boucher

EDINBURGH UNIVERSITY PRESS

© Matthew Sharpe and Geoff Boucher, 2010

Edinburgh University Press Ltd
22 George Square, Edinburgh
www.euppublishing.com

Typeset in Sabon
by Servis Filmsetting Ltd, Stockport, Cheshire, and
printed and bound in Great Britain by
CPI Antony Rowe, Chippenham and Eastbourne

A CIP record for this book is available from the British Library

ISBN 978 0 7486 3803 1 (hardback)
ISBN 978 0 7486 3804 8 (paperback)

Contents

Expanded Contents List

Abbreviations

AF   Slavoj Žižek, 'The Abyss of Freedom', in S. Žižek and F. W. J. Schelling (eds), *The Abyss of Freedom/Ages of the World* (Ann Arbor: University of Michigan Press, 1997)

CHU   Slavoj Žižek (with Judith Butler and Ernesto Laclau), *Contingency, Hegemony, Universality* (London: Verso, 2000)

CND   Slavoj Žižek, 'Concesso non dato', in Matthew Sharpe, Geoff Boucher and Jason Glynos (eds), *Traversing the Fantasy: Critical Responses to Slavoj Žižek* (London: Ashgate, 2005), pp. 219–56

CS   Slavoj Žižek, 'Carl Schmitt in the Age of Post-Politics', in Chantal Mouffe (ed.), *The Challenge of Carl Schmitt* (London: Verso, 1999), pp. 18–37

DSST   *Did Somebody Say Totalitarianism? On the Abuses of a Term* (London: Verso, 2001)

ES   Slavoj Žižek, *Enjoy your Symptom! Jacques Lacan in Hollywood and Out*, 2nd edn (London and New York: Routledge, 2001 [1992])

FA   Slavoj Žižek, *The Fragile Absolute – Or, Why Is the Christian Legacy Worth Fighting For?* (London and New York: Verso, 2000)

FP   Slavoj Žižek, 'The Fetish of the Party', in W. Apollon and R. Feldstein (eds), *Lacan, Politics, Aesthetics* (Albany, NY: State University of New York Press, 1996)

FRT   Slavoj Žižek, *The Fright of Real Tears: Krzysztof Kieslowski between Theory and Post-theory*. London British Film Institute Publishing, 2001)

FTKN   Slavoj Žižek, *For They Know Not What They Do: Enjoyment as a Political Factor* (London and New York: Verso, 1991; 2nd edn, 2002)

HH   Slavoj Žižek, 'Herschaftsstruktur Heute', in Hugh Silverman and M. Vögt (eds), *Über Žižek: Perspektiven und Kritiken* (Vienna: Turia, 2004), pp. 210–30

HTR   Slavoj Žižek, *How to Read Lacan* (New York: W. W. Norton, 2007).

IBK   Slavoj Žižek, *Iraq: The Borrowed Kettle* (London: Verso, 2004)

IDLC   Slavoj Žižek, *In Defence of Lost Causes* (London: Verso, 2008)

IR   Slavoj Žižek, *The Indivisible Remainder: An Essay on Schelling and Related Matters* (London and New York: Verso, 1996)

LA   Slavoj Žižek, *Looking Awry: An Introduction to Jacques Lacan through Popular Culture* (Cambridge, MA, and London: MIT Press, 1991)

MC   Slavoj Žižek, 'Multiculturalism, or, the Cultural Logic of Multinational Capitalism', *New Left Review*, 225 (Sept.–Oct. 1997), 28 ff.

ME   Slavoj Žižek, *The Metastases of Enjoyment: Six Essays on Woman and Causality* (London and New York: Verso, 1994)

OB   Slavoj Žižek, *On Belief* (London: Routledge, 2001)

OV   Slavoj Žižek, *On Violence* (London: Picador, 2008)

OWB   Slavoj Žižek, *Organs without Bodies: On Deleuze and Consequences* (New York and London: Routledge, 2003)

PD   Slavoj Žižek, *The Puppet and the Dwarf: The Perverse Core of Christianity* (Cambridge, MA, and London: MIT Press, 2003)

PF   Slavoj Žižek, *The Plague of Fantasies* (London and New York: Verso, 1997)

PV   Slavoj Žižek, *The Parallax View* (Cambridge, MA: MIT Press, 2006)

RL   Slavoj Žižek, 'Repeating Lenin'. www.lacan.com/replenin; first posted 2001

SI   Slavoj Žižek, 'The Spectre of Ideology', in S. Žižek (ed.), *Mapping Ideology* (London: Verso, 1994)

SO   Slavoj Žižek, *The Sublime Object of Ideology* (London and New York: Verso, 1989)

TN   Slavoj Žižek, *Tarrying with the Negative* (Durham, NC: Duke University Press, 1993)

TS   Slavoj Žižek, *The Ticklish Subject: The Absent Centre of Political Ontology.* (London and New York: Verso, 1999)

WDR   Slavoj Žižek, 'Welcome to the Desert of the Real', *South Atlantic Quarterly*, 101/2 (2002), 385–9

WDR   Slavoj Žižek, *Welcome to the Desert of the Real: Five Essays* (London and New York: Verso, 2002)

WDLT   Slavoj Žižek, 'With Defenders Like These, Who Needs Enemies', in Paul Bowman and Richard Stamp (eds), *The Truth of Žižek* (London: Continuum, 2007), pp. 197–255

Introduction

Žižek and Politics

Slavoj Žižek is without question one of the most important and provocative contemporary thinkers. Yet his work has radically divided critics and commentators, often along political lines. On the one hand, his work has been compared with the biggest names of French post-structuralist theory like Michel Foucault, Jacques Derrida and Gilles Deleuze, for its scope, insights and significance. Although he began publishing in English only in 1989, by 2006 Žižek was already a highly influential figure in social theory, continental philosophy, cinema studies, literary and cultural studies. He is rightly celebrated for his introductions to the French psychoanalyst Jacques Lacan, and his use of Lacanian psychoanalysis to interpret popular culture.

Beyond the academy, too, Žižek is well known as a cultural commentator, film critic and Marxist sociologist. He writes on an astonishing variety of topics, ranging from the Iraq war, fundamentalist terrorism and the global financial crisis to the questions raised by biotechnology or the films of Alfred Hitchcock, James Cameron, David Lynch and Krzysztof Kieslowski.

On the other hand, Žižek demands that his work be taken seriously as a Lacanian intervention in political philosophy and social theory. He has always argued that his theoretical positions lead to radical political conclusions. His opening interventions in cultural and theoretical debates announced the need to significantly extend democratic politics through deep reforms. As of 2008, in a further radicalisation, Žižek declared himself a 'Communist' and 'dialectical materialist', and called for a sweeping cultural and political revolution. Not surprisingly, then, his work is often represented as not only fiendishly difficult theoretically, but highly controversial politically. For some, Žižek is to be celebrated for keeping open the possibility of an emancipatory political alternative, in defiance of the liberal-democratic consensus on the 'end of history'. For others, Žižek deserves denunciation for serial offences, including

1

irresponsible provocations and political vacuity, moral blindness and totalitarian leanings, contradictory argumentation and slipshod referencing (e.g. Harpham 2003; Sharpe et al. 2005; Bowman and Stamp 2007).

Unlike many other intellectuals, Žižek thrives on this controversy. He relentlessly pumps out provocative ideas and polemical rejoinders, as if causing political division were the aim of the exercise. To this end, Žižek's work scorns many of the technical academic conventions. There is first of all the already infamous Žižekian style – swooping effortlessly from Lacan to Lenin and back, via a digression on the paintings of Malevich or a scene from Hitchcock, and like sequences. There is the self-conscious rhetorical devices Žižek uses: rhetorical questions ('is this not . . .?') and set phrases ('Of course, this is . . . what we see here . . .') that signal bewildering shifts in the argumentative logic of the chapter or article (e.g. Boynton 1998; Myers 2003: 4–5; Clemens 2005). Then there is Žižek's seeming lack of interest in many of the pieties of Western academic life – the obsessive attention academics pay to details such as footnotes and clarification of the argument (Gilbert 2007: 64–6, 69), or the concern with what Žižek calls the 'boring standard reproaches' (*PV* 5) to psychoanalysis, involving technical arguments about its limitations; and the methodological reflections that prevent any particular discipline, including philosophy, from acting as a master key to the social totality. Sidestepping these sorts of concerns, Žižek's texts involve a series of bold engagements with the major questions posed by contemporary history and politics.

So Who is Slavoj Žižek?

Slavoj Žižek holds doctorates in both philosophy (University of Ljubljana) and psychoanalysis (University of Paris VIII). He did his doctorate in psychoanalysis under intellectual luminaries Jacques-Alain Miller and François Regnault. He has a formidably, almost uniquely, gifted mind, with an astounding grasp of contemporary theory. Žižek has written books and articles in Serbo-Croatian, Slovenian, French, English and German. And he has written an extraordinary amount of them: intellectual engagements with everything from the history of opera, popular culture and contemporary theory, to modern philosophy, European cinema and political events. There are some fifty books, at least fifteen of them in English, at the last count – for it is hard to keep up with someone who regularly produces in excess of 200,000 published words in a two-year period. Then there are more than a hundred articles. Recently, there have been two two films, *The Pervert's Guide to Cinema* (2005), exploring Žižek's theories on the link between film and ideas, and *Žižek!* (2007), a zany extended interview and fan piece on the master himself. Žižek has been translated into some twenty languages and is mandatory reading on university courses around the world. There are at least ten secondary books on Žižek already and an international refereed journal, the *International Journal of Žižek Studies*. The number of secondary responses continues to grow, as the academic world struggles to keep up with Žižek's own extraordinary productivity.

Žižek is currently (2009) the International Director for the Birkbeck Institute for the Humanities at the University of London. He is also a senior researcher at the Institute of Sociology at the University of Ljubljana and a professor with the European Graduate School. Žižek is now regularly top billing on the transatlantic lecture circuit, a fact that has earned him the accolade or denunciation of being an 'academic rock-star' and an 'intellectual celebrity' (Boynton 1998; Mead 2003).

Žižek's prolific output and the ongoing controversy around his ideas is the sign of a remarkable intellectual, engaged in a constant, politically committed work-in-progress. Žižek's academic works continually challenge us to think through and beyond our preconceptions, including questioning ideas that we have received from Žižek himself (Kay 2003; Butler and Stephens 2005). And he uses his academic success to launch popular interventions which aim to generate moral shock about injustice, oppression, and complacency.

In the ceaseless ferment of Žižek's work, this dual commitment to rethinking ideas and to employing them in the service of political emancipation has remained constant. Žižek grew up and gained his first doctorate in Slovenia, which until 1991 was part of the Socialist Federal Republic of Yugoslavia. Tito's Yugoslavian government claimed to represent a 'self-managing socialism', relatively independent of Brezhnev's Russia. One consequence of this independence was the relative openness of Yugoslav culture to the intellectual and popular culture of the West, which the young Žižek avidly devoured. An intellectual maverick, Žižek turned to the important, but politically right-wing philosopher Martin Heidegger as an antidote to the Marxist orthodoxy of the ruling bureaucracy, and by the 1980s Žižek was a political dissident in former Yugoslavia. Despite difficult political conditions in intellectual life, Žižek eventually managed to get his doctoral degree and a university post. In the mid-1980s, Žižek shifted to Paris, where he studied the work of the French psychoanalyst Jacques Lacan under Lacan's son-in-law and literary executor Jacques-Alain Miller for his second doctorate. By the time Žižek appeared on the English-speaking academic scene in the late 1980s, he had mastered the work of the great German philosophers Immanuel Kant, George Wilhelm Hegel and Martin Heidegger, together with that of the famed generation of post-war French theorists, Jacques Lacan, Louis Althusser, Jacques Derrida, Julia Kristeva, Claude Lévi-Strauss and Gilles Deleuze. Characteristically for Žižek, when the Socialist Federal Republic of Yugoslavia broke up in 1990–1, Žižek ran for office as a presidential candidate against the former socialist party's nominees, while at the same time delivering the intellectually brilliant lectures that are reproduced in book form as *For They Know Not What They Do* (1991; 2nd edn 2002) (Dews 1995; Osborne 1996; Wright and Wright 1999; Parker 2004: 11–35).

Within the English-speaking academic world, Žižek made his name, and his fame, with a stunning series of works published between 1989 and 1994: *The Sublime Object of Ideology* (1989), *Looking Awry* (1991), *For They Know Not What They Do* (1991), *Enjoy your Symptom!* (1992), *Everything You Always Wanted to Know about Lacan (But Were Afraid to Ask Hitchcock)* (1992), *Tarrying with the Negative* (1993) and *The Metastases of Enjoyment* (1994). Part of the reason these works were so striking was Žižek's effortless mastery of all the theoretical authorities in cultural studies, comparative literature and continental philosophy. Žižek also brought a surprising new perspective, minted in the particular intellectual circumstances of his native Slovenia. This perspective has always centred around two of the most difficult, but also most often maligned and misunderstood, thinkers: Hegel, the nineteenth-century philosopher of 'dialectics', and Lacan, arguably the most brilliant, and certainly the most obscure of Freud's successors. *Looking Awry*, *Everything You Always Wanted to Know* and *Enjoy your Symptom!* advertise themselves as 'Introductions to Lacan' by reference to popular culture and Hollywood cinema. They have already become required reading for students trying to comprehend Lacan's difficult concepts, as they are applied in film theory, philosophy and cultural studies. *The Sublime Object of Ideology, For They Know Not What They Do, Tarrying with the Negative* and *Metastases of*

Enjoyment are, by contrast, independent theoretical treatises in their own right.

In each of these books, Žižek makes the intimate connection between the high theory and his political conclusions clear. For Žižek, his 'return to Hegel' via Lacanian psychoanalysis reveals that 'Lacanian theory is perhaps the most radical contemporary version of the Enlightenment' (*SO* 7), whose aim is political emancipation. Seemingly aligning himself in these works with the radical-democratic project of post-Marxism, Žižek indicated that the project underlying his synthesis of Lacanian psychoanalysis and Hegelian dialectics was the extension and deepening of political democracy, against the restriction of democracy to parliamentary manœuvres, interest-group negotiations and free market economics (*SO* 6).

Yet by 2001 Žižek had reversed this position on the extension and deepening of democracy. In what seemed to many a major rethink of his entire project, Žižek declared that the demand for more democracy was part of the problem. What is needed, he now believes, is not post-Marxist 'radical democracy' or civic republicanism, but a return to the Marxist dictatorship of the proletariat. Žižek's most important theoretical works from *The Ticklish Subject* (1999), through 'Repeating Lenin' (2001), *Did Somebody Say Totalitarianism?* (2001), *On Belief* (2001) and *The Puppet and the Dwarf* (2003), to *The Parallax View* (2006) and *In Defence of Lost Causes* (2008), have all supported this 'dialectical materialist' position. Žižek's adversaries now are not just political liberals and the so-called 'P[olitically] C[orrect] multiculturalists' of the postmodern academy. They include his former post-Marxist allies Ernesto Laclau, Judith Butler, Étienne Balibar and Jacques Rancière.

Žižek's basic project of bringing high theory to produce a new form of Leftist politics has remained completely consistent. But it is fair to say that he has progressively radicalised his political conclusions through an ongoing process of self-correction or redirection, and fierce debate with his faint-hearted (as he paints them) former allies (e.g. *CHU*; *TS* 127–51) In other words, for Žižek, the real question we should ask is not 'why is Žižek's work so divisive?' For Žižek, the true puzzle is: why are today's academic 'radicals' so hopelessly complicit with the free market and political liberalism? Why is Žižek almost alone in calling for revolutionary opposition to global capitalism, with the possible exception of Alain Badiou (*IDLC* 1–8)?

It is tempting and plausible to explain Žižek's political shift from

radical democracy to revolutionary vanguardism in terms of a difference between two political situations or conjunctures. Between 1989
and 2000, the situation was characterised by the 'victory of liberal
democracy' and the 'triumph of capitalism'. It was crucial to resist
the 'New World Order' of a monolithic post-Communist consensus
on the death of alternatives to political liberalism and free-market
economics. Although radical democracy at first represented an alternative project, it soon became enmeshed in the turn away from real
confrontation with the reigning ideology, and got bogged down in
multiple struggles for cultural recognition within an identity-political
framework. Ultimately, the New Left post-Marxists, with their
identity politics, were unable to provide an effective opposition to
the 'blackmail' of the reigning liberal ideology, which consists in the
idea that a militant defence of democracy or the market is the limit
of all possible political action – anything more radical leads directly
to totalitarian atrocities.

Yet, after 2001, the global capitalist world order revealed its ter-
rifyingly violent underside in the 'War on Terror'. Not only did the
West refuse to acknowledge its own role in creating the conditions
for the rise of fundamentalist terrorism. The Bush administration
also demonstrated that the paradoxical flipside of its ideological
advocacy of democracy against all radical ideas is in fact the suspension of human rights in the practical defence of parliamentary liberalism and the world market. Torture, rendition, political assassination,
pre-emptive strikes and illegal warfare were all back on the agenda
as part of the 'triumph of capitalism' and the 'victory of liberalism'.
For Žižek, this has called for a radical response that went beyond
the demand for an expansion of democracy – it calls for something
approximating to a new socialist revolution. One index of this
change in Žižek's politics is his shift from defending radical democracy (a 'residue of bourgeois ideology' (*FTKN*, p. xviii)) to new talk
of a renewed proletarian dictatorship (*IDLC* 412–19). Another is
his abandonment of the term 'social antagonism' for the idea of
'class struggle' (*CHU* 90–135). Yet another is his rejection of the
opposition between 'totalitarianism' and 'democracy' as inherently
misleading and anti-radical (*DSST*).

As far as Žižek is concerned, the division among the critics and
commentators is merely a 'symptom of the political deadlock' today.
In a classic case of the psychological mechanism of displacement,
political concerns about his work appear in the form of theoretical objections, so that the academic critics can protect their radical

credentials (CND; HH; WDLT) This political deadlock, meanwhile, involves a widening gap between what is objectively needed (a new socialist revolution) and what seems subjectively possible (protest and identity politics).

As for Žižek's theoretical project, this remains as it was announced in *For They Know Not What They Do*. There Žižek said that his work was composed of

> three centres of gravity: Hegelian dialectics, Lacanian psychoanalytic theory, and contemporary criticism of ideology. . . . The three theoretical circles are not, however, of the same weight: it is their middle term, the theory of Jacques Lacan, which is – as Marx would say – 'the general illumination which bathes all the other colors and modifies their particularity'. (*FTKN* 3)

A critic might reply that something *has* changed in these 'three centres of gravity': the source for the 'contemporary criticism of ideology' has gone from post-Marxism back to Marxism. But, for us, this is not the decisive thing to note, and we agree with Laclau and Parker that Žižek's Marxism is a tricky thing (Laclau 2000b: 195–206; Parker 2004: 94–101). The key thing uniting Žižek's three apparently unrelated theoretical 'centres of gravity' is his central philosophical contribution – namely, his rehabilitation of the notion of the modern subject. It is because Lacan supplies an immensely sophisticated theory of the subject that, for Žižek, Lacan's ideas 'bathe all the other colors and modify their particularity'.

And it is precisely here, in the theory of the subject, that something crucial *has* changed theoretically. As Žižek himself concedes, the crucial intellectual shift that subtends the political opposition between his early, radical-democratic work and his recent, revolutionary vanguardist work is the shift from the 'subject of desire' to the 'subject of the drives' (*FTKN*, pp. xvii–xviii, xxxi–xxxii). It is in Žižek's two distinct concepts of the subject that we can locate the key to his political shifts.

The Dilemmas of Enjoyment as a Political Factor

Žižek's most radical and interesting innovation in the theory of ideology is to have proposed that unconscious 'enjoyment' is a political factor (cf. Dean 2006). Enjoyment (*Jouissance*, in Lacan's original French) is a psychoanalytic term that means something very different from pleasure. Enjoyment is what is 'beyond the pleasure principle':

it involves obscene forms of satisfaction that are experienced as unpleasure; it is how subjects 'get off' in ways that disgust them and that they consequently disavow, pretending to themselves that they only have this repulsive experience thrust upon them unwillingly. Consequently, enjoyment, which Žižek ultimately identifies with the Freudian death drive and designates as 'the Real' (to be contrasted to the reality of ordinary experience), involves the satisfaction of the bodily drives. This manifests itself through apparently 'daemonic' compulsions to repeat, through anxiety-generating yet strangely fascinating experiences (from the sublime to the obscene), and through the mutely persistent symptoms that the subject stubbornly clings to, despite all their protests and complaints about how they hate this problem in their lives.

Enjoyment is, for example, what locks the subject into one apparently unsatisfactory relationship after another with, for instance, those controlling boyfriends or hypercritical girlfriends. It is what subjects are 'getting off on' amid all their apparent misery, and it is why, every time they resolve to put a stop to this sort of relationship, what they in fact do is get in deeper, or find another person with whom to repeat the pattern. Humiliating and degrading as it is, there is something 'in it' for the subjects, even though what this 'something' is completely escapes them. Ask them, and they will vehemently deny its existence, maintaining instead that, despite the fact that they are desperately unhappy once again, there is no pattern whatsoever, it is all the fault of the other person. And, besides, they are just about to change everything, and so on.

It is Žižek's masterstroke to have successfully applied this psychoanalytic insight into human behaviour to politics. Political life, from the perspective of much contemporary theory, is based on identification with ideologies, and, specifically, on identification with the ideological keywords, such as 'democracy', 'freedom' or 'America', that hold ideologies together. Symbolic identification with these ideological keywords, or 'master signifiers', shapes the identity of subjects as citizens of a political community. The subject recognises itself as 'a social democrat', or 'a good Australian', because he or she has integrated this master signifier into its subjectivity in a decisive way. The subject is able to identify with (a) master signifer(s) in this way because ideologies are always propagated through institutions. The institutional rituals of civic life are a form of ideologically saturated socialisation into the accepted values and ideals of the political community. According to this theory, political change must happen because subjects discard one master signifier and replace it with another. When this occurs, subjects' political or 'symbolic' identification changes, and with it their political orientation and actions. A subject starts life, for instance, in a staunch Labour Party household where 'social equality' is the family watchword. But then something – something that it is the business of the theory to clarify and explain – happens, and they adopt a new master signifier, 'individual liberty'. Presto! – everything changes in the subject's existence. They join the local branch of the Conservative Party, start dating a corporate executive, take up using the masculine pronoun instead of gender-neutral language and get involved in a screaming match at the next family Christmas.

But Žižek notices two things about political life that upset this picture of ideological and political change. The first is that, even when subjects are thoroughly disenchanted with an ideological master signifier, they do not necessarily adopt a new one. Generally speaking, they just carry on as before, only in the context of a cynical distance towards their professed values and ideals. Žižek's own former Yugoslavia provides a perfect example of this. Žižek observes the way that, in the 1980s, nobody actually accepted the official Communist ideology. Everybody privately complained about the lack of credibility of the party apparatus. Yet everything continued just as before.

The second thing Žižek notes against the idea that politics is solely about subjects' conscious identifications with public ideals like 'liberty' or 'socialism' is that, once subjects do adopt a new ideological master signifier, once again this seldom makes a big difference to what they actually do. The new regime announces sweeping reforms in the name of their freshly minted political ideals. But this announcement is followed by the return to power of the former bureaucracy, together with a trenchant revival of all the old habits of everyday life, and the gradual strangulation of the promised reforms. Again, the break-up of former Yugoslavia is a striking illustration of this process, where the democratic ideals professed by the new governments quickly became mere ideological smokescreens, behind which elements of the old apparatus inflamed existing national rivalries into savage conflicts. What is it, beyond symbolic identification with master signifiers, that provides the extraordinary inertia in ideological shifts and that holds the potential to derail progressive change into political violence? This is Žižek's key question. Žižek's answer is: enjoyment – the death drive.

In his first book in English, *The Sublime Object of Ideology*, Žižek uses the mythological figure of the Fisher King from Wagner's opera *Parsifal* as a sort of theoretical metaphor to understand what is in play here (*SO* 76–9). In the Grail Legend, the Fisher King is the custodian of the Chapel Perilous. Every year, he is supposed to perform a ceremony involving the Holy Grail, to bring fertility to the land. Now, if we follow the old school, Cambridge myth-and-ritual interpretation of this as a pagan rite in which the king is supposed to make love to the high priestess in a holy marriage ceremony, thereby symbolically guaranteeing the return of spring, then the next bit makes perfect sense. The Fisher King is incompetent in the institutional ritual he is supposed to conduct, because he has forgotten the meaning of the symbols that belong to the ceremony. Accordingly, the ceremony is carried through as rape, rather than as marriage, the Holy Grail is lost and the land is laid waste as a consequence. The Fisher King is mysteriously wounded in the upper thigh with a ghastly cut that will not heal. Every year, he painfully performs the now meaningless ceremony. But the results are always the same – until a perfect knight arrives to return the meaning of the sacred symbols, heal the King, recover the Holy Grail and restore the land.

For Žižek, this wonderfully romantic scenario is in reality a sort of thought experiment through art. What would human conduct look like, if we could get past the screen of the symbolic meanings that we ascribe to all our actions? It would look like the Fisher King's doomed rite: endless, compulsively repeated institutional rituals, performed in the name of high symbols (like purification of the community to guarantee the spring), whose actual effects are the paradoxical pleasure-in-pain registered in the body as the result of the habitual act. The sexual content of the bodily satisfaction is delicately indicated in the legend by the location of the wound (in the 'thigh'), as is the ultimately fantastic character of the divine object in the name of which all this is done (the 'Holy Grail' = symbol of the eternal human wish for absolute completion and total satisfaction). Finally, the legend indicates the dimension of unconscious fantasy in the way that, with the symbols restored, the sublime object at the centre of the ritual blazes forth as a token of an other-worldly redemption. With the symbols restored to their fullness of meaning, the Holy Grail becomes the mystical referent of the ideal of purity that governs the ceremony, and the suppurating wound of sexual satisfaction is magically transformed into the regenerating power of sacred marriage.

Perfect nonsense, of course – but, for Žižek, *every* ideology is like this, at its heart. Every ideology involves a rich universe of symbolic meaning organised around some central ideal(s), or master signifier(s), underneath which is the Real of subjects' unconscious enjoyment in their subjection. This *Jouissance* is gained through performance of the institutional rituals that this ideology justifies. A master signifier such as 'America' integrates the political community of the USA through the performance of collective rituals such as elections and mobilisations. Participation in the institutional ritual brings a strange sort of satisfaction, a sense of communal belonging, to all its members. This master signifier necessarily conjures up, unconsciously, a sublime object that would represent the ultimate fulfilment of the dreams of community implied in the ideal of America – the sort of imagined community represented in wishes for a Manifest Destiny, for instance. Such subjects hope, unconsciously, that, if the real meaning of the ideals that founded America could be recovered, then the spring would return. As it is, however, the subject is wounded, inexplicably smitten with the dreadful inability precisely to put into words what it is that America represents. And so they carry on with the institutional rituals of the political community, groping amid the culture's shared symbols for some combination that would at last flare into meaning and restore the lost sense of unity and purpose. It always seems that somebody has ruined or threatened the Thing that America really stands for (or any Nation, Žižek would suggest) – that great hope that the ideal names and the rituals invoke. From time to time, a candidate for the role of perfect knight comes along – but quickly turns out to be all-too-human. In the meantime, the subjects get on with the business of opposing those enemies within and without who would steal or destroy any chance of recovering the Nation's Holy Grail (what Žižek calls 'the National Thing' (e.g. *TN* 201–5)).

For Žižek, political socialisation 'wound' the subject with a loss of enjoyment. The meaningless institutional ritual that accompanies the symbolic performance of ideological ceremonies (for example, voting) engenders a partial satisfaction, experienced as unpleasure, that Žižek calls 'surplus enjoyment'. This 'surplus enjoyment' is, as it were, the left-over enjoyment from the supposed loss that happened when the subject adopted that ideology in the first place (e.g. *SO* 49–53). This unconscious representation of lost enjoyment and the hope of its eventual restoration is what Žižek calls the 'ideological fantasy'. So, for Žižek, surplus enjoyment is not only how the subject

11

'gets off' on the institutional ritual – it is also constructed by the social fantasy and symptomatic of the subject's continuing adherence to ideology. Žižek associates the subject's symptomatic allegiance to the institutional ritual with Lacan's term 'sinthome', an archaic French spelling of 'symptom' that designates 'a certain signifier which is not enchained in a network, but is immediately filled, penetrated with enjoyment', something that is 'a little piece of the real' (SO 77–8). Subjects cling to this 'wound', to the institutional ritual, because it is ultimately what they are in the social world. If they lose the institutional ritual through what Žižek calls 'traversing the fantasy', then they lose their social identity, and have to begin all over again. For Žižek, then, the task of ideology critique is to investigate both the symbolic meanings promoted by an ideology and the symptomatic ways that subjects 'enjoy' the institutional ritual, thanks to the social fantasy that sustains the ideology (SO 125).

Žižek develops and elaborates this set of insights in striking ways that we will explore in this book. But notice that, powerfully insightful though it is, there is a political dilemma built into this position. It explains the irrational hold on subjects that ideology has. But, in this account, ideology always threatens to become too tenacious. If the hold of ideology lies in unconscious enjoyment, then how are subjects supposed to adopt new ideologies? How can they transcend the institutional practices of the old ideology, whatever their good (conscious) intentions? Enjoyment is something that by definition persists, that remains stuck in the same place, despite all the superficial changes in symbolic arrangements. How, then, do subjects alter an unconscious enjoyment that structures their actions, but whose existence they deny? How can subjects be persuaded to 'traverse the fantasy', when this involves the loss of their social identity?

We might argue that institutional changes must affect the enjoyment of subjects, and so develop a theory of how the dynamics of social institutions subtly affect the psychology of individuals who live and work within them. Alternatively, we could develop a theory of enjoyment, arguing that, since the surplus enjoyment structured by social fantasy is conjured up by the social ideals that the ideology promotes, an analysis of social ideals will yield the key to grasp the ways in which that ideology hooks subjects into it in unconscious fantasy. This is the path taken by Žižek.

But now the dilemma reappears again: what is the fulcrum, the point on which the lever for any liberating political change turns? Should political movements seek to 'traverse the fantasy' of the dominant ideology, by making symbolic changes that drain off the symptomatic enjoyment of those still captured by the institutional rituals of the dominant ideology? In other words, should political movements seek radically to undermine the unconscious appeal of the dominant ideology? Or should political movements seek to get subjects to identify with their symptomatic enjoyment and direct this energy against the dominant ideology itself? In other words, should political movements seek to tap into the unconscious as a radical force to explode the dominant ideology? In Žižek's Lacanian terms, the opposition here is between symbolic identification and the Real of enjoyment – that is, between the Symbolic and the Real. Logically speaking, there are two, mutually exclusive alternatives:

- We might try a radical alteration of the Symbolic – seeking not a new ideological master signifier, but an unprecedented reform of socio-symbolic and institutional arrangements, one that would disperse the mirage of the sublime object that is conjured up for subjects by the institutional rituals and that structures the unconscious enjoyment of the subject. We might, in other words, try to convince the Fisher King to realise that the Holy Grail does not exist. Such an approach, which Žižek calls 'traversing the fantasy', aims at liberating the desire of the subject. Instead of being stuck fast on the meaningless institutional ritual, hung up on a fantasy object, the subject is freed up to desire in new ways, to adopt new symbolic identifications that really do result in practical changes.
- Alternatively, we might try to tap into the Real, into the power of the death drive, and seek to set it against the existing institutional rituals and symbolic identifications. This alternative would correspond to convincing the Fisher King that the real Holy Grail is in his 'thigh', and that the power to restore fertility in the kingdom lies not in the missing sacred symbols but in a radicalised performance of the act. Accordingly, the King should smash the Chapel Perilous and found a completely new community in the wasteland. This alternative, which Žižek refers to as 'identification with the *sinthome* [symptom]', seeks to liberate the drive of the subject. The political subject rejects all symbolic identifications and institutional rituals, and regards themselves as the waste product of symbolisation, an outcast from the political community. Žižek holds that this opens up the possibility of tapping into the unprecedented power of the subject to transform the world.

Here, regeneration happens, not by fixing the old order, but by destroying it, and by replacing it with a new Symbolic Order.

This opposition between 'traversing the fantasy' and 'identifica-tion with the *sinthome*' reflects an ambiguity at the heart of Žižek's position. Žižek's opposition between the 'subject of desire' and the 'subject of the drive' (*FTKN*, pp. xi–cvii), aligns with the opposition of traversing the fantasy and identifying with the *sinthome*. These ideas name the two options he has taken, in trying to unite his theory with concrete politics, since bursting on the scene in the mid-1980s. As we indicated above, at first Žižek embraced a radical-democratic framework. But since around the turn of the millennium (or between 1996 and 1999 in any case), Žižek has opted for a revolutionary vanguardist position, modelled on the idea of 'identification with the *sinthome*'. Each of the options reflects one horn of a dilemma built into Žižek's greatest insight, into enjoyment as a political factor. It will be our task in what follows to examine how and why Žižek's position has changed, with what implications for Žižek's politics.

A Critical *Introduction*

The aim of *Žižek and Politics*, then, is to spell out, in as plain lan-guage as possible, all Žižek's key theoretical notions, as they bear on his politics. The book is an introduction, aimed at students and interested non-specialists, as well as established readers in the rarified realm of 'High Theory'. In *Žižek and Politics*, the reader will learn about Žižek's own key terms or master signifiers:

- the Ego Ideal, the Symbolic Order, the big Other, and the superego;
- the nature of transgressive enjoyment, and the role it plays in political life;
- the critique of 'ideological fantasies', master signifier and 'sublime objects of ideology';
- the modern or 'Cartesian subject', and Žižek's critique of the 'post-structuralist' orthodoxy that claims to have 'deconstructed' it;
- Žižek's ideas concerning the importance of social conflict in political life and its implications for the project of emancipation and the institutions of democracy;
- Žižek's remarkable reading, in the middle of the 1990s, of Romantic philosopher Gottfried Schelling's theology or theogony,

and the way it stands as a marker for the decisive changes in Žižek's work and politics;

- Žižek's later, pessimistic theory of culture as involving 'the decline of the paternal function' and the consumerist 'society of enjoyment';
- Žižek's shift from his earlier, radical-democratic politics, to his later, revolutionary, authoritarian vanguardism;
- Žižek's later turn to political theology, and a politicised species of Christianity.

But *Žižek and Politics*, true to its subtitle, is also a *critical* introduction. In clarifying Žižek's ideas we aim also to explain why there is such bitter debate involved in the reception of his work. We locate the division in critical reception in polarised responses to the radical shift in Žižek's work, from the subject of desire and a radical-democratic politics, to the subject of the drive and a revolutionary vanguardist politics. Accordingly the book proposes a new understanding of Žižek that goes beyond previous introductions. We interpret the conflict among the critics as the symptom of a division within Žižek's work itself.

We proffer this new, critical interpretation now because the critical response to Žižek has been characterised by a kind of 'time lag'. This is partly because of the frenetic pace of Žižek's publishing. It also reflects the genuine novelty of his contributions to philosophy, political theory and the other fields in which he intervenes. Finally, Žižek himself has reached the point where he too claims that he has radically changed direction since 1996–7.

Since 2002 there has been an increasing stream of engagements with Žižek's work: critical monographs, edited collections and introductory works. In addition to a growing list of articles and book chapters on Žižek, there is a series of valuable introductions by Sarah Kay (2003), Tony Myers (2003), Ian Parker (2004) and Jodi Dean (2006). Most of the introductions take Žižek's 'three centres of gravity' as the organising principle of their work, setting forth his interpretation of Hegel, Lacan and Marx in successive chapters. The critical books on Žižek have followed a different logic: Matthew Sharpe (2004) and Marcus Pound (2008) have produced book-length critical engagements with Žižek's social theory and theological positions, respectively. Adrian Johnston's *Žižek's Ontology* (2008) is a remarkable reconstruction of Žižek's philosophical ideas as what Johnston calls a 'transcendental materialism'.

Then there are three edited collections of essays on Žižek the hard-hitting content of which have elicited full-length replies by Žižek. Matthew Sharpe, Geoff Boucher, and Jason Glynos's *Traversing the Fantasy* (2005) contains both psychoanalytic and philosophical critiques of Žižek's work by figures such as Peter Dews and Ian Buchanan. James Bowman and Richard Stamp's *The Truth of Žižek* (2007) pulls no punches in its responses to Žižek's theoretical work and political positions. Erik Vogt and High Silverman's *Über Žižek* (2004) contains a probing essay by Mark de Kesel, among others. The foundation of *The International Journal of Žižek Studies* in 2006 was further testimony to Žižek's status as one of the world's leading intellectuals.

A distinctive feature of Žižek's work is the way he has always constructed his own positions in dialogue – or rather, in polemical debate – with other contemporary thinkers. By 2009 there also exist polemical exchanges between Žižek and a series of intellectual luminaries, Ernesto Laclau, Judith Butler, Terry Eagleton, Yannis Stavrakakis, Sean Homer, Simon Critchley, Peter Dews and more. Žižek's prolonged engagement with figures on the French intellectual Left such as Étienne Balibar, Jacques Rancière, Jacques-Alain Miller and Alain Badiou is conducted across many of Žižek's books. Žižek has also made sallies at psychoanalytic thinkers Richard Boothby, Jonathan Lear and Jacob Rogozinski. Then there are Žižek's continuing engagements with key contemporary thinkers such as Jacques Derrida, Gilles Deleuze, Michel Foucault, Richard Rorty, Jürgen Habermas and Daniel Dennett – although these are arguably less direct exchanges than Žižek's brilliant, heterodox interventions from outside into ongoing debates.

However, one feature of the ongoing academic work of 'working through' what one critic has called the 'Žižek effect' (Resch 2005) stands out. Much of the work before 2004 was devoted to patiently deciphering Žižek's work, which we will see can be tricky enough. Yet, since that time, more and more authors – witness those collected in *The Truth of Žižek* – have well and truly traversed the fantasy that Žižek is an unimpeachable theoretical and political authority, whom we can but hope to understand but never criticise. Since 2004, indeed, the vast majority of writing on Žižek has become increasingly critical. As we commented, Žižek has now been accused of nearly every theoretical and political sin readers can imagine: everything from supporting Joseph Stalin and Chairman Mao to not footnoting properly, and producing readings of other philosophers that really should not pass muster in the academic world. The exceptions include the work of Scott Parkin, Rex Butler, Adrian Johnston and Jodi Dean, together with that of many of the authors who have contributed to *The International Journal of Žižek Studies*. These figures have sought to balance their criticism of some aspects of Žižek's politics with their appreciation of his contribution to psychoanalytic and political theory. That is also the perspective we aim for.

The point is that the preliminaries in the work of 'Žižek reception' are finished. Twenty years on from *The Sublime Object of Ideology*, it is now time to begin the process of bringing together the disparate critical threads and charges that have been arraigned against Žižek since 2004. This is the critical aim of *Žižek and Politics*.

Our Method: Žižek and Political Philosophy

Much of the supposed novelty and the difficulty surrounding Žižek's work really has to do with the lack of any historical perspective that is a consequence of our postmodern condition. Theoretical fashion often treats the latest celebrity Theorists as if they had sprung fresh from Zeus' thigh, or come down in the last shower. By contrast, we intend to assess Žižek's work against a larger philosophical and historical background, as a thinker who offers a political philosophy that can and should be assessed in the terms proper to that discipline. Žižek has, after all, often argued that we should be wary of today's craze for 'the new', the 'most radical', and so on – so paradoxically sometimes the most radical thing to do is to assess all this alleged novelty against more lasting standards.

Political philosophy begins from the opinions of citizens about the rightness of the political regimes in which they live, the distribution of the goods and the obligations of citizenship. Political philosophy's goal is to ascend from these opinions, towards views about what is possible and desirable based on new insights into what is lastingly true. Its origin lies in the unavoidable fact of political life, that people's political opinions disagree, and that this disagreement can often be bitter or even violent. What the political philosopher seeks to do is to discover some higher standard with reference to which we could assess all competing opinions about what is possible and desirable.

The standard to which political philosophers are inevitably drawn are competing accounts of the human condition. Once we know what kind of creatures we are, we can decide how we ought to organise our political lives, and what measures we can feasibly adopt to change our political regimes for the better. The history of political philosophy has provided numerous accounts of the human condition: we are rational political beings, or we are god's creatures, or we are cunning and dangerous animals, or we are naturally asocial individual pleasure maximisers, or we are inescapably social communal beings. Political philosophers have duly opted on the basis of their accounts of the human condition for different political ideals: from the utopia of a state run by philosophers to societies in which free markets regulate almost all social life, from socialist states in which all are equal to highly hierarchical aristocracies or monarchies with Kings as the earthly representatives of God. The political philosopher's account of human nature leads to a description of political ideals that the philosopher holds to be desirable (because they accord with human nature), tempering these ideals against a considered reflection upon what is possible in any particular historical time or regime.

Fortunately, we can unpack a lot of Žižek's ideas about human nature, political community and social ideals, and make some decisions ourselves about the possibility and desirability of the two basic positions (radical-democratic and revolutionary vanguardist) that he takes. Žižek explicitly advocates a conception of the human condition based on Lacanian psychoanalysis, according to which the kernel of the human condition is the death drive. Surplus enjoyment, or the death drive, he tells us explicitly:

> defines the human condition as such: there is no solution, no escape from it; the thing to do is not to overcome, to abolish it, but to learn to recognise it in its terrifying dimension and then, on the basis of this fundamental recognition, to try to articulate a *modus vivendi* with it. (SO 5)

So Žižek's claim to have theorised 'enjoyment as a political factor' is not just a claim to have noticed something interesting about political ideologies. It is a claim about how the most basic element in human nature affects political communities. This claim is so fundamental that he repeats it many times in his books, in the form of an anthropological observation about the North American first nation of the Winnebago, which Žižek clearly feels applies to all human societies:

> [The Winnebago] is divided into two subgroups, 'those who are from above' and 'those who are from below'; when we ask an individual to draw . . . the plan of his village (the spatial disposition of cottages), we

18

obtain two quite different answers, depending on his belonging to one or the other subgroup. Both perceive the village as a circle, but for one subgroup, there is, within this circle, another circle of central houses, so that we have two concentric circles, while for the other subgroup, the circle is split in two by a clear dividing line. In other words, a member of the first group (let us call it 'conservative corporatist') perceives the plan of the village as a ring of houses more or less symmetrically disposed around the central temple, whereas a member of the second ('revolutionary antagonistic') subgroup perceives the village as two distinct heaps of houses separated by an invisible frontier. The central point of [this anthropological observation] is that this example should in no way entice us into cultural relativism, according to which the perception of social space depends on the observer's group membership: the very splitting into the two 'relative' perceptions implies a hidden reference to a constant – not to the objective, 'actual' disposition of buildings, but to a traumatic kernel, a fundamental antagonism that inhabitants of the village were unable to symbolize, to account for, to 'internalize' and come to terms with; an imbalance in social relations that prevented the community from stabilizing itself into a harmonious whole. The two perceptions of the village's plan are simply two mutually exclusive attempts to cope with this traumatic antagonism, to heal its wound via the imposition of a balanced symbolic structure. (*CHU* 112–13; *FA* 51; *TS* 221–2)

So Žižek's philosophical anthropology means we are driven by the death drive, compelled to repeat the institutional rituals of our political communities, in a fantasmatic bid to recover the enjoyment supposedly lost when we gained our social identities by adopting shared ideals and accepting shared prohibitions. But, Žižek adds, this ideological 'fantasy' of the loss of enjoyment gets projected onto those who, in society, have adopted other social ideals. In ideological fantasy, it is always *they* who have stolen the enjoyment (*TS* 201–5). According to whether the subject has adopted dominant or subordinate social ideals, their perception of *how* the others have stolen the subject's enjoyment will differ drastically. This leads to the split he describes between 'conservative-corporate' and 'revolutionary-antagonistic' visions of the social whole. Notice, though, that this division in society is absolutely *necessary*: there is no 'enjoyment as a political factor' without the fantasy of the 'theft of enjoyment', and, without enjoyment as a political factor, there are no social ideals and, hence, no society, because social ideals bind groups into collectivities.

Žižek's account of human nature is also, notably, one whose conclusion is that all political communities are inherently antagonistic or divided. This is why he speaks of social life in terms of the experience of 'a traumatic kernel [and] a fundamental antagonism' that cannot be symbolised. If political passions run hot, but subjects themselves cannot explain why, this is because 'society as a Corporate Body is the fundamental ideological fantasy' (*SO* 126). But in fantasy it is always the fault of the other group that social harmony is mysteriously prevented.

Unsurprisingly, Žižek's conception of human nature as centred on the death drive and political community as inherently riven by social antagonism shapes what he thinks is possible and desirable in politics. More surprisingly, he reaches two distinct conclusions on this matter. In his work from 1989 to 1995 he advocates finding a better way to live with this traumatic fact through the structural reform of political communities. This coincides with his radical-democratic politics and his concentration on the subject of desire. After 1996 Žižek seems to advocate the elimination of social antagonism through the creation of a radically new sort of political community. This coincides with his revolutionary vanguardist politics and his interest in the subject of the drive.

One task of the critical aspect of this book is to indicate our judgement on which of these positions is more possible and most desirable, while supplying readers with sufficient information to reach their own conclusions.

Reading Žižek: The Politics of Žižek's Style

Although we think that the ultimate cause of the divided reception Žižek's political ideas have received is a division in Žižek's own work, there is no doubt that, on the surface, the main irritant is his peculiar style. It is certainly hard to think of a contemporary thinker about whom there is more elementary disagreement as to 'what he stands for'. Many critics take Žižek's frequent invocations of the Marxian legacy seriously. Žižek, they argue, is a radical Marxist, who pits the 'old', class Left against the 'new', multiculturalist Left. According to other critics, Žižek has no political position. Žižek's Marxism is a merely polemical, strategic ruse to pit against his 'PC multiculturalist' foes within the academy. Some argue that Žižek's work evinces the longing for a new, closed form of tyrannical regime, wherein Žižekian philosophers would advise or themselves be the new, legally unchecked Princes. According to yet others, Žižek is a reactionary: an anti-feminist, or an anti-Semitic theorist, masquerading as a man of the Left (Berger 2001; Herbold 2005).

There is no doubt that many of Žižek's most controversial provocations can be traced to his intellectual style as a contrarian. As Terry Eagleton (2006) notes, the guiding rule for Žižek's positions seems to be their unfashionability. So, the moment a position (such as radical democracy) becomes popular, Žižek drops it for another (such as his vanguardist Marxism). Žižek works hard, in other words, to appear as outlandish and fascinating – as 'the liberal's worst nightmare' – for a certain gaze, usually the 'PC multiculturalists' or 'postmodern deconstructionists' he delights in outraging. To a certain extent, this posture of the exotic Other is an elaborate trap for unwary (or prejudiced) readers. This trap, however, involves rather more than just the ruse of a series of inflammatory games designed to smoke out the reader's hidden liberalism or ethnocentric stereotypes about the Balkans. This is merely a decoy for the real game, which is a certain unquiet that Žižek's provocations aim to cause. When Žižek makes his increasingly radical political assertions, can we take him seriously? Is this bluff, double-bluff, or blind man's bluff, with Žižek as the most blind?

Certainly, Žižek's style is characterised by what rhetoricians call 'parataxis', which means that Žižek's reflections on politics are never sustained in ways we might expect from a leading philosopher. By parataxis, we mean a rhetorical style that suppresses the logical and causal connections between clauses in a sentence, paragraph, chapter or work. The distinction between syntax (which includes logical and causal connections) and parataxis (which suppresses them) can be illustrated easily. It is the difference between 'the dog hid because of the thunder' (which is syntactical) and 'a burst of thunder; the dog quaking' (which is an instance of parataxis). A paratactic work such as Žižek's leaves it to the reader to infer what the connection between the ideas is. Žižek's critique of ideology, his expositions of political theorists and his analyses of historical political events pass readily into the analyses of films, ads, sexual difference, metaphysics and theology, almost anything – usually with only a characteristic phrase or a rhetorical question to connect them. This has provoked the response that Žižek often uses political examples to illustrate theory, rather than being interested in using theory to illuminate politics (Laclau 2000b: 195–206).

Žižek often says contradictory things, and proceeds wholly on an exegetical basis, as a mere commentator on the ideas of others. Also, like Jacques Lacan, Žižek often seems to criticise his own positions, as if he had no fixed or final positions at all (*ME* 173). It is, for instance, very difficult to think of any writer who, more than Žižek, presents texts that enjoin readers radically to transgress or to *enjoy!* – although he is ruthless in attacking this post-structuralist imperative in other theorists. It is equally tough to think of anyone who, more than Žižek, has reduced politics to ethics, even though Žižek complains about everyone else today that they do just this (*CHU* 127) – in Žižek's case, he goes about this by trying to derive his model of political action from the psychoanalytic clinic. Žižek also infamously repeats passages of himself, without acknowledging the citation, in a way probably never before published, facilitated by the copy-and-paste function of the modern word processor. Žižek's texts often end with a whimper, rather than the 'bang' of any conclusion, patiently worked towards (Laclau 1989: p. vii).

Then, there are different types of Žižek texts. As Žižek's profile has grown, Žižek has made a name writing columns on the events of the day in the *London Review of Books*, the *New York Review of Books* and a variety of 'e-zines' on the web. In these articles, Žižek often presents a quite moderate, left-liberal front: he is for a unified Europe, against the ideological use of terrorism to justify US torture or imperialism, for a two-state solution in Palestine, against any too-cynical dismissal of the progressive significance of Obama's election – the list goes on.

The text of many of these articles appears, sometimes in *verbatim* chunks, in what Žižek has called in interview his series of 'B' texts: shorter, more popularly accessible pamphlets such as *On Belief* (2001), *Welcome to the Desert of the Real* (2002), *Iraq: The Borrowed Kettle* (2004) and *On Violence* (2008). Then there are Žižek's longer, more scholarly 'A' productions such as *Parallax View* and *In Defence of Lost Causes* published in 2006 and 2008, or *The Ticklish Subject* of 1999, each exceeding 300 pages. In these texts Žižek's more episodic, moderate commentaries on the events of the day are interlaced with his readings of leading and historical thinkers, and his continuing work of exposing the difficult ideas of Hegel, Schelling and Lacan. The unusual thing is that it is above all in these most academic texts that Žižek presents his most radical or 'counter-hegemonic' political prescriptions: prescriptions that might surprise readers who have come to the texts through Žižek's more public presentations. These prescriptions have become more and more strident since 1999, culminating with *In Defence of Lost Causes* in 2008.

How are we to make sense of this *oeuvre*? It is tempting to say that no one has ever written books like Žižek. As his fame has grown, Žižek's output has grown as rapidly, and his patient respect for academic conventions has widely lapsed. This speaks to the dismissive conclusion that Žižek's contradictions are caused because he is writing more quickly than anyone can possibly think. Perhaps Žižek is one of those people Freud famously described as 'ruined by success'. Or perhaps Žižek is a sociological phenomenon: the victim of the postmodern, globalised lecture circuit, and the cult of personality that seems like the 'institutional unconscious' of parts of the humanities academy (Gilbert 2007)? Against this casual dismissal of Žižek, however, when we look back on the history of political philosophy, Žižek's rhetorical devices are far from being new.

Žižek has himself warned that, beneath the user-friendly surface of his texts, there is a position deployed with scant regard for all the wealth and warmth of humanistic concerns. In Žižek's *In Defence of Lost Causes*, we are warned that 'it is up to the reader to unravel the clues which lie before her' (*IDLC* 8). *The Parallax View* similarly advertises the 'cruel traps' Žižek sets for the reader who is trying to decipher what he means (*PV* 11). Then there is one open confession of his toying with audiences he has little respect for – by fabricating a reading of a modernist artwork in *Fright of Real Tears* (*FRT* 5–6; WDLT 197–8). Far from shrinking from such a controversial device, Žižek then goes on to repeat the bluff almost *word for word* in an apparently serious context, discussing paintings by Malevich, Hopper and Munch (*FRT* 106; Quinn 2006: 2).

So what can be at play in this version of philosophical esotericism, the practice of concealing or partly concealing one's true meaning? What might the politics and motivation of such rhetorical trickery be?

The uncanny thing is that all the features of Žižek's texts – self-contradiction; repetition with small variations; the presentation of his own ideas in the guise of commentaries on other people; paratactic shifts between topics without apparent rhyme or reason; the failure to conclude or to sustain 'linear' argumentation; even the resulting confusion among commentators – have been seen often enough in the history of political philosophy, from Plato down to Nietzsche. These writing techniques were used by philosophers who knew that their political opinions stood at right angles to accepted opinion, so they could not possibly present them in a simple, readily accessible way. That would be to risk persecution: either public ostracism, or, in closed societies such as the former Yugoslavia, imprisonment or worse. Additionally, philosophers have often felt that philosophy and common sense are in tension, so that those who hold to popular opinions are generally thought of as dupes. For many pre-modern political philosophers, the difficult logic of their discourse is a way of losing the dupes in a maze, while signalling to the elite few who can follow a series of conclusions about which it would be politically dangerous to speak openly.

We will show in this book that, as Žižek's position becomes more politically controversial, as he shifts from radical democrat to revolutionary vanguardist, his conception of what is possible and desirable in politics becomes increasingly distant from contemporary popular opinion. Accordingly, Žižek's style is at least in part a form of camouflage. To use a more contemporary example, like the old Communist parties in the West, his texts seem to have their front organisations, open to the general public, while the more radical arguments are for the inner elite willing and able to understand and take them on. As Ian Parker has noted, Žižek has made some very frank statements about his Lacanian dogmatism and in praise of the 'Stalinist' rule he attributes to Jacques Alain-Miller within the Lacanian psychoanalytic community (Parker 2004: 120–1). The critical reader is entitled to wonder whether there is a certain positioning of himself towards authority in Žižek's texts – a valorisation of the 'romance' of dogmatism or orthodoxy – whose political consequences can only be of a certain kind.

The Two Žižeks

Our major argument about the division in Žižek's work and his politics structures the book. Our claim is that there are, conceptually speaking, effectively *two* Žižeks: the Radical-Democratic 'Žižek$_1$' and the Revolutionary-Vanguardist 'Žižek$_2$'. These Žižeks are divided by a remarkable moment in Žižek's career. This was the moment, between 1996 and 1997, when Žižek delved into the Romantic philosopher Gottfried Schelling, and his rather esoteric account of how God gave birth to the world (AF; *IR*; Johnston 2008).

We argue the following. Žižek's insight into enjoyment as a political factor presents him with the dilemma we posed above. The horns of the dilemma – reliance on the Symbolic and advocacy of a radical-democratic politics, or a leap into the Real and the embrace of revolutionary vanguardism – generate Žižek's two different periods, the early and the recent. Schelling's Romanticism was the catalyst that

Enlightenment versus Romanticism

The distinction between Enlightenment thinking and anti-Enlightenment Romanticism can be schematically summarised in the following terms:

- For the Enlightenment, the link between human nature and ideals of political freedom is rationality. Through reason, the subject will arrive at what is possible and desirable in a political community.
- By contrast, for Romanticism, the bridge between human nature and social freedom is to be crossed using some irrational force – the Imagination, unconscious fantasy, the non-rational drives and so forth.
- Philosophical Romanticism holds that human rationality is not the deepest or most characteristic human trait, and that – indeed – human rationality is always underlain and undermined by forces, affects or truths accessible only to artistic experience or religious faith.

prompted Žižek to change tack, switching from the one horn of his dilemma to the other. The result is the dramatic difference in the theoretical, ethical and political conclusions that Žižek reached between 1989 and 1995, compared with those of 1996–2009.

Of course, this is in large measure an *analytical* distinction between two Žižeks, and not a substantive difference. We do not think that Žižek has become a different person, or that elements of the anti-democratic revolutionary vanguardist position were not present within the earlier, radical-democratic phase (and vice versa). But we do mean that the dominant structure of his thinking has changed. Where, formerly, the anti-democratic, revolutionary vanguardist elements were strictly subordinated to a radical-democratic politics, from 1998 onwards they have become dominant. The radical-democratic elements, meanwhile, now tend to appear only when Žižek is defending himself from critical accusations that what he advocates is neither desirable nor possible.

There are several registers of this change from 'Žižek$_1$' to 'Žižek$_2$' in Žižek's books.

- From a deeply *ironic* theory of ideology that sets out to show the depth of our underlying heteronomous commitments to symbolic-shared norms and ideals (Chapter 1), to a deeply *cynical* theory that pessimistically discloses the Real undersides of all our symbolic commitments, in what Žižek terms the 'obscene superego injunction to *enjoy*!' (Chapter 4).

- At the political level, from a 'Žižek$_1$' theory that gestures towards a new theory of democracy (Chapter 1), grounded in a more realistic account of human desire and subjectivity (Chapter 2), to a 'Žižek$_2$' radical critique of liberalism, democracy and (or at base *as*) capitalism that issues in increasingly uncompromising advocacy of 'vanguardism' (the idea that a revolutionary 'vanguard' should take over power), authoritarian government and the political use of terror (Chapter 5).

- At the ethical level, from Žižek$_1$'s at least implicit, and avowed, Enlightenment interest in autonomy, individuals' and societies' rational self-determination, to Žižek$_2$'s Romanticist concern for authenticity, the ideal that individuals and societies commit themselves resolutely to the particularistic 'ideological fantasies' or 'sinthomes' that shape their ideological commitments.

- At the level of Žižek's framing theory of the human condition or 'philosophical anthropology', from Žižek$_1$'s remarkable early retrieval of the finite, socially shaped Hegelian–Lacanian subject of desire from theoretical unfashiability (Chapter 2) to Žižek$_2$'s account of the subject as the bearer of an uncanny, infinite or even diabolically evil death drive, recalcitrant to all symbolic ideals ('Žižek's Vanishing Mediation'; Chapter 6).

- At base, from Žižek$_1$'s optimistic commitment to using psychoanalytic reason to drain the 'ocean' of the drives through the talking cure (to invoke Freud), to the pessimistic Žižek$_2$ idea that psychoanalysis instead provides us with a theoretical 'insight' into the centrality of the death drive in politics realistic enough to see clearly how the most we can do is learn without illusion to struggle within the drives' irrational tides. (This is why we will suggest that the later Žižek is Freudo-Hobbesian: since Thomas Hobbes was the early liberal philosopher who argued that, since human beings are naturally aggressive and envious towards their neighbours, what they above all need is a state so powerful that it can quell subjects by using terror.)

We hope there are many questions the reader feels drawn to ask at the end of this Introduction. They can be answered only by the body of this book. The final question the reader might want to ask is this: how exactly do the authors think that Žižek's encounter with

Schelling and philosophical Romanticism crystallise all these apparent changes?

Our answer will be that, when Žižek turns to Schelling, he explicitly falls into a philosophical trap shared by many contemporary theorists in the so-called cultural turn. This trap was fatefully presaged by the Marxist theorist György Lukács in the 1920s. This is the trap of positing or proposing a 'subject–object' – in Žižek, the 'Other', or 'Capital' – as the topic of his theoretical analysis. What do we mean?

Žižek tells us directly in his two analyses of Schelling's theology, *The Indivisible Remainder* (1996) and *The Abyss of Freedom* (1997), that God himself (a subject) gives birth to the world or Symbolic Order (the object/ive world) from out of himself. The world as we know it is as it were 'God in the mode of Otherness': which he created as a way to resolve what Žižek tells us was a horrific, prehistorical dilemma ('the rotary motion of [His] drives'). The details of this creation narrative will be explained in 'Žižek's Vanishing Mediation'. For the moment, the key thing is that Žižek wants to argue that this strange theology can be used to explain not simply how God created the ordered world we experience. He also proposes, more or less explicitly, that it can tell us how human subjects themselves can (and implicitly always *have*) created the political regimes or Symbolic Orders (democracies, monarchies . . .) in which they live in radical, violent founding Acts that give political shape to their 'death drive'. In a word, Žižek₂ has a theological conception of human subjectivity and politics (Chapter 6). It is little wonder, with such a framing view of the human condition, that his earlier, at least strategic nods to democratic theory disappear.

Žižek's Schellingerian turn, *Žižek and Politics* will argue, lies at the heart of Žižek's push towards a deeply pessimistic, anti-pluralistic theory of culture (Chapter 4), and his ultra-Leftist political vanguardism (Chapter 5). More than this, we also think it retrospectively provides the clue to understanding the theoretical presupposition of Žižek's infamous paratactic style (remember we saw in the previous section its implicit anti-democratic politics). Our idea is that Žižek *can* only propose to shift so effortlessly between politics, ethical or moral theory, the analyses of cultural or ideological artefacts (such as films, advertisements, literature, and so on), a psychoanalytic philosophy of the subject, and (increasingly after 1996) theology for this very good reason: namely, *at base, Žižek is committed to the notion that all these theoretical fields have the same basic structures, which can all be analysed using the same terms and methodology.*

Each of these theoretical fields, that is, are so many 'expressions' of the one underlying 'subject–object', which Žižek typically calls 'the big Other', in his Lacanian terms. To indicate what we suspect strongly is the deeply flawed nature of this presupposition: this means that Žižek wants his readers to accept that political systems (with all their plurality of people, classes and groups, institutions and their differing histories) have meaningfully 'identical' structure as the subjectivity of individual people who live within them. This subjectivity, Žižek also wants his readers to accept, can in turn be studied in the same terms as the theological 'subjectivity' of God. And this is why we can (and Žižek regularly does) answer political questions by 'cutting' paratactically to theology or the ethics of the psychoanalytic clinic; answer questions about the nature of subjectivity by recourse to political causes and cases, and so on.

To be direct, we think these Žižekian presuppositions cannot hold up to critical reflection. In particular, we are going to argue in Chapter 4 that Žižek's drift from his critique of ideology to a pessimistic, (neo)conservative philosophy of culture involves his failing to distinguish between the subjective Ego Ideal and the objective Other or Symbolic Order (see also Chapter 1 for definitions of these terms). And we are going to argue in Chapter 5 that Žižek becomes utterly incapable of theorising the nature of economics and the role it plays in politics, because he tries to think of the two in explicitly psychoanalytic categories: that is, exactly as if these systems were somehow like the 'internal' agencies within a giant 'subject–object' called 'global Capital'. In each case, these theoretical elisions lead him towards the more radical and tendentious political prescriptions for which he has been most widely criticised.

But all this is a long way off yet. We need first to begin by examining Žižek$_1$, a task in whose context we are also going to define for readers the key terms of Žižek's political philosophy.

Part One

Žižek$_1$

Chapter 1

Žižek and the Radical-Democratic Critique of Ideology

Looking Ahead

Žižek's Lacanian analysis of ideology is probably one of the most important contributions to descriptive political theory since the 1980s. Žižek's theory of ideology adeptly employs his 'Lacanian dialectics'. This is a unique synthesis of Lacanian psychoanalysis and Hegelian dialectics, which allows Žižek to grasp the contradictions in ideologies and understand their hold on us. These are the points we will clarify in this chapter.

- We will explain how this Lacanian dialectics works, using some of Žižek's most striking examples, beginning from Žižek's responses to the collapse of historical Communism in 1989 and to the terrorist attacks of 11 September 2001.
- Secondly, we will look at one of Žižek's most powerful insights into ideology, the unconscious logic of the so-called theft of enjoyment, as a central mechanism of all ideologies. This also shows his ability to expose the libidinal 'underside' to ideology through illuminating the unconscious logic at work within it.
- Finally, we will show the logical connections between Žižek's critique of ideology and his early, radical-democratic political tendency. Žižek criticises the irrational beliefs beneath apparently rational ideals as the bulwarks of injustices today.

Slavoj Žižek and the New World Order

Slavoj Žižek's *The Sublime Object of Ideology* appeared in 1989. In this year, exactly 200 years after the beginning of the French Revolution, the Berlin Wall fell. With the collapse of historical Communism as a result of economic stagnation and democratic revolution against the Party dictatorship, the Soviet Union broke apart into a host of nations. The East European states of the Soviet Bloc rejected their Communist governments. Žižek's native Slovenia seceded relatively peacefully from Yugoslavia in 1991. Žižek stood as a presidential candidate in the democratic elections that followed and narrowly missed winning office. The West looked confidently to the former Communist countries, looking to see the West's faith in the value of liberal capitalism vindicated in full.

In the USA, then-incumbent President George Herbert Bush caught the moment famously. Bush described the emerging global situation as a 'New World Order', characterised by the worldwide spread of liberal democracy and free-market economics. The pre-eminent intellectual statement of the times came from the neoconservative Francis Fukuyama. In *The End of History and the Last Man* (1992), Fukuyama argued that the fall of the Berlin Wall signalled the end of human history. The long series of violent struggles between competing conceptions of the best political regime was over. The Western coupling of (neo)liberal economics and parliamentary democracy was the only legitimate form of government remaining. Socialism, one more blood-stained god that had failed, would now join the absolute monarchs of early modernity and their quarrelling feudal forebears – in the dustbin of history. In liberal parliamentarism and free markets, the deep political aspiration for mutual recognition protected by the rule of law is fully realised.

How does Žižek stand vis-à-vis this new 'post-ideological' consensus? His position is typically provocative and controversial. Žižek argues that 'in a way . . . Francis Fukuyama was right, global capitalism IS the 'end of history' (RL 12). Today, politics is conceived of in terms of the 'post-political' management of society and the economy, precisely because the West thinks of itself as having entered a 'post-ideological' condition. The 'bipartisan consensus' on free markets and liberal societies is based on the perception of social reality as something neutral and unproblematic. Different political parties now compete on the basis of their style of management (or even on the basis of the personalities of their leaders). In his debate with Ernesto Laclau and Judith Butler in 2000, Žižek put it this way:

> Today's predominant consensus . . . [sees] the age of ideologies – of grand ideological projects like Socialism or Liberalism – [as] over, since we have entered the post-ideological era of rational negotiation and decision-making, based upon the neutral insight into economic, ecological, etc., necessities . . . This consensus assumes different guises, from the neoconservative or Socialist refusal to accept it and consummate the loss

of grand ideological projects by means of a proper 'work of mourning' . . . up to the neoliberal opinion, according to which the passage from the age of ideologies to the post-ideological era is part of the sad but none the less inexorable process of the maturation of humanity. (*CHU* 323–4)

So Žižek's orienting political contention about today's world is that, since 1989, we have been living in a period of unprecedented global consensus. In the New World Order, it somehow seems easier for people to imagine the world being destroyed by some catastrophic natural event than for them to imagine any political alternative to the reign of global capital (SI 1). Parliamentary politics in the developed countries has gravitated to the Right. Žižek shares the scepticism of critics on the Left about whether the 'opposition' to the Right posed by the so-called Third Way politics of the Democrats and the New Labour parties is worthy of that name. He sees their coupling of free-market economics with the democratic promotion of 'values' and a 'consultative' way of governing as something of a front, concealing a different message, to the big end of town: 'we will do the job for you in an even more efficient and painless way than the conservatives' (MC 35).

But Žižek's position is not only provocative. By highlighting the way that the lack of opposition to capitalism is reflected within the academy, he controversially accuses many supposedly radical theorists of complicity with the 'post-ideological' consensus. Although the Right constantly alleges that the supposedly 'anti-Western', 'postmodern', 'adversary culture' within the universities is responsible for some sort of decline of the West, Žižek thinks that 'radical' intellectual circles today do not really oppose the new globalising order at all. Thus Žižek agrees with right-wing critics that a 'post-modernist' or 'post-structuralist' consensus emerged in the humanities in the West after the 1970s. He unhesitatingly uses terms such as 'politically correct' (or PC) to describe the liberal postmodern consensus in the humanities. But Žižek disagrees with the Right that this postmodernist consensus is politically radical.

For Žižek, the key element of the new 'PC multiculturalism,' or 'postmodernism' is its rejection of Marxism as an 'essentialist' or 'economically reductive' philosophy, and the supplanting of class politics by 'identity politics'. Class struggle and economic issues have largely disappeared from political debates in the West, Žižek notes. 'Culture wars' about issues to do with race, sexuality and gender, and the ethical questions being raised by today's advances in the biogenetic sciences, have taken their place. For this reason, Žižek suggests that the postmodernists' celebration of difference, 'becoming' (change), otherness and the new postmodern plurality of lifestyles and subcultures is 'radical' only from the perspective of the cultural conservatives they oppose. In the same era in which neoliberal economics has taken on an unprecedented political importance, Žižek complains that the New Left has been directing progressives' focus away from what really matters in shaping public life.

Think, by contrast, of what occurs as soon as the prospect of any far-reaching change affecting the economy is raised. Žižek proposes that we soon find that a 'politically correct' *Denkenverbot* (prohibition against thinking) operates to suppress questioning of global capitalism. And, despite the fashionable 'anti-hegemonic' rhetoric, this happens in the postmodern academy just as much as in the mainstream media. Žižek notes that philosophers as different as Jürgen Habermas and Jacques Derrida 'would probably adopt the same left-of-centre liberal democratic stance in practical political decisions'. We should not be fooled by their 'great passionate public debates', then, nor by the Right's outrage against their 'relativism',' 'permissiveness', 'adversarial culture', and so on (*CHU* 127–8). In fact, Žižek proposes, the underlying premises of the 'postmodernist', academic New Left are profoundly conservative. Far from providing any real ethical or political resistance to the neoliberal, free-market consensus, postmodernism is merely the cultural logic of global capitalism. As Žižek says:

> the moment one shows a minimal sign of engaging in political projects that aim seriously to change the existing order, the answer is immediately: 'benevolent as it is, this will necessarily end in a new gulag.' The 'return of ethics' in today's political philosophy shamefully exploits the horrors of the gulag or holocaust as the ultimate bogey for blackmailing us into renouncing all serious radical engagement. (*CHU* 127)

Although Žižek agrees with the description of today's Western politics as 'beyond Left and Right', then, he in no way accepts the Fukuyama-style conclusions drawn by theorists of the 'Third Way'. Thinkers such as Anthony Giddens and Ulrich Beck celebrate this condition of political apathy as a more peaceable, post-ideological 'second modernity'. But scratch the surface, keep an eye on popular culture or even the news, Žižek suggests, and it soon becomes clear that all is not well in the post-cold-war order. Let us look at how this is so, and how Žižek proposes we should understand the unrest or 'discontents' he detects beneath the glittering surface of the multinational, multicultural, postmodernist, capitalist global consensus.

The Spirit is a Bone, Globalisation is Fundamentalism

The terrorist attacks of 11 September 2001 were interpreted by many commentators as the end of the New World Order. Within weeks, the 'War on Terror' was declared. Conventional wars in Afghanistan and Iraq followed. The new mantra of the Western media was that, after '9/11', 'everything has changed'. Ominous invocations of what the neoconservative Samuel Huntington called 'the clash of civilisations', between the Judaeo-Christian and Muslim worlds, replaced celebrations of an end to historical struggles. The liberal-democratic West faced a new, external threat: militant Islamic fundamentalism. In the face of this new enemy, many of the civil liberties and political rights that the 'post-historical' West had come to take for granted were rolled back. From the White House, George W. Bush answered the question widely asked after 9/11, 'why do they hate us so much?' with the plaintive: 'they hate our freedoms'. This idea represents a modification of the Fukuyama 'end of history'. While most of the world moves forward through liberal democracy and free markets, some reactionary enclaves deliberately reject modern freedom and opt for fundamentalist totalitarianism.

Žižek's position represents a basic challenge to this sort of complacency. He insists that underneath the post-political consensus of the global order lies fundamental discontent. The so-called dark phenomena of the second modernity – religious fundamentalism, ethnic hatreds, virulent sexism and violent homophobia – are not something coming from outside global capitalism. These supposedly external threats to the West's way of life appear to be the result of 'hatred of our freedom', so fundamentalist terrorism seems like the opposite of liberal democracy. But, once we contextualise these phenomena, Žižek argues, they turn out to be effects of the social 'contradictions' (inner problems and tensions) of global capitalism. Furthermore, his position suggests that they are in some important sense preprogrammed into the world order by the unconscious beliefs underlying *Western* ideologies. Specifically, the appearance of the fundamentalist Other as the negation of the post-political consensus on liberal democracy and free markets is the way that the effects of contradictions *within* Western social reality appear as an external threat arising from *without*. This sort of reversal of perspective is something like Žižek's 'basic operation' in ideology critique, so it is worth paying attention to the way he argues this striking case.

According to the post-political orthodoxy of everybody from Third Way social democrats to moderate Republicans, the Western way of life is inclusive, because liberal societies are tolerant of difference. Religious convictions, cultural styles, consumer preferences and goals in life are the private business of liberal individuals, who therefore tolerate the fact that others have different personal beliefs and aspirations. But what that means, Žižek points out, is that the celebration of difference by postmodern theorists, multicultural politicians and 'politically correct' academics is a celebration of those private differences that do not impact on the public sphere. The moment that the cultural other steps over the line and begins to express his religious convictions, for instance, in the form of demands for the public regulation of dress codes for women, this multicultural other suddenly morphs into a fundamentalist bigot, if not a fully fledged Islamic terrorist.

For Žižek, the post-political consensus in the West is an effort to suppress 'social antagonism' – the sorts of volatile disagreements about basic values and social institutions that lead to real political opposition. Against this conceptual and political background, we can understand why, in typically frenetic fashion, Slavoj Žižek was among the first commentators to respond to 11 September 2001. What would become *Welcome to the Desert of the Real* (2002) developed out of a paper Žižek initially published only days after the terrorist attacks. The title of Žižek's book is taken from the Wachowski brothers' 1999 blockbuster *The Matrix*. It is the invitation offered by Morpheus (Samuel L. Jackson) to the messiah figure 'Neo' (Keanu Reeves) after Neo has chosen to 'unplug' from the illusory world generated by the computer program, the 'Matrix', which maintains the semblance of an untroubled and peaceful world. With the post-political illusions of universal prosperity and generalised happiness created by the Matrix shattered, Neo must confront the dark reality of a post-apocalyptic world, where machines harvest human beings for energy to sustain themselves (*WDR* 15). For Žižek, this film stunningly anticipated America's situation immediately before and then after the terrorist attacks. Like the Matrix, the post-political illusion of a global consensus on liberal democracy and free markets actually concealed the appalling reality of global exploitation of the developing world by a rapacious global capitalism. Accordingly, Žižek argues that on 11 September, America experienced not something unprecedented, but a wake-up call, an unwelcome 'welcome' to the ongoing reality of the vast majority of the human population:

> Cruel and indifferent as it may sound, we should also, now more than ever, bear in mind that . . . the US just got the taste of what goes on around the world on a daily basis, from Sarajevo to Grozny, from Rwanda and Congo to Sierre Leone . . . America's 'holiday from history' was a fake: America's peace was bought by the catastrophes going on elsewhere. (WDR 388; *WDR* 16)

Žižek's list of the sites of ongoing violent conflict in the world is not wholly unmotivated. As a Slovenian, Žižek had witnessed close at hand the rise of neofascist parties within the former Yugoslavia, and the outbreak of ethnic conflicts after the end of the Communist era. According to Žižek, 'the re-emergence of nationalist chauvinism', in the form of the Balkan war and ethnic cleansing by Milosovic's Serbs, was a direct consequence of the excessively rapid insertion of former Yugoslavia into the capitalist economy (*TN* 211).

9/11 presented the USA with a choice, Žižek argues: 'will Americans decide to fortify their "sphere", or risk stepping out of it' by reconsidering the effects of its foreign actions and policy on the wider world (WDR 389)? The American Executive's response was an unequivocal 'No' to any suggestion that it might have any responsibility for generating the conditions that make terrorist atrocities seem morally acceptable to desperate, radicalised people. For the Bush administration, the terrorists' acts were embodiments of an inconceivable, 'purely Evil Outside', visited on a wholly inno-cent nation (WDR 387). Yet, Žižek asks us, is it enough merely to dismiss Bush's ideologically motivated oversimplification? Does not Bush's 2001 attempt to position the terrorist attacks as acts visited upon an innocent America from outside simply mirror the standard way Western commentators and politicians comprehend all the 'dark phenomena' haunting our post-political 'second modernity'? And does not the Bush doctrine's elevation of Bin Laden and al-Qaeda to figures of inscrutable Otherness have some unsettling implications for the way postmodernists celebrate absolute Otherness as a relief from the supposed tyranny of modern Western rationality?

Žižek's answer to the last two questions is direct: 'Yes, it does.' Confronted with the rise of ethnic violence, and the growing popu-larity of far Right politics in Europe and elsewhere, Third Way theorists such as Beck and Giddens argue that these phenomena rep-resent relics of bygone, more violent periods in human history. The implication is that they will surely disappear, given time. Consider the predominant Western view on the Balkans conflict, as involving irrational 'ancient hatreds' that were temporarily held in check by the Communists' reign and that can now be solved only by the modernisation of former Yugoslavia.

Žižek's view stands this dominant interpretation on its head. On the one hand, the move to *externalise* any causes of political discontent or trauma is one of the founding devices of all political ideologies. If the cause of our problems comes from outside – say, from the Kosovars, Jews, Muslims, Freemasons, and so on – this means that we can avoid facing the possibility that *we* might be implicated in the phenomena we denounce. A war against this enemy or intruder into our way of life supplants the need for internal struggle or political reform. On the other hand, Žižek thinks that the predominant Western stance on phenomena like fundamentalism and terrorism is descriptively false: the new global order's problems do not represent the relics of bygone periods, visited on an innocent West from outside. To see why, we need to introduce one of Žižek's two most important influences: German Enlightenment philosopher G.W. F. Hegel.

G. W. F. Hegel

Georg Wilhelm Friedrich Hegel (1770–1831) shares with his predecessor Immanuel Kant a claim to being the greatest modern philosopher. In a series of magisterial works, Hegel constructed a new system of philosophy, whose claim to 'absolute knowledge' makes him the *bête noir* of contemporary theoretical fashion. Hegel's thought is notoriously difficult. But the main elements that Žižek relies upon – Hegel's insistence on totality, the idea of a philosophy of contradictions (or 'unity of opposites') and the radical negativity of the subject (see Chapter 2) – can be spelt out reasonably clearly.

- Hegel's founding notion is that 'the truth is the whole'. Hegel holds that no phenomenon (no thing, event or person) can truly be grasped in isolation. In reality, Hegel argues, every phenomenon is formed through a network of relations that constitute – that is, give form and reason to – it. To take an everyday example, if we see a man or woman shouting angrily in the street, merely perceiving this tells us nothing about *why* he or she might be shouting so.

To do this, we would need to know about the relationship between this action and a whole set of other things: whether or not he had just lost his job or his wife, someone had stolen his wallet, and so on. Hegel holds that everything is contextually determined, in other words, so to understand the world reasonably is to situate things in their larger context.

- The context that determines all the other local contexts at a particular moment in history Hegel calls the 'totality'. Such totalities (including political regimes, or even the global international order today) are the widest network of interrelations between things, processes and actions within which every event, thing or person is located.

- Secondly, for Hegel, every totality contains dynamic 'contradictions', tensions between different parts, things, processes and people, and these 'contradictions' are what drive it forward. Hegel's doctrine that the 'truth is the whole' hence also involves the claim that this truth is in process, always changing or historical. Philosophical thought must comprehend the dynamic 'contradictions' in totalities – for instance, in Marx's Hegelian understanding of capitalism, the contradictions between the interests of the bourgeoisie and the workers.

- For Hegel, in particular, it is necessary to see the 'unity of opposites', or how particular processes, events or things – even enemies – which might seem wholly opposed are actually shaped by their relations *with* their seeming opposites. What at first appears as the 'external opposite' of a phenomenon, Hegel holds, may always in reality be part of the same changing totality that shapes what it is: so, although the bourgeois may lament organised labour, their own identity (and economic interests) depend on what they oppose. This is the Hegelian idea of 'the unity of opposites', identified in what Hegel calls 'speculative judgements' attentive to the contextual determination, and dynamic development, of particular phenomena in the world.

How, then, does Žižek's recourse to Hegel affect how he understands the 'dark phenomena' of the contemporary period, such as terrorism, fundamentalism, neofascism and the rising number of sexual and other pathologies amongst postmodern Western subjects? When we understand these phenomena as external 'relics' visited upon us from outside, Žižek argues, we remain at the ideological level. Placing these phenomena in their total context means seeing them as *the result of internal contradictions*. They are intrinsic, if unintended, by-products of the deregulation and globalisation of liberal capitalism, its 'exportation' to the societies of the developing world and its extension throughout everyday life within the developed world.

So, for instance, Žižek argues that the Balkan conflict of the 1990s was not a relic of a bygone period. It was 'the first clear taste of the twenty-first century . . . the prototype of the post Cold War armed conflicts' (*TN* 223). Why? Because the authoritarian nationalist movements in Serbia and Croatia that caused the conflict are a *response* to the rapid-fire globalisation of the former Yugoslavia after 1989. These 'chauvinistic nationalisms' operated as 'a kind of 'shock absorber' against the sudden exposure to capitalist openness and imbalance', Žižek argues (*TN* 210). As difficult as this is for Westerners to confront, Žižek's argument is that we need to understand even groups like the Taliban or al-Qaeda in today's War on Terror as 'a kind of 'negative judgement' on liberal capitalism' (*TN* 224). This means: they are reactions against Western liberal capitalism, *shaped or 'mediated' by what they oppose*, rather than wholly external counter-forces that abstractly 'hate our freedom'.

> The truth articulated in this paradox . . . is that . . . far from presenting a case of exotic barbarism, [even] the 'radical evil' of the [Maoist guerrilla movements, the Kampuchean] Khmer Rouge and the [Peruvian Shining Path] is conceivable only against the background of the constitutive antagonism of today's capitalism. (*TN* 224)

To be provocative, we might say that Žižek's political version of Hegel's speculative judgement, Hegel's assertion of the unity of opposites in his provocative claim that 'the spirit is a bone', is 'globalisation is fundamentalism'. Fundamentalism is that phenomenon in which the West gets its own truth back from the non-capitalist world in an inverted, violent form.

Of course, Žižek rejects nineteenth-century philosophies of historical progress of the sort rehashed by Fukuyama after 1989. He is an astute observer of the new types of political and social problems that liberal capitalist societies face today. Žižek's thought resists all attempts unthinkingly to 'wash our hands' of responsibility for the malaises that trouble our world. In Hegel's terms, such a position is that of the 'beautiful soul', whose complaining about the horrors of the world serves to conceal their own implication in the mess they lament. Žižek is fond of reciting the Hegelian idea that evil lies also in the gaze that, looking around, sees evil everywhere *else*.

This is a modernist, Enlightenment position – and one that is clearly on the progressive Left, as his analysis of the fallout from 9/11 shows. It is an Enlightenment position in that Žižek's Hegelian reading of the darker phenomena of today's world calls upon us to have the courage to take a philosophically enlarged responsibility for the world in which we live. What appears to be irrational and wholly Other, Žižek argues, is never so wholly irrational as a too-abstract perspective imagines. If Žižek is right, it is not that the religious fundamentalists, ethnic nationalists and reactionary sexists are massed, like barbarians at the gates of Rome, in external opposition to the enlightened modern West. The Western Enlightenment itself has yet to complete its own exposure of the unreason at the heart of modernity. For the radical-democratic Žižek (Žižek$_1$), a Lacanian dialectics – a combination of psychoanalysis and Hegel – can grasp, and help us to transcend, the irrational discontents of Enlightenment reason. Instead of denouncing the Enlightenment as a new prison, as postmodernism does, Žižek proposes rationally to understand the 'dark phenomena' of the contemporary world as caused by the internal limitations of an Enlightenment that has not gone far enough. The specific claim is that, when Enlightenment rationality becomes the servant of capitalist domination, then it engenders irrational anti-Enlightenment forces.

From Hegel to Psychoanalysis

The second major theoretical inspiration of Žižek's political theory is psychoanalysis. Žižek vigorously opposes the positivist view that sees in Freudian psychoanalysis a new obscurantism. Sigmund Freud and his successor Jacques Lacan's postulation of an unconscious side to the human psyche is part of the Enlightenment effort rationally to understand even our darkest fantasies. Freud's ambition, captured in the slogan that 'where the [unconscious] id was, there the I shall come to be', is reflected in the nature of the 'talking cure'. The psychoanalytic wager Žižek accepts in full is that, although we often 'know not what we do', reason can and should be brought to bear upon our pre-rational sexual and aggressive drives, both to understand them and to alter their expressions.

Žižek's adoption of psychoanalysis to understand political phenomena wherein subjects 'know not what they do' stands in a long tradition of psychoanalytic social theory. In *Metastases of Enjoyment* (1994), Žižek situates his work in the lineage of 'Freudo-Marxism' begun by the Frankfurt School thinkers: particularly Adorno, Marcuse and Habermas (*ME* 7–28, 167–217). These Western Marxists (also heavily indebted to Hegel) turned to psychoanalysis to explain why the workers of Europe did not embrace socialist revolution in the 1930s, but turned in numbers to fascism. The wager of 'Freudo-Marxism' is that psychoanalysis can supplement Marxism. It can provide a theory of human motivation deep enough to explain the appeal to irrational sacrifice and the fatal attraction subjects seem to feel towards forms of political authoritarianism (*ME* 16–22). The hope is that insight into these sources of motivation – and the way political regimes appeal to them – will allow us to counteract these reactionary political forces in future.

According to Žižek, the irrationality of an ideology involves the split between what people say that they know and what they unconsciously believe, as expressed through their actions. For instance, under Tito's version of Stalinism in the former Yugoslavia, what Žižek calls 'ideological cynicism' was rife. The Party claimed to rule in the name of the common good. But people knew that, behind the scenes, factional struggles raged, with different groups competing to capture power (*SO* 157–8). The strange thing was that official Yugoslav ideology effectively named the ruling bureaucracy itself as the final obstacle to be removed, if full socialist 'self-management' was to be achieved. In this situation, rational knowledge called for the replacement of the bureaucracy by popular sovereignty. But this very bureaucracy demanded that everybody conform in their actions to the latest official shift in the party line. Thus, the ideology of 'self-management' required cynical distance from the party line combined with irrational conformity to the institutional rituals of the bureaucracy.

Accordingly, Žižek detected a paradox at the heart of the ruling ideology in former Yugoslavia, the paradox of rational knowledge combined with irrational (conformist) deeds. The attitude of Yugoslav subjects did not fit Marx's famous formula for how ideologies work, by deceiving or misrepresenting the truth. Instead, subjects 'knew very well, but nonetheless, they were doing it' – namely, acting in ways that reproduce unjust social arrangements. Subjects knew very well that the state really *was* the enemy of workers' self-management. Yet this knowledge did not affect their loyalty to the status quo. They acted as if they did not know, as if there was no reason to challenge the authorities to make good on their promise to cede power. As Žižek puts it in *The Sublime Object of Ideology*, what was in play here was a kind of 'enlightened false consciousness' or 'ideological cynicism'. Such ideology 'no longer has the pretension . . . [of being] a lie experienced as truth [by duped subjects] . . . It is no longer meant, even by its authors, to be taken seriously' (*SO* 28, 30). Its formulation, by contrast to Marx's famous definition of ideology, would be: *they know very well what they are doing, yet they are doing it anyway.*

Žižek's analysis of ideological cynicism adds subtlety to the post-Marxist critique of political ideologies. It indicates the deep, even paradoxical ways that people can be convinced to support political parties, movements or regimes that betray their true interests. It also speaks powerfully to the political situation and lived experience of subjects in Western liberal-capitalist societies. Mass media exposés of political corruption and incompetence are a regular feature of democratic politics, with the consequence that most citizens are cynical and apathetic. Everybody knows that global capitalism involves shocking poverty and misery in the developing world, that the later modern state is largely captive to private interests and lobby groups, yet nobody does anything about this. The institutional routines of parliamentary democracy and the market society go on as before:

> It is as if in late capitalism 'words do not count', no longer oblige: they increasingly lose their performative power: whatever someone says is drowned in the general indifference: the emperor is naked and the media trumpet forth the fact, yet no one seems really to mind – that is, people continue to act as if the emperor were not naked. (SI 18)

Žižek's notion of ideological cynicism allows him to powerfully critique the idea of a post-ideological world, where the sober business of economic administration, coupled with identity politics, has supplanted passionate conflicts between different political ideologies such as liberalism, communism or social democracy. As Žižek rightly notes, no one truly 'taken in' by a political ideology has ever consciously thought that they were the dupes of a set of 'ideological', which is to say 'false' or deluded, beliefs. Few people can happily accept the idea that they are dupes or fools – instead, they accuse everyone else of being ideological victims, while proclaiming themselves 'post-ideological' or 'non-ideological'. Ideological delusion, in other words, belongs to the peculiar class of things that people take exclusively to happen to everybody else – a little like dying of cancer or in a car accident. So, when our Third Way politicians tell us that they are no longer socialists, but beyond all ideology, Žižek argues that *they are in fact expressing the arch-ideological position.*

When Žižek draws on Jacques Lacan's psychoanalytic account of the subject, split between conscious self-awareness and unconscious fantasy, it is to give a theoretical account able to explain the way that subjects act politically on unconscious beliefs, despite the full conscious awareness of what they do. And, for him, Lacan's understanding of the unconscious as shaped around fantasies concerning the beliefs and motivations of the Other(s) provides the most extraordinarily powerful theoretical framework to map how this is so.

Ideological Identification and its Vicissitudes

Let us now develop Žižek's contribution to the Marxian legacy of ideology critique by drawing on his psychoanalytic theory. This will involve understanding Žižek's debt to Louis Althusser's understanding of ideology and spelling out the different registers of Lacan's claim that 'the unconscious is the discourse of the Other'.

ŽIŽEK WITH ALTHUSSER

Alongside Hegel and Lacan, Žižek is most directly indebted for his understanding of political subjectivity to the French Marxist Louis Althusser, whose revolutionary work on ideology in the late 1960s made a profound mark on literary and cultural studies more broadly.

Žižek's account of ideology develops each of Althusser's insights into ideological interpellation, ideological misrecognition and the institutional ritual that sustains ideology, by means of Lacanian psychoanalysis. Althusser's account (1971: 121–86) of interpellation and of ideology as the 'imaginary relation of the subject to their real conditions of existence' was already shaped by his reading of Lacan's ideas. Žižek extends the Althusserian theory of ideology by explaining the libidinal investments that subjects have in their unconscious beliefs.

Althusser suggested that the way ideologies work was grasped by the seventeenth-century theologian Blaise Pascal in his provocative description of religious conversion. For Pascal, religion was not

Althusser's Theory of 'Interpellation' and the 'Materiality' of Ideology

In his famous piece 'Ideology and Ideological State Apparatuses', Louis Althusser announces a dramatic shift away from orthodox Marxist accounts. By contrast with Marx's account of 'false consciousness':

- Althusser develops a famous account of how individuals become the subjects of ideology through 'interpellation,' or their 'hailing' by the state apparatus in the process of socialisation. When the individual recognises herself in the call of this ideological authority, she supposes that the political authorities are a grand Subject ('God', 'nation', 'the Party', and so on) capable of legitimately calling her to account.
- Ideologies do not primarily involve accounts (whether true or false) about 'how the world is', so much as accounts of who individuals are, how they 'fit' into the political world. Ideologies misrepresent subjects' *relations* to the world by representing a functional social role (as a worker or citizen, for instance) as something freely adopted by them. As a structuralist, Althusser argues that what is politically decisive is the structural places we each hold (as fathers or mothers in kinship structures, workers or financiers in the economic structures, and so on). The paradox is, however, that people will perform these roles only *if they think, in doing so, they are freely realising their subjective potential.* For Althusser, the autonomous individual is a result of ideological misrecognition.
- Ideologies are always embodied or institutionalised in 'state apparatuses', such as the media, schools, universities, corporations. This is why Althusser insists that ideology is 'material' in nature, not purely ideal or 'in people's heads'. If an ideology (for example, the neoliberal belief that market exchange is the 'natural' and 'best' way to organise social relations) is to stay in people's heads, it must first of all shape peoples' daily, lived material practices. Only in this way will this way of seeing themselves and the world seem 'natural' and unquestionable to them.

a matter of faith, but a question of obedience to the religious ceremony: 'Kneel down and pray, and you will believe.' Žižek suggests that Pascal's formula needs only a further distinctive twist – 'kneel down and pray, *and you will believe you knelt down because of your belief*' – to grasp the extent to which even subjects' deepest beliefs are shaped by the 'external' institutions and repeated practices of their daily lives (*SO* 12, 40).

Žižek also radicalises Althusser's emphasis on how ideologies lead people typically to misrecognise their functional roles in the sociopolitical and economic structures of their societies. Developing his analysis of the politics of cynical ideology, Žižek proposes that a new term, ideological *dis-identification,* should supplement Althusser's ideas of interpellation and identification. Since subjects must think they are free (not to obey) if they are to peacefully conform to authority, Žižek's idea is that political regimes must always, 'between the lines', allow subjects ideas and practices that allow them to 'dis-identify' with the regime, and entertain the belief that they are not *solely* political subjects (*CHU* 103; *ES* 186; *PF* 27).

Sometimes, Žižek talks about dis-identification in terms of the 'inherent transgressions' a political regime must allow its citizens, if it is to command their assent (*CHU* 218; *ME* 72; *PF* 29). Žižek here agrees with Michel Foucault's famous insight that political regimes can never succeed by being solely repressive, or only 'saying No'. They must also tacitly 'say Yes' to avenues and activities – such as humour, intoxicants, prostitution, clubs, bars, holidays and carnivals, sporting events and wars – wherein subjects are able to 'let off steam' and enjoy activities that are usually 'off limits', or not tolerated in public life. Žižek's Lacanian word for the type of libidinal investment at stake in these inherent transgressions that sustain our ideological dis-identification is 'enjoyment'. As we will see below, enjoyment – and subjects' beliefs about it – are decisive in Žižek's descriptive account of how regimes keep our lasting consent.

The cornerstone of Žižek's move beyond Althusser, however, lies in how Žižek brings insights to his revised account of ideological interpellation taken from the psychoanalytic account of subjectivity developed by Lacan. Situating Žižek in terms of our schema of what makes for a political philosophy, this account of subjectivity is Žižek's philosophical anthropology or account of human nature. On it will pivot all his accounts of what is politically possible or desirable.

ŽIŽEK BEYOND ALTHUSSER, WITH LACAN

In the Introduction to this book, we have already seen that Žižek argues that the split between the symbolic meaning of social ideals and the institutional ritual that sustains these social ideals is the key to understanding how the unconscious operates in political ideologies. Žižek gives a masterful elaboration of this basic insight in the central chapter of *The Sublime Object of Ideology* (*SO*, ch. 3). Žižek's position, as we see it, can be represented as follows:

Symbolic meaning = explicit terms of ideology: ideological misrecognition
Key terms: Ego Ideal = master signifier = social ideal

Institutional ritual = unconscious enjoyment
Key terms: unconscious fantasy = social/ideological fantasy = inherent transgression of the social ideal

Lacanian psychoanalysis argues, intriguingly, that a person's sense of identity – her ego – involves not one, but two components. On the one hand, there is what Lacan calls a person's 'ideal ego'. This is the way the person would like others to see her. It corresponds in Lacanian theory to the *imaginary* register of human experience. By this technical term, Lacan means, most broadly, that this level of our identity is at first modelled on loved others we perceive around us, whose behaviour we strive to mirror in order to win their love, and stabilise our sense of who we are. But then there is a person's 'Ego Ideal'. This component of the ego involves *symbolic* identification. The Symbolic is the register of language and culture, and symbolic identification means the internalisation of cultural norms through identification with figures of symbolic authority – paradigmatically, the parents. A person's Ego Ideal is the perspective from or in which she would like to be seen as the person she hopes to be.

We can grasp how central symbolic identification is to our self-identity by looking at Žižek's amusing vignette on 'Jean-Jacques judged by Rousseau'. The philosopher Jean-Jacques Rousseau actually felt that his ego was watched and judged by his father's name, and that he had to do something big to satisfy the expectations built into this highly idealised paternal image. 'Jean-Jacques judged by Rousseau', then, is just the man, Jean-Jacques Rousseau, but considered as the forename supervised by the surname. The forename designates the ideal ego, i(o) in the Lacanian 'algebra', whereas the surname denotes the Ego Ideal,

I(O), the moment of symbolic identification, the point of the supervisory gaze, 'the agency through which we observe and judge ourselves' (*SO* 108). Žižek explains that

> imaginary identification is identification with the image in which we appear likeable to ourselves, with the image representing 'what we would like to be', and symbolic identification is identification with the very place from where we are being observed, from where we look at ourselves so that we appear, to ourselves, as likeable, worthy of love. (*SO* 105)

In the Lacanian 'algebra', although the Ego Ideal is the result of symbolic identification, it is designated as the Imaginary Other, I(O), which means that it represents, for the subject, the ideal unity of the entire Symbolic Order, the point that makes the social order into a closed totality of meaning. Imaginary identification is subordinated to symbolic identification: 'imaginary identification is always identification on behalf of a certain gaze in the Other' (*SO* 106).

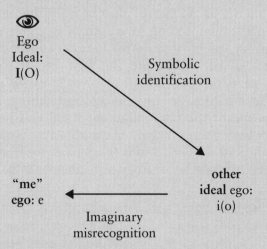

Figure 1.1 *Jean-Jacques (e) is trying to impress his deeply admired friend Denis Diderot (i(o)) with what a great philosopher he, Rousseau, is. But who does he think gazes lovingly on him when he does so? (Not poor old Diderot!)*

The key thing is that the Ego Ideal, as its name suggests, involves the dimension of what Freud terms 'idealisation' and Lacan the Symbolic Order. A person's Ego Ideal is less any real individual person than some idea or ideal with which the person deeply identifies. The Ego Ideal centres upon a 'master signifier', a point of symbolic identification that, in itself, is just a signifier, but one that, in the psychic economy of the subject, plays a special role: it is a signifier without a signified. It 'quilts the field' of a certain context, but it itself has no meaning. 'Rousseau', after all, 'the Rousseau family', is just a name, just a combination of sounds. By organising the entire family heritage, however, by lending some unity to the dispersed familial narrative, it seems to be saturated with meaning – especially for the subject, Jean-Jacques Rousseau. More precisely, what the family name does, for Rousseau, is to specify his place in society as a place of excellent achievements and the highest ideals. In other words, the Ego Ideal holds the place of the Symbolic Order in the psychic economy of the subject. It allocates the subject a position in society, a symbolic mandate with social authority that is defined as deriving from a socio-cultural totality: I(O).

The big Other, or Symbolic Order, meanwhile, the network of linguistically mediated socio-cultural rules, is beautifully illustrated by Žižek:

> During the last election campaign in Slovenia . . . a member of the ruling political party was approached by an elderly lady from his local constituency, asking him for help. She was convinced that the street number of her house (not the standard 13, but 23) was bringing her bad luck – the moment her house got this new number, due to some administrative reorganization, misfortunes started to afflict her (burglars broke in, a storm tore the roof off, neighbours started to annoy her), so she asked the candidate to be so kind as to arrange with the municipal authorities for the number to be changed. The candidate made a simple suggestion to the lady: why didn't she do it herself? Why didn't she simply replace or repaint the plate with the street number herself by, for example, adding another number or letter (say, 23A . . .)? The old lady answered: 'Oh, I tried that a few weeks ago . . . but it didn't work – my bad luck is still with me, you can't cheat it, it has to be done properly, with the relevant state institution.' The 'it' which cannot be duped in this way is the Lacanian big Other, the symbolic institution. (*TS* 326)

In Žižek's Lacanian terminology, the Ego Ideal involves a passionate attachment to a symbolic 'big Other' (with a capital O). It is worth emphasising that the Lacanian Other refers to the entire socio-cultural network of rules and customs. Although this is some-times personified in subjects' imaginations as a figure of symbolic authority (say, father or mother), the Other does not just mean another person.

Many of Žižek's most striking original political insights are appli-cations of this Lacanian psychoanalytic understanding of identity. In Žižek's Lacanese, the subject is 'decentred' because its most impor-tant, symbolic identifications are with external social ideals that are 'experienced as an order [the big Other] which is minimally reified, externalized' (RL 16). Žižek's most extended account of his view of the way that what subjects know, feel and desire is decentred comes in *Plague of Fantasies* (PF 106–22).

Knowledge, Desire and Affect as 'of the Other'

- *Knowledge.* Lacan emphasised how, if psychoanalysis is to work, the analysand must suppose that the analyst knows – or will be capable of knowing – the meaning of her symptoms, dreams and bungled actions. The transferential relationship, wherein the ana-lysand 'transfers' on to the analyst her expectations about how others see her, depends on this expectation of the analyst as an 'Other supposed to know'. The analyst is in this way effectively supposed, by the analysand, to be like an external bearer of her innermost knowledge. (This is one reason why Lacan gnomically calls the unconscious 'the discourse of the Other' in subjects.)

- *Affects, emotions.* Žižek maintains that our emotions are much more deeply structured by our perceptions of Other(s) than we imagine. The type of phenomenon he has in mind is captured in the observations that laughter and crying are somehow 'conta-gious'. Žižek's classic example is the so-called canned laughter in sitcoms, which seems really to have struck Žižek when he arrived in the West. Why do the producers put this laughter of some invisible Other(s) there, Žižek asks, if not to signal to us at home when we should laugh, or effectively to laugh for us, relieving us of the burden? 'Even when I watch a TV mini-series with canned laughter . . . even if I do not laugh, but simply stare at the screen, tired after a hard day's work, I nevertheless feel relieved after the show' (*PF* 109). Žižek calls the phenomenon in play here 'inter-passivity' (cf. Pfaller 2005). Žižek's claim is that an Other can effectively, passively, feel for us, in our place. Additional examples Žižek cites are 'weeper women', who ritually cry at funerals in some societies and the chorus in classical tragedies that again weep and moan for us (*PF* 109).

- *Desire.* For Lacan, famously, desire is the desire of the Other. The claim, like most of Lacan's key claims, condenses several different registers. At what he calls the 'Imaginary' level, wherein we shape our self-image by identifying with others, there are phenomena like fashion – wherein what people desire as 'hip' or 'cutting edge' is shaped by what everyone else is wearing, and hysterical desire, wherein subjects feel drawn only to 'taken (wo) men'. One step up into the Symbolic Order, we encounter the way what people desire is shaped by social expectations and conventions: I desire to be a doctor, because it is a prestigious position commanding respect, is well paid, and so on. Finally (at the level of what Žižek calls 'the Real'), Žižek and Lacan cite St Paul's famous declaration that 'without the Law, Sin falls dead' as anticipating the deepest psychoanalytic register of the idea that 'desire is desire of the Other'. 'Desire as the desire of the Other' in this sense refers to the evident, 'fatal attraction' people have towards what is prohibited, transgressive, transcendent, off limits, *because it is off limits*. Desire in this register is related to the Freudian death drive, in so far as its satisfaction always points the subject 'beyond Law' towards what we fantasise has been lost to us as civilised, 'castrated' subjects.

Having explained how individuals' conscious self-identity depends on a passionate attachment to the Other that is unconscious, Žižek advances to his second step in the argument. Here, he talks about the 'Real of enjoyment' and unconscious fantasy. As Žižek's 2001 title *On Belief* indicates, however, the most politically important factor in his account of the decentred subject of ideology is belief. As we shall see, Žižek's key notion of the ideological *fantasies* that undergird subjects' political commitments turns upon his notion that belief, too, is always belief in 'the Other'.

We have seen that, for Žižek, individual self-identity is decentred, because, although the subject may be aware of who they would like to be (their ideal ego), their symbolic identification, or Ego Ideal, is profoundly unconscious. As we stated, the Ego Ideal concerns not only symbolic authority – the social ideals that the subject identifies with – but it also holds the place, in the psychic economy, of the big Other. The Ego Ideal, on behalf of the big Other, allocates the subject a place in the socio-political totality, and it gives the subject a social mandate, a definite role to play in worldly affairs. For the subject, as the example from Slovenia shows, the big Other, the socio-political totality, functions as if it were personified – for instance, classic instances of the big Other are God and Fate. When the subject symbolically identifies with the figure of Jesus and engages in the institutional rituals of the Christian Church, this Ego Ideal holds the place, for the subject, of God, and it assigns the subject a place in the totality of Creation with a definite social mandate (as a believer supposed to 'love thy neighbour' and obey God's commandments).

Žižek proposes that the fundamentally unconscious component of this set of beliefs concerns what God finds satisfying about the conduct of the faithful – what God 'enjoys'. The problem is that, in the unconscious, what the big Other enjoys might be something that the subject would deny if this were presented to them as a conscious proposition. For instance, it might be the case that, for a believer, God enjoys the extermination of unbelievers. Equally, the subject unconsciously supposes that those with different Ego Ideals, with different social ideals, religious convictions and moral values, serve strange big Others, alien gods. The unconscious logic runs as follows. If God demands the extermination of the unbelievers, then these Others, these other gods, might well demand the annihilation of the believers in our, the true faith. The gods of the others seem to demand an obscene enjoyment that makes these others profoundly dangerous. This is, of course, a classic instance of what psychoanalysis calls 'projection', the attribution to another of one's own aggression, as a rationalisation for the anxiety that the presence of the other evokes. Žižek's argument, then, is that unconscious belief centres on beliefs about the 'enjoyment of the Other'. The word 'Other' here should be taken in the double sense: it is *our* big Other that we hold these unconscious beliefs about, but we always project these beliefs onto another's Other. When, for instance, non-Muslim Westerners begin speculating about the dangerous and fanatical beliefs of Muslims (that they think that suicidal terrorist attacks will earn them a bevy of virgins in Heaven as a reward for killing unbelievers, for instance), this tells us a lot about the unconscious beliefs held by the non-Muslim Westerners (see Chapter 6).

Ideological Fantasy: The Others Supposed to Believe and Enjoy

Žižek maintains that subjects' political identities and choices are based upon a set of fundamentally unconscious beliefs or – in Žižek's neologism – ideological fantasies. Žižek argues that humans' beliefs, like our desires and affects, are shaped to a far greater extent than we consciously recognise by our suppositions about *what others believe and enjoy.* This truth gives rise to much of the seeming irrationality of political behaviour, which Žižek thinks his Lacanian development of the critique of ideology can uniquely clarify. We can approach Žižek's position by reflecting upon a strange yet mundane observation. The vast majority of people of all political persuasions consider themselves to be fundamentally decent. Human beings overwhelmingly, if not universally, share a set of moral commitments: to their families, friends, local communities, and so on. Yet, for all the talk of our post-political age, people on the Left and Right continue to divide heatedly about issues such as immigration, national identity, abortion, and gay and minority rights. At the same time, as Žižek might remind us, outside the developed countries, over thirty civil wars rage in which people continue to show themselves as willing to suspend ordinary morality in the name of political commitment as they were in Homer's day. History's pages are drenched in the blood of the slain in political struggles, wars, civil wars, *coups d'état* and revolutions. What is Žižek's Lacanian position on this difference between politics and morality?

It is this, apparently paradoxical, hypothesis. Politics is such a uniquely passionate, divisive dimension of our social being, because people's competing ideas about what is just are centrally shaped by individuals' beliefs concerning Other(s), groups and people whom they may never have directly encountered. Let us explain why.

Consider how beliefs *per se*, as opposed to the things we know, concern ideas the truth about which we may have reasons for doubt: for example, the existence of God or an afterlife. If certainty was available about such things, belief would not be required. For this reason, a person's beliefs are among the most intimate and fragile parts of their individual identity. How, then, are people's beliefs formed and shaped? Žižek's answer is that, far more than we usually suspect, our beliefs are shaped by our supposition concerning what others believe. Where we cannot personally know, Žižek thinks we tend to 'outsource' our beliefs: according to the famous hysterical logic of 'I'll have what she's having'. An example to which Žižek returns is of people who believe in God 'through' their priests. The average believer does not know the deep theological meanings of the sacraments. But this is no problem: the Church provides a group of people, the priests, who *do* know the meaning of these things, and so can in this sense *believe for the ordinary believers*. The purest case of this (which Žižek takes from Hegel) is of ordinary church attendees in medieval Europe. The vast majority of these people could not have understood more than a few words of the Latin tongue in which the Church services were carried out.

These strange cases are not exceptions to the rule of how belief works, according to Žižek. He argues that most subjects, even in our enlightened modern societies, do not know what is 'signified' by the key terms of modern political ideologies: terms such as 'the nation', 'the people', 'the market', or 'the general will'. What politically matters is only that each individual supposes that *Other(s)*, or at least the political or group leaders, know the meaning of these terms and of the political Cause. The reader can perhaps then see how this Žižekian notion of 'belief as belief through the Other' sits with Žižek's idea that conscious cynicism about political authorities is fully consistent with political conformism: people mirror the behaviour of others, even if it would seem to go against their rational self interest.

In the light of this set of reflections on unconscious belief, it is not surprising that Žižek says that: 'Perhaps the most succinct definition of ideology was produced by Christopher Hitchens when he tackled the difficult question of what the North Koreans effectively think about their "beloved leader", King Yong II':

> 'mass delusion is the only thing that keeps the people sane'. This paradox points towards the fetishistic split at the heart of any functioning ideology: individuals transpose their belief onto the big Other (embodied in the collective) which thus believes in their place – individuals thus remain sane *qua* individuals, maintaining the distance towards the 'big Other' of the official discourse. (RL 16)

Žižek's hypothesis that we believe through the Other, when we subscribe to an ideology, and that this externalised belief shapes how we actually behave, is striking. But, as we have expounded it up to now, it says nothing about the logical or 'discursive' structures of ideologies we subscribe to. Nor does it speak to the issue of what might draw us to identify with them in the first place. Psychoanalysis's

When Cynicism Meets Belief of the Other

According to Žižek, today's predominant cynicism generates an over-whelming political conformism in the developed countries. His explanation involves this hypothesis concerning the decentred nature of our beliefs. How?

- Although *I* am not personally taken in by the ideological 'bullshit', I *believe through the Others, whom I suppose do truly believe*. These Others are the dupes; I keep my inner distance. The paradox is not simply that I act as if I did not keep such a distance. It is that *these others also maintain this position regarding me*. So, for them, *I* will figure as such an 'Other supposed to believe'. And so social conformism is maintained, even though privately, each person keeps their 'inner distance' (*PF* 107; RL 7; *SO* 185–6).
- This is why Žižek is so attracted to the strange fairy tale of the emperor with no clothes: so long as no one states the obvious, things continue working fine. Stalinist Communism, according to Žižek, was a living exemplification of such a peculiar, functional political regime.
- In a typically incisive critique, Žižek, for instance, argues that the standard liberal critique of neoconservative political philosopher Leo Strauss – of not believing in the religious creeds Strauss recommends as necessary for others – misses the mark. Strauss, despite his conscious distance to the great monotheisms, *believed through the vulgar Others whom he supposed needed to believe* (*IBK* 166–71). This is why his political position defends orthodoxy against the openness of liberal society, every bit as strongly as if he was a 'true believer'.

promise to political theory has always involved its claim to deeper insight into the motives for people behaving as they do. Why do subjects 'enjoy their nation as if it were themselves', to invoke the title of one of Žižek's best pieces? Žižek's answer involves his central theoretical notion of ideological fantasies, and sublime objects of ideology.

Žižek addresses these issues most powerfully in an analysis 'close to home' for him, one that is already deservedly famous. It concerns the relationship between the 'chauvinistic nationalisms' – Serb,

Croat, Slovenian, Albanian – that emerged after 1989 in the former Yugoslavia, to fuel the war of the 1990s. According to Žižek, all ideologies turn around certain 'sublime objects' of subjects' belief. These are objects named by what Žižek calls the 'master signifiers' of a particular regime, master signifiers like 'the American people', 'the Soviet Cause', 'freedom', 'the Serbian/Croatian/Albanian nation'. The sublime objects referred to by these master signifiers are of a different kind from the types of objects you might physically meet or bump your head against. When Žižek dubs them sublime, the first thing he means is that these objects are at once more elusive but also more *elevated* in subjects' minds. They are thus transfigured because they are the central elements in what Žižek calls ideological fantasy: the powerful, founding set of beliefs about Our Regime that any political system aims to generate in subjects. It would be unusual if someone *could* say exactly what 'the American people' was, or what 'our way of life' was really all about, as readily as they might describe some object in the palm of their hand (*TN* 125–6). The closest a person might get to accurately describing some sublime ideological object, like 'the Slovenian Nation', would be to invoke certain, emotionally charged experiences: the Olympic victory of a sporting hero, the moment of national succession from Yugoslavia, or a national celebration. Here again Žižek's political materialism is in play. People *enjoy* their ideological commitments in such 'ineffable' moments – and this is a visceral, passionate Thing. 'You had to be there' is something a political subject often says to an uncomprehending outsider.

But here again (it will not surprise you!) a final paradox beckons. On the one hand, in ideological fantasy, political groups' sublime object(s) of ideology are celebrated as inalienable to them – Our Thing essentially, or Our Essence objectified. On the other hand, however, ideological fantasy typically positions these sublime objects of ideology as under threat from the outside, as if they were only *too* alienable. Ideologies do not simply shape the commitments of loyal subjects, and their internal solidarity to the group or regime. Ideologies also shape groups' sense of their relations to others, outside the group. Žižek's central idea here is that ideologies do this by constructing fantasies of Others supposed to enjoy the hardships 'we' experience, whom we take to have access to the enjoyment we have forgone.

Here is a passage where Žižek illustrates his meaning by reflecting on the Balkan conflict of the 1990s:

The late Yugoslavia offers a case study . . . in which we witness a detailed network of 'decantations' and 'thefts' of enjoyment. Each nationality has built its own mythology narrating how other nations deprive it of the vital part of enjoyment and possession of that which would allow it to love fully . . . Slovenes are being deprived of their enjoyment by 'Southerners' (Serbians, Bosnians) because of their proverbial laziness, Balkan corruption, dirty and noisy enjoyment, and because they demand bottomless economic support, stealing from Slovenes their precious accumulation by means of which Slovenia could already have caught up with Western Europe. The Slovenes themselves, on the other hand, are supposed to rob Serbs because of their unnatural diligence, stiffness and selfish calculation; instead of yielding to simple life pleasures, Slovenes perversely enjoy constantly devising means of depriving Serbs of the results of their hard labour, by commercial profiteering, by reselling what they bought cheaply in Serbia. Slovenes are afraid that Serbs will 'inundate' them, and that they will thus lose their national identity. Serbs reproach Slovenes with their 'separatism', which means simply that Slovenes are not prepared to recognise themselves as a sub-species of Serb. (*TN* 204)

The Other Supposed to Thieve our Enjoyment

While Žižek first developed his analysis with reference to the East European example, the scope of his idea concerning Others supposed in ideological fantasy to be thieving Our Enjoyment is much wider, as a critique of how ideologies work in general.

- For today's predominant neoliberalism, for instance, the welfare 'bludgers' and 'moms' are the Others supposed to enjoy illicitly.
- By contrast, for what remains of the Left, capitalism *per se* is predicated on the extraction of surplus value at the extent of objectifying, commodifying and exploiting honest workers' capacities.
- In the war on terror, the Muslim fundamentalists are the 'Other supposed to enjoy': consider the fascination with the idea that the 9/11 hijackers were moved by the thought of a sexual paradise in which each would get access to virgins in the afterlife, and so on.

People's beliefs concerning enjoyment, Žižek argues – the only 'substance' Lacanian psychoanalysis recognises (*SO* 72) – is a political factor of the first importance, if we are to understand how they believe and act. Yet political theory hitherto has largely overlooked or misunderstood it.

The 'formula' Žižek borrows from Lacan's account of the individual fantasies shaping peoples' neuroses to formalise our collective ideological fantasies concerning enjoyment of/and the Other is:

$$\$ \lozenge (a)$$

The $\$$ here stands for political subjects, united by their identification with a sublime object of ideology, (a). Between the $\$$ and the (a) stands the 'losange' $(\lozenge)$, which indicates a relation of mutual exclusion: the subject 'fades', is eclipsed, should they come too close to this fantasy object, should they 'get what they really want'. In the background, then, we all unconsciously imagine some Other(s) devoted to thieving this sublime object of ideology from us, enjoying our hardships. To repeat, Žižek's supposition is that, because an individual's symbolic Ego Ideal is shaped by his identification with the social Other, it is legitimate to speak in this psychoanalytic way of 'ideological fantasies'.

We will also be reflecting on the prescriptive implications of Žižek's conception of ideology and ideological fantasy as we proceed. There is a certain descriptive proximity of Žižek's theory to conservative authors in the history of political philosophy, from Burke to De Bonald and De Maistre, who also stressed the extent to which the aesthetic and irrational components of human experience is politically decisive. This shows that, from the start, Žižek could have 'gone either way' politically – towards the pessimistic ideas that inform Žižek's most recent revolutionary vanguardism; or in the radical-democratic direction Žižek initially followed. This direction, as we will now see, was shaped by his earlier commitments to Kant and Hegel, and his brilliant rereading of their work through a Lacanian lens. The key move was to argue that the enjoyment ideologies tell us has been thieved or lost by the Other(s) supposed to enjoy *was always already lost*: or, in Hegel's phrase, 'it only came to be in being lost'.

And so we return here to the first of Žižek's insights examined in this chapter: the Enlightenment commitment to take on expanded responsibility for phenomena we are tempted to posit as beyond our control, irrational and unaccountable. To critique an ideology on this model is like 'traversing the fantasy' in clinical psychoanalysis. Although politics and the psyche are *not* the same, they are linked by the ideologies that form personal and public subjectivities. Žižek's critique of ideology directs us to see that, whatever the objective wrongs Other(s) may have dealt us, we have responsibility for how we have symbolised or 'come to terms' with our fate. Our ethical task, the ethical task of psychoanalysis and of ideology critique for the radical democratic Žižek, is to aspire to deal with Others in a way that is not shaped by fantasies about their theft of our enjoyment (SO 124–8). The ground of this ethics is what we will see next, Žižek's Lacanian reconstruction of German Idealism's theory of the subject. So this is what we turn to now.

Chapter 2

Retrieving the Subject: Žižek's Theoretical Politics

Introduction: Žižek's Ticklish Subject

The opening of *The Ticklish Subject* (1999) is vintage Žižek:

> A spectre is haunting Western academia . . . the spectre of the Cartesian subject. All academic powers have entered into a holy alliance to exorcise this spectre: the New Age obscurantist (who wants to supersede the 'Cartesian paradigm' towards a new holistic approach) and the post-modern deconstructionist (for whom the Cartesian subject is a discursive fiction, an effect of decentered textual mechanisms); the Habermasian theorist of communication (who insists on a shift from Cartesian method-ological subjectivity to discursive intersubjectivity) and the Heideggerian proponent of the thought of Being (who stresses the need to 'traverse' the horizon of modern subjectivity culminating in current raging nihilism); the cognitive scientist (who endeavors to prove empirically that there is no unique sense of Self, just a pandemonium of competing forces) and the Deep Ecologist (who blames Cartesian mechanist materialism for providing the philosophical foundation for the ruthless exploitation of nature); the critical (post-)Marxist (who insists that the illusory freedom of the bourgeois subject is rooted in class division); and the feminist (who emphasizes that the allegedly sexless cogito is in fact a male patriarchal formation). Where is the academic orientation that has not been accused by its opponents of not yet properly disowning the Cartesian heritage? And which has not hurled back the branding reproach of Cartesian subjectivity against its more 'radical' critics, as well as its 'reactionary' adversaries? (*TS* 1)

There is a lot here. First, Žižek is paraphrasing the famous opening challenge of Marx and Engels' *Communist Manifesto*, underlining his Marxian credentials (see Chapter 1): as he puts it, 'keeping open' a heritage that, since 1989, has virtually disappeared from the universe of intellectual and political respectability (*IDLC* 4–9).

Secondly, Žižek's remarkable intellectual gifts are on display. In particular, there is his capacity to condense into one or two passages more conceptual content than other authors struggle to (re)produce in entire chapters. Part of the charm of reading Žižek is such passages.

They demonstrate a remarkable taxonomical *élan*, backed by Žižek's considerable philosophical learning. It is possible to feel at times that you have suddenly gained a clear perspective on an entire field that might otherwise have taken weeks, months or years to master.

The third thing the opening of *The Ticklish Subject* shows is Žižek's remarkable appeal to new students. Žižek's philosophical rhetoric, and, as such, what can be called his 'theoretical politics', are on display. Žižek presents his work as a kind of 'minority report' on the contemporary theoretical world. There is a romance to this self-presentation. Žižek is the East European, straight-talking outsider who can say things forbidden to other perspectives, and who can perceive the commonalities between staid opponents in the oft-closed universe of Western academic theory. A comparison here with the progenitors of the 'hermeneutics of suspicion', Karl Marx, Friedrich Nietzsche and Sigmund Freud, suggests itself, or even with Niccolò Machiavelli, whose scandalous frankness continues to captivate readers to this day.

We saw in Chapter 1 the importance in Žižek's theory of ideology of Lacan's notion of the Other(s) supposed to know, in shaping subjects' desires and political commitments. Reading Žižek's work, though, it is tempting to coin another notion: the 'Other supposed *not* to know'. For it is hardly an exaggeration to say that all Žižek's work is set up in polemical rivalry with a set of Others supposed to be ignorant. For Žižek, the Others in question represent a 'PC [politically correct] multiculturalist' or 'postmodern deconstructionist' consensus. Its theoretical champions are the great French 'post-structuralists': Jacques Derrida, Michel Foucault, Gilles Deleuze and Emmanuel Levinas. To be fair, when he attacks 'PC multiculturalism', most often he is not critiquing any one of these figures, so much as a kind of dominant or 'hegemonic' vulgate derived from these thinkers' works in Anglo-American cultural studies and continental philosophy. The key *doxa*, or set of unquestioned assumptions, of this consensus that Žižek opposes are these.

- That the modern Enlightenment associated with philosophers such as Descartes, Kant and Hegel, with its hopes that scientific and rational progress could build more peaceable and humane societies, has failed. According to the dominant perspective, the Enlightenment's founding assumptions – first among them being the sovereignty of the 'Cartesian subject' – are directly implicated in the great atrocities of the twentieth century, including Nazism and the holocaust, Stalinism and the gulags.

- That Enlightenment thought and modern science are not the product of an 'enlightened' break with pre-modern, mythical or religious ways of thinking, as its champions argue. The modern enlighteners and scientists are supposedly the last, consummate representatives of a much deeper set of Western prejudices. For Žižek, as we saw in the quotation above, whether this prejudice is figured as a 'logocentric' desire to comprehend the totality, or a more apparently 'political' critique of the Enlightenment, is only a question of theoretical preference.

- That, as a consequence, everybody must observe the prohibition on thought (*Denkenverbot*) against any radical political agency, against which we saw Žižek protest in Chapter 1. The positive side of this new reformism or conservatism is praise of local, minoritarian, strategic, reformist political movements. Grand political projects to build a better society are out of the question. What is needed for a renewed Left is a 'rainbow' alliance of a plurality of social movements that respond to the multiple injustices visited on racial, gender and sexual minorities, as well as socioeconomic inequalities.

From the opening pages of *The Sublime Object of Ideology*, Žižek has challenged all these dominant academic opinions. Importantly, however, there is a serious philosophical position behind the polemics. Žižek argues that his position turns on a defence of the Cartesian subject, and is a continuation of the modern Enlightenment, despite its myriad critics. Recalling Žižek's critique of ideology can help us from the start to see why.

Žižek's critique of ideology starts from the position that Žižek's master, Jacques Lacan, rightly identified with the eighteenth-century Enlightenment thinkers such as Rousseau and Voltaire. This is the creation of a 'state of knowledge that is not a homage to power' (Lacan 1971: I. 12). The aim of Enlightenment thought is to free the subject from that pseudo-knowledge, which merely serves the interests of the powerful, and to enlighten the subject as to its real interests. The ambition of the Enlightenment radicals was a society composed of individuals who obeyed only those governments and laws in accord with their free exercise of reason. Unsurprisingly, the Enlightenment thinkers, like Žižek, were political radicals in their day – although postmodern thought very often forgets this.

Žižek's Lacanian critique of ideology identifies the webs of unconscious beliefs concerning the Other(s) and their enjoyment, beliefs that bind subjects to political regimes. That is, Žižek extends the Enlightenment critique of ideology by exposing the unconscious ways that the subject can remain hostage to the unjust rule of powerful others, even in the 'enlightened' age (*SO* 79–80). The subject supposes that the Other guarantees the social order and assigns the subject a social identity. So, even when subjects resist power, they fear shaking this Other too totally, lest they lose the bases for their own identity. Žižek tells us how subjects, instead of exercising free and rational agency, more often invest their most passionate, pre-reflective energies in propping up the same unjust social order that the ideology protects.

Put differently, Žižek's critique of ideology aims at overcoming heteronomy. It shows why, once subjects have peeled away or 'traversed' the layers of ideological fantasy, they must be brought to understand that the Other, which subjects suppose guarantees the order and justice of their political regimes, 'does not exist' (*FTKN* 152–6; *SO* 114–24; *TN* 231–7). This means that a political regime is never a fully self-consistent, independent whole, into which people are born but about which they can do nothing. In the radical democratic Žižek (1989–*c*.1995), the political ideal that animates Žižek's work is the modern notion of autonomy: rational self-determination by self-legislating individuals, in opposition to our dependent, heteronomous subjection to the socio-political Other.

The opening of *The Ticklish Subject*, with which we began this chapter, declares the philosophical basis of this Enlightenment position. This lies in Žižek's rehabilitation of the modern, 'Cartesian' subject. This notion of the subject was inaugurated by René Descartes's famous argument that 'I think, therefore I am' (*cogito ergo sum*) was the one idea of which he could be absolutely certain. Descartes intended to reconstruct philosophy on this basis – doing away with reliance on superstition, tradition, common sense and the dogmas of the powerful. For the post-structuralists, however, following the right-wing German philosophers Friedrich Nietzsche and Martin Heidegger, the Cartesian subject or *cogito* is the most problematic of all modern ideas. Its deeply unethical core is evident in Descartes's arrogant claim that his philosophical revolution would make moderns 'masters and possessors of nature'. For the post-structuralists, the modern subject represents the most complete embodiment of the Western, patriarchal dream of a fully transparent, masterful Self. The self-assertion of this modern subject accordingly leads to modern humanity's violent rejection of its own shaping historical, material, social, embodied and gendered preconditions. In this way, the post-structuralists maintain, the modern subject stands beneath modern technological manipulation and destruction of the natural world, and modern totalitarian regimes' ruthless suppression of their political opponents.

Žižek, by contrast, argues that modern philosophy's central notion of the Cartesian subject represents a real break with the West's previous philosophical and religious heritages. Moreover, it is necessary politically, as the basis for us to conceive ways of over-coming the multiple ways political domination works, which post-structuralist theory ably identifies. In terms of the parameters shaping political philosophies that we established in our Introduction, then, we can say that Žižek's philosophy of the 'ticklish subject' has the pivotal place in his thought that philosophical anthropologies (visions of the human condition) had in older political philosophies. The way Žižek understands the Cartesian subject frames what Žižek can think is politically desirable, and informs his views concerning the possible ways these political ideals can be achieved.

The problem according to Žižek is that the modern subject as theorised by Descartes, and then by the great 'German Idealist' phi-losophers Immanuel Kant and Georg Wilhelm Hegel, is nearly as universally misunderstood as it has been reviled. Against the reign-ing theoretical consensus, Žižek contends that the Cartesian subject has a forgotten 'unacknowledged kernel' (*TS* 2). This is one that anticipates the psychoanalytic discovery of the unconscious, and that Žižek accordingly claims his Lacanian perspective allows him to dis-close or uncover. So in this chapter we will explicate this vital philo-sophical core of Žižek's politics: his Lacanian-'Cartesian' account of the subject. But, in order to do this, we will start by looking in more detail at Žižek's powerful criticisms of the leading post-structuralist authorities in the theoretical academy *c*.1985–90, ascending from these brilliant critical engagements to his rereading of Descartes, Kant and Hegel in the middle and later sections of the chapter.

Žižek's Criticism of 'Post-Structuralism'

Žižek advances many criticisms of different political and theoretical aspects of the leading post-structuralist theorists' ideas throughout his career. Nevertheless, it is possible to say that Žižek's criticism of the post-structuralist authorities his work challenges so powerfully has four elements.

1. Philosophically, the post-structuralists' critique of modern philosophy simply misunderstands the notion of the subject developed by Descartes, Kant and Hegel. Specifically, the post-structuralists make the mistake of identifying the ego with the subject, thus overlooking the unconscious.
2. In fact, the notion of the subject developed by Kant, Hegel and later by Lacan not only avoids the barbs of the post-structuralist critiques. It also anticipates the key critical points Foucault, Derrida and others make against Western philosophy in their defence of difference.
3. The post-structuralists misrecognise, and therefore cannot explain, their own 'position of enunciation'. This means, in non-technical terms, the position from where they speak – their own commitments – and make their criticisms of the modern subject and modernity.
4. Politically, the post-structuralists' emphasis on difference, others and otherness, becoming or change, minorities and 'minoritarian' or pluralist approaches to politics is not intrinsically politically progressive or even subversive. It reflects the cultural logic of late capitalist consumerism (see Chapter 3).

Taken together, (1)–(3) represent a devastating philosophical attack on the post-structuralist orthodoxy that dominated much of Anglo-American Theory before Žižek's emergence. If Žižek is right, the leading theoretical lights of Anglo-American cultural studies and continental philosophy c.1989 misunderstand the modern philosophical lineage they claim decisively to refute. They have been tilting at windmills, tearing down a straw man. More than this, in a wonderful irony, the philosophy of the subject developed by the German idealists would enable us to understand how the post-structuralists also misunderstood their *own* positions.

Let us now look at Žižek's arguments in detail.

Forgiving Foucault: From the Other to the Subject

Michel Foucault's work has played a key role in recent debates in political theory, historical sociology, cultural studies and queer theory – the list goes on. Žižek's engagement with him is as such very important in marking his difference from other contemporary Theorists.

Foucault, Genealogy, Political Theory

- Foucault's genealogical works criticise the way previous political philosophies had understood power (Foucault 1979, 1990).
  Political philosophers since Plato treat power as a kind of quality or
  substance a person or people can possess and then exercise on
  other people. So, from the Greek classics onwards, philosophers
  distinguish the different political regimes principally by recourse
  to the question of who and how many people possess sovereign
  power (*krasia*): one (as in monarchies and tyrannies), a few (as in
  aristocracies and plutocracies) or many (as in democracies).
- By contrast, Foucault argues that political theorists' focus on 'sovereign power' misses the multiple ways people are subjected to
  political discipline and control in their daily lives.
- Foucault contends that power is exercised in the ways that institutional routines shape subjects' identities and forms of knowledge.
  This extends from the way hospitals, asylums and prisons are
  built so that their inhabitants can be under constant surveillance,
  to the way we are encouraged by the modern 'human sciences' to
  think about our bodies, our individual biographies and our sexuality, and to the series of minute or 'micro' exercises that regiment
  children from a young age in educational institutions.
- Foucault stresses that power, viewed in this neo-Nietzschean
  way, is not simply negative or repressive, prohibiting people's
  behaviours. Power is productive, Foucault argues: it shapes
  people's behaviours and sense(s) of identity from the ground
  up, rather than being imposed on them from the outside. Indeed,
  Foucault at times argued that power even produces its own resistances, so extensive is its hold in later modern societies.

So what does Žižek say concerning Foucault's remarkable
Nietzschean intervention in political theory?

First, Žižek questions the sufficiency of Foucault's emphasis on
uncovering the 'micro' or 'capillary' ways that subjects are disciplined and oriented by power in their everyday lives. Žižek does not
challenge that Foucault's famous analyses expand our sense of how
power works. Foucault's analyses of the many minute ways that
people's bodies and behaviours are shaped and disciplined in hospitals, schools, prisons, and so on readily complements Žižek's own

materialist emphasis on the way that people's beliefs are generated by their repetitive material practices (Chapter 1). More than this, Foucault's emphasis on how power *produces* individuals' sense(s) of identity reflects Žižek's emphasis on how deeply ideologies shape people's political selves. It is comparable to Žižek's psychoanalytic idea that power is never simply negative, since ideologies work by permitting or even prescribing 'inherent transgressions' to subjects.

However, Žižek thinks that the Foucauldian emphasis on uncovering the 'decentred,' plural or capillary operations of power in society misses something. This is the dimension that Žižek's psychoanalytic approach to ideology unearths – namely, how people *perceive* (or misperceive) the operations of power upon them, and how this (mis) perception is necessary if they are to be politically 'disciplined and surveilled'. On this issue, Žižek's approach is much closer to traditional political philosophy than Foucault's. Žižek might concede that multiple political forces can act to shape people's political identities and beliefs. The point for him is that individuals each nevertheless tend to *(mis)perceive* the political regime they live in as 'a single, reified Other' (the I(O) of the mathemes): 'the social system', 'the human condition', 'what everyone thinks', and so on (RL 16)

Žižek also challenges the crucial corollary to Foucault's emphasis on the multiple, decentred operations of power, in the way we think about political agency: who and how people can act to change the regimes in which they live. Foucault famously argued that, when we correctly understand modern, disciplinary power, we will see that 'the subject we are invited to free' by the Enlightenment is constituted, or wholly shaped, by the very same plural, micro-operations of power we aim to 'release' her from (Foucault 1979: 30). Žižek is not the only critic to note that this position can lead to a pessimistic conclusion. If power shapes even its own 'resistances', as Foucault sometimes claimed, it is difficult to see that there is much space for independent political actions or agents. To deny any independence to subjectivity is to pose a real question as to what agency we can look to, to resist or transform unjust regimes. It is to arrive at a pessimistic determinism.

The more positive reading of Foucault, taken up by many in the New Left, aligns his view with contemporary celebrations of the 'decentred,' plural postmodern subject, in the world of the new media and the Internet. Foucault also argues that moderns are each exposed to multiple discourses, capillary powers and modes of 'subjectivation'. Hence, we should rid ourselves of any nostalgia for a single, unified identity:

In 'post-structuralism', the subject is usually reduced to so-called subjectivisation; he is conceived as an effect of a fundamentally non-subjective process; the subject is always caught in, traversed by pre-subjective processes [for instance, Foucauldian power, but in other theorists, the play of language] . . . and the emphasis is on the individuals' different ways of 'experiencing', 'living' their positions as 'subjects', 'actors', 'agents' of the historical process . . . The great master of such analyses was, of course, Foucault . . . (SO 189–90)

And here we can see why Žižek's critique of post-structuralism was so exciting at the end of two decades of sometimes uncritical reception of Foucault and Derrida in the English-speaking world. Žižek does not deny the post-structuralist claim that our personal identities are very largely 'socially constructed'. Žižek also accepts the Foucauldian claim that social identity is determined by multiple social influences. For each of us, our ego or 'self-image' truly is constructed out of many 'different partial identifications,' as we travel through life (TS 330). Žižek, however, denies that these true observations undermine the notion of modern subjectivity, as this was developed by Descartes, Kant, then Hegel.

The key point that Žižek rejects is that, as *subjects*, as opposed to egos, or 'selves,' we are *wholly* socially constructed. We can imagine the multiple partial identifications that make up a person's self as like the layers of an onion. The 'Cartesian subject' in this image, by contrast to any one of these layers, is like the void or 'nothing' in the middle, Žižek contends (PF 140–1). It underlies all these different contents. It is not identical with, or 'reducible to', any one or more of them. So, Žižek says, when we talk about the 'decentred subject' or 'multiple subject positions' within post-structuralist theory, this

does not mean there are simply more Egos/Selves in the same individual, as in MUDs [multi-user domains]. The 'decentrement' is the decentrement of the [Cartesian subject] (the void of the subject) with regard to its content ('Self', the bundle of imaginary and/or symbolic identifications) . . . The subject is 'split' even if there is only one unified 'Self', since this split is the very split between [the Cartesian subject] and Self . . . (PF 141).

The Subject versus the Ego/Self

The Subject: $	The Self or Ego
(Empty, non-substantial: the subject is the only vanishngly present 'I' of the act of speaking, distinct from the Ego)	(Substantial. Imaginary or Symbolic identity – the 'me' – composed of identifications with significant others)

The key thing for the moment is that Žižek, on the basis of a distinction between the subject and the Self or Ego that we will develop further below, claims that Foucauldian-style attacks on the modern subject are misdirected. Žižek's subject is far from being a substantial individual, Ego or Self that seeks to be the 'master and possessor' of everything that resists its identity. In fact, it *itself* resists such 'subjectivisation'. The ironic result is that many of the post-structuralist 'critiques of the philosophy of the subject' in fact end by actually (mis)recognising what Žižek thinks this subject is. The irony is that they do so under the names of what supposedly radically resists modern philosophy: Otherness, the Other, difference, *différance*, resistance, the virtual and so on. In short, Žižek's

> answer to the question asked (and answered in a negative way) by such different philosophers as Althusser and Derrida – 'can the gap, the opening, the void which precedes the gesture of subjectivization, still be called "subject"' – is an emphatic 'Yes!' – . . . the subject prior to subjectivization is not some idealist pseudo-Cartesian self-presence preceding material interpellatory practices and apparatuses, but the very gap in the structure that the imaginary (mis)recognition of the interpellatory Call endeavours to fill. (*CHU* 119)

We will take the next step in our ascent towards Žižek's reclaiming of the Cartesian subject from post-structuralism by examining what he has to say about another theoretical doyen of the 1990s, Jacques Derrida.

ŽIŽEK'S DERRIDA: TRANSCENDENTAL SIGNIFIEDS OR SUBLIME OBJECTS OF IDEOLOGY?

Jacques Derrida emerged in the late 1960s with a series of crucial works establishing the (anti-)philosophical tenets of 'deconstruction'. Žižek has consistently critiqued Derrida's work, and way of reading modern philosophy.

The first thing Žižek alleges concerning Derrida's remarkable reading of Western ideas is that Derrida misunderstands his own 'position of enunciation'. Deconstruction, like Foucauldian genealogy, presents itself as a subversive, highly risky, avant-garde operation. It challenges philosophers' pretension to establish a pure theoretical 'metalanguage' able to comprehend everything under the sun. However, Žižek notes, one always knows with deconstructionist texts who the bad guy is (logocentrism, traditional philosophy) and the types of move the post-structuralist will make against it:

Derrida: Deconstruction and the Critique of Western 'Logocentrism'

- Deconstruction is based on a grand critique of Western philosophy, from Plato through to NATO. For Derrida, philosophers have tried to combat this possibility of meaning being 'disseminated' beyond their control by constructing philosophical systems. These systems aim to lay out closed, stable systems of meaning, which make everything transparent to the mind of the philosopher, just as if she were talking to herself.
- At the base of each philosophical system, Derrida claims, there is always a founding 'transcendental signified': a central concept, like 'the Ideas' of Plato, or 'God' in the medievals (Derrida 1976, 1982). This stands above and gives everything else its place and meaning. For Derrida, the modern subject inaugurated by Descartes's *cogito sum* is the latest (and in many ways the most notorious) example of such a transcendental signified.
- Derrida's key claim is that the 'logocentric' dream of Western philosophers runs at right angles to a true understanding of the nature of language. The meaning of signifiers in any language is 'differentially constituted', an idea crucial to Derrida's famed notion of *différance* (with an 'a'). Every particular word or concept signifies only by virtue of its place in the language's structure (like so many pieces of a puzzle), which is determined by its differences from all the others. The key Derridean caveat is that, because language is an open order, the arrival of a full and complete meaning is endlessly deferred.
- In this light, Derrida disputes all philosophers' attempt to elevate particular signifieds (the Ideas, God . . .) to a transcendental status as the false attempt to treat these signifieds as if they were *not* differentially constituted. For this reason, Derrida's deconstructive texts show how philosophers' systems cannot and do not succeed in elevating transcendental signifieds above the differential play of linguistic signifiers. Deconstructive texts are hence typically more poetic than traditional philosophers', open to the play and slippage of meaning that language's differential nature allows.

The whole effort to evade the purely theoretical form of exposing our ideas and to adopt rhetorical devices usually preserved for literature masks the annoying fact that at the root of what the post-structuralists are saying there is a clearly defined theoretical position, which can be articulated without difficulty as a pure and simple metalanguage . . . to put it bluntly, the position from which the post-structuralist can always make sure of the fact that 'there is no metalanguage' . . . is the position of metalanguage at its purest. (SO 154–5)

The deeper basis of this Žižekian claim that deconstruction's way of reading 'runs a little too smoothly' concerns Žižek's Lacanian adaptation of structuralist linguistics. As with his critique of Foucault, Žižek effectively agrees with Derrida's post-structuralist critique of transcendental signifieds. We saw in Chapter 1 how Žižek also directs our attention to concepts such as God, the Nation, the People, and so on, which allegedly stand out from the ordinary run of other concepts. Žižek calls the things that such concepts name 'sublime objects of ideology'. The 'signifiers' that name them, words like 'God' – or, to use a modern example, 'the Party' – are what Žižek terms 'master signifiers': in his Lacanian notation, S_1. Derrida's position is that the sublime appearance of self-presence, certainty and splendour that an idea like God connotes for believers conceals how this concept, 'God', cannot truly be self-sufficient. To understand 'God', Derrida argues, we must use other signifiers and concepts – despite the dreams of mystics to attain unmediated access to the Godhead.

Žižek again is very close to this Derridean notion when he argues that the master signifiers of political and theoretical ideologies are in truth 'empty signifiers'. Of course, from the perspective of a true believer, God or the People are Ideas full of extraordinary meaning, so sublime they cannot even be put into ordinary words. In Lacanian terms, these words intimate for political subjects the enjoyment ordinarily off limits to speaking, civilised subjects. Žižek designates this sublime 'stuff', this enjoyment, with the Lacanian notation (a), for the famous Lacanian 'object petit a', the object-cause of desire.

Ideological illusion: how master signifiers appear to interpellated subjects

S_1	master signifier (e.g. 'Australia')
(a)	sublime signified: the enjoyment at the core of our way of life (e.g. 'Australianness')

In the diagram, word and meaning, master signifier and sublime signified, are represented as divided from one another by what Lacan calls the 'bar resisting signification'. Lacan's insight into the operation of language in the unconscious is very similar to Derrida's *différance*: the final signification, the ultimate signified of the master signifier, S_1, is permanently deferred and thus 'barred' from consciousness. But in the unconscious, the sublime object of this master signifier, the enjoyment signified, forms an ultimate horizon of meaning or transcendental signified of the master signifier, the object (*a*).

Žižek's critique of ideology – and his theory of language – like Derridean deconstruction, shows that this sense of 'transcendental signification' or sublime meaning, which attaches to master signifiers, is a lure. No person by himself knows the content of 'our' master signifiers: 'Australian-ness', and so on. This is why subjects' beliefs concerning the beliefs of the Other are so important for Žižek. The devil is in the detail of why Žižek argues that the master signifiers are 'empty signifiers'. Where Žižek differs from Derrida is that what this lure conceals is not the infinite slippage of *différance*. It is nothing other than the dreaded Cartesian subject, for Derrida the transcendental signified *per excellence*.

How Master Signifiers 'Represent the Subject for Other Signifiers'

Žižek's key argument, in contrast to that of Derrida, involves the Lacanian assertion that the master signifiers (S_1), in truth, represent the (Cartesian) subject ($\$$) for all the other signifiers (in his Lacanian notation: S_2). So the Cartesian subject, not the infinite dissemination of signifiers, which supposedly undermines it for ever, is what the sublime appearance of Derrida's 'transcendental signifieds' conceals.

- At a first level, Žižek holds, master signifiers 'represent the subject' in so far as they are the key words with which we identify politically. A communist, for example, will identify with master signifiers such as 'the people' or 'the dictatorship of the proletariat'. These words 'represent' his political beliefs.
- But why does this signifier, 'the people,' represent the subject, not for other subjects, but *for the other signifiers?* Well, here Žižek

- draws on work by Ernesto Laclau and Chantal Mouffe (Laclau and Mouffe, 1985). When a communist attests belief in 'the people,' this signifier will affect how they interpret a whole host of other, politically ambiguous signifiers. So: 'freedom' might mean 'freedom from the chaotic sway of inhuman market forces'; 'democracy' might mean 'people's control of Soviets'; 'equality' might mean 'the equal distribution of social wealth, beyond the formal legal fictions of the liberal world,' and so on.
- The key thing is how, by contrast, a liberal's identification with a signifier like 'liberty' will mean that each of these other signifiers will have quite different meanings: 'freedom' will mean primarily 'freedom to trade'; 'democracy' 'the right to vote in representative elections';, or, in neoliberalism, 'the right to invest money freely'; 'equality' will signify 'the formal equality of all to trade and own property, protected by the rule of law', and so on.

Seeing what Žižek borrows in his early texts from post-Marxists Laclau and Mouffe allows us to approach the second, more difficult idea captured in his difficult Lacanian formula: 'master signifiers represent the subject for other signifiers.' We have seen how the master signifiers are, by themselves, empty. They do not signify but they function, according to Žižek. And they function by 'quilting', or tying together, other signifiers (SO 87–9). The sublime objects of ideology they invoke are fantasmatic, in Žižek's psychoanalytic term. Their fascinating, august appearances conceal how, say, 'the People' does not exist as an untouchable, stable, fully self-consistent substance. But recall also what we learnt from Žižek's critique of Foucault: that the subject as Žižek conceives it is, also, not a substantial thing. Bringing these two thoughts together, Žižek argues that the Cartesian subject – a non-substantial subject that can give or withhold its political assent to ideologies and regimes – 'is' the hidden, true referent of the master signifier(s) at the heart of all political ideologies:

Critical theory: how master signifier(s) 'represent the subject' for other signifiers

S_1	master signifier (e.g. 'the People')
$	the empty, non-substantial subject, agent of belief and possible action(s)

This does not mean that the Cartesian subject as Žižek sees it is a Transcendental Signified, as Derrideans might triumphantly rejoin. What it means is that, where ideologies function by holding up sublime, substantial objects ((a): the Nation, the People, etc.) before us that demand our passive obedience, Žižek's critique of ideology functions by showing that our belief as subjects is the only 'substance' these sublime objects of ideology have. The philosophical point is that this agency is not a stable, unchanging and self-transparent, pre-existing substance. The political point is that, as subjects, humans can challenge and change the master signifiers and sublime objects political regimes hold up before them.

But to clarify all this properly, let us now look directly at Žižek's remarkable retrievals of the great modern philosophers, Descartes, Kant, then Hegel.

Changing the (Cartesian) Subject: Cogito, not Sum

We are beginning to see how, for Žižek, the Cartesian subject is not the fully self-assured 'master and possessor of nature' of Descartes's *Discourse on Method*. Žižek agrees that such a self-transparent, all-controlling subject deserves all its multiple feminist, post-structuralist, ecological and other criticisms. The issue is that, for him, the subject is what Žižek calls in the essay 'Kant with (or against) Sade' (Wright and Wright 1999: 291), an out-of-joint onto-logical excess, gap or *clinamen*. We have seen, from his critique of Foucault, that the subject is not identical to the substantial imaginary and symbolic identifications we each take on. From Žižek's critique of Derrida, we have seen how the subject is the active agency whose beliefs sustain ideologies' semblance of sublime, substantial power. The basis of these notions, however, is Žižek's remarkable Lacanian rereading of the much-maligned modern philosophy of the subject.

Although Žižek tends to identify himself philosophically as Hegelian, for reasons we will see, Immanuel Kant's critique of human reason's limits and capacities is deeply important in Žižek's early work. According to Žižek, nearly two centuries before the post-structuralists, Kant had produced a devastating critique of meta-physical philosophy in general, including Descartes's *cogito ergo sum* ('I think, therefore I am') and related definition of the subject as *res cogitans*, a thinking thing that could be master and possessor of nature.

In his 'Transcendental Dialectic' in *The Critique of Pure Reason*, Kant criticised Descartes's argument that the self-guaranteeing 'I think' of the *cogito* that resists Descartes's method of doubt must be a *sum*: namely, a substance or thinking thing (*res cogitans*). For Kant, to be precise, the *ergo* or 'therefore' involved in Descartes's *cogito ergo sum* is a false inference (*TN* 59–61). For Kant (as for Žižek), the 'I think' of the subject must be 'capable of accompanying' all the subject's perceptions of ordinary, 'empirical' objects. But this is all Descartes establishes when he famously contends that, even when he doubts everything else, he cannot without self-contradiction doubt that it is *he* who is doubting. All the *cogito* is here, Kant famously argues, is a purely formal 'unity of apperception': in more mundane language, a place, opening or screen whence empirical things can appear and take on meaning, be affirmed, denied, doubted, loved, hated, and so on (*TN* 13–15).

To put the same thought differently, for Kant there is a qualitative gap between the *cogito* (or the 'I think' of the subject) and the 'I am' involved in any substantial selfhood an individual might take on. The subject that sees objects in the world cannot see herself seeing, any more than a person can jump over her own shadow. As Kant puts it, in words Žižek cites:

> Through this I or he or it (the thing) which thinks, nothing further is repre- sented than a transcendental subject of the thoughts = X. It is known only through the thoughts which are its predicates and of it, apart from them, we cannot have any concept whatsoever. (Kant 1993: A346; *TN* 15)

So Žižek agrees with Kant that, as subjects, we can never know what Thing we are 'in the Real,' at the very point from whence we speak about, and perceive, the world. This is why each of us must seek clues to our identity in our social and political life, asking the question *che vuoi?* (what do you want?) of Others and shaping our desires, affects and beliefs around our suppositions concerning them (see Chapter 1). In an already famous analysis in *Tarrying with the Negative*, Žižek hence contends that the director's cut of Ridley Scott's 1980s film *Bladerunner* show the truth of the Cartesian subject (*TN* 9–12). For, within this version of the film, the main character Deckard (whose name even sounds like Descartes, Žižek notes (*TN* 12)) literally does not know what he is: in truth, he is a robot-replicant (a thinking Thing!) that misperceives itself to be a flesh-and-blood human being (*TN* 11–12).

One of the key things Žižek thinks Hegel clarifies, which Kant

The Subject of Enunciation versus the Ego of the Enunciated Content

For Žižek following Kant, then, the following two vital distinctions are aligned:

The subject   versus The Self or ego
The cogito ('I think') versus The 'I am' as (thinking Thing')

Žižek's wager is that the post-structuralist and other contemporary attacks on the 'modern subject' only target the Self, ego, or 'I am' on the right-hand side. Following Lacan, Žižek however adds a further aligned opposition, drawing on the technical language of linguistics:

The subject or 'I' of
the enunciation   versus The 'me' of the enunciated
(the act of speaking)   (how the 'self' is described in what is said)

When we speak, Žižek follows Lacan, there is the active, speaking subject of (the act of) enunciating the sentence – to take a famous example, the subject who says to someone, 'I am a liar'. And then there is the 'I' that appears, through the pronoun, *in* what is said – and who appears to whomever reads or hears this enunciated sentence as a 'lying thing' or 'thing that lies'.

wavered about, is how the type of profound self-ignorance exemplified by Deckard in *Bladerunner* is not a regrettable fact about our nature as subjects – as if we are in truth a kind of Thing, which it so happens is (presently) unknowable to us. No, the subject as subject is not a Thing at all, which is why it cannot be known:

> what Hegel effectively accomplishes is a kind of reflective inversion [of Kant's idea that the subject is unknowable] . . . the 'unknowableness' of the subject qua Thing is simply the way the understanding (mis)perceives the fact that the subject 'is' a non-substantial void – where Kant asserts that the subject is an unknowable, empty X, all one has to do is confer an ontological status on this epistemological determination: the subject is the empty nothingness of pure self-positing . . . (*IR* 124)

Or, in other Hegelian terms, the subject *is* the bearer of a 'negativity': the uncanny ability to stand back from, understand and actively change (or 'negate') what is given to it through the senses. This conception of the subject as a negativity is why Žižek repeatedly cites in his books the disturbing passage from the young Hegel describing the modern subject, not as the 'light' of the modern Enlightenment, but 'this night, this empty nothing that contains everything in its simplicity . . .' (e.g. AF 8; ES 50; FTKN 87).

We will return to Žižek's remarkable reading of Hegel below. Before we do so, however, we need first to pursue how Žižek reads Kant's analysis of the sublime in art and nature, in *The Critique of Judgment*. This analytic both (1) ties in with his account of the subject, and (2) informs Žižek's central political concept, of the 'sublime' objects of ideology that fascinate and capture subjects. It is thus necessary to our developing story.

From the Sublime to the Subject, Aesthetics to Politics

For Žižek, follwing Kant, we rightly call things sublime when they are so large or powerful that we cannot quite 'take in' what we see. The classic examples, dear to the Romantics, are rearing steeds, powerful storms, troubled oceans, fearsome hurricanes and the like. As Žižek rightly stresses, however, Kant's account of what is involved when we rightly explain 'that is sublime!' involves more than meets the eye (*TN* 45–58). For Kant, the force or size of these sublime objects painfully impresses upon us the limitation or 'finitude' of our own perceptual and physical powers. The mystery is that this painful experience is also somehow pleasurable: as with Lacan's notion of *Jouissance*, which involves excessive enjoyment, always verging on pain and transgression. How Kant explains this enigma is vital to seeing how Žižek understands the basis of ideological illusion, and how we can overcome it.

Žižek's model for how to traverse this illusion comes from his reading of Kant's other, the 'mathematical' sublime. Things are mathematically sublime on Kant's terms when they are so immeasurably large that they can astonish us, like the empty infinities of space whose thought terrified the theologian Blaise Pascal. These sublime objects, Kant holds, invoke for us not our moral freedom, but a possibility still dear to our scientists today: that of developing a 'Theory of Everything'. Yet, Kant argues, we can never achieve such a synoptic understanding of the whole physical universe. To do so would involve occupying an impossible 'position of enunciation', outside the universe. The phenomenal world, at least in so far as it appears

The Dynamic Sublime and the Stuff of Ideology

- As Žižek details in *Tarrying with the Negative*, Kant's intriguing claim is that, when we see some seemingly limitless or overpowering things, this humbling experience serves to intimate to us something very different from what we might imagine. This is that, within ourselves, *we* have a capacity whose infinite power trumps any power(s) we witness in nature: namely, the power associated with the faculty of our Reason.

- Kant's analytic of the 'dynamic' sublime (great storms, cyclones, volcanic eruptions, and so on) hence effectively asks us to consider: what is the power of a mighty hurricane, compared to the power of our own Reason, which can in moral experience (according to Kant) draw us to put what is right above our love for self, friends, family and all other worldly goods (cf. *TN* 49)?

- It is the recollection of this infinite power of Reason within us, for Kant, that the sublime objects' 'humiliation' of our perceptual powers occasions, and this (self-)reflective judgement is what gives us the peculiar aesthetic pleasure in the sublime.

- Specifically, the 'dynamic' sublime involved in perceiving the overpowering might of nature serves to recall us to our higher moral calling, for Kant. When, prompted by the dynamic sublime, we reflect upon the 'infinite' power of the rational moral law to call us to give up on everything that gives us pleasure, Kant argues that we can see how we ourselves must be what he calls 'Noumenal', free, supersensible Things or Selves, in but not fully *of* the physical, 'phenomenal' world (*TN* 54–7).

- The point for us here is that, as the term 'sublime object of ideology' might suggest, Žižek's analysis of the sublime political objects (God, the People, Democracy, and so on) at the heart of political ideologies follows the logic of Kant's analytic of the dynamic sublime. Our political ideologies present these objects as untouchable things for us to revere and identify with. Žižek, by contrast, argues that we should reflectively see, behind their captivating-sublime features, projections of our own capabilities as subjects. Yet Žižek disputes Kant's claim that the freedom our experience of sublimity intimates reflects that in truth we are 'made of special stuff': a sublime or Noumenal Self, above ordinary causality. This for him is the *über* form of ideological illusion.

to us, Kant's analysis suggests, always remains internally divided, inconsistent, inaccessible to our total comprehension – or, in Žižek's Lacanian term, 'not-all' (*TN* 54–6).

Žižek's notion, vis-à-vis the sublime objects of political ideologies, such as 'the People' and so on, is that we should respond to them in the same way Kant responds to the 'mathematical antinomies'. That is, we should resist seeing these sublime objects ideologically, as intimating to us some super-sensible dimension of political experience – as Kant thinks the dynamic sublime intimates our Noumenal Freedom. Instead, we should accept the possibility that the Other of the political regimes in which we live 'does not exist' or is 'not-all', like Kant's physical universe. This maxim 'the Other does not exist', vital to Žižek's politics, means that the regimes (or Others) we live in are always similarly internally divided or inconsistent – or, as Žižek adapts this Marxian term controversially to these seemingly very different, Kantian–Lacanian considerations, it is always riven by 'class struggle'.

The Substance is Subject: The Inner Hegelian Kernel of Žižek's Dialectics

Perhaps Žižek's most difficult, 'speculative' thought of all about the Cartesian subject, which links this philosophical doctrine to politics, is this. The void or lack that 'is' the subject, which we have seen is also what underlies the sublime force of the master signifiers, *is* the void or lack in the ideological Other(s) by virtue of which they 'do not exist'.

If the political regimes we inhabit remain 'not-all' – that is, subject to internal division, political conflict, antagonism or 'class struggle' – the ultimate reason is because their 'substance' is rendered incomplete by *us ourselves*, as subjects. As subjects in Žižek's sense, our uncanny freedom above all includes the capacity abstractly to reject or 'traverse' regimes' ideological fantasies, which usually conceal how the Other does not exist as the untouchable, sublime systems we often hope and imagine. As Žižek puts it in *Tarrying with the Negative*: ' "subject" is ultimately but a name for the externality of the Substance [or the Other] to itself, for the "crack" by way of which the Substance becomes "alien" to itself, (mis)perceiving itself through human eyes as the inaccessible-reified Otherness' (*TN* 30).

The Sublime, Ideological Fantasy and the Subject

So let us bring these abstract reflections back to the political ground.

- Recall from Chapter 1 the formula of the ideological fantasy: $\$ \lozenge$ (*a*). In the ideological fantasies that Žižek argues undergird our unconscious attachments to political regimes, the subject ($\$$) (mis)perceives himself as a passive agent, standing opposed to sublime-fantasmatic objects (*a*) that captivate his allegiance.
- We can now add that to traverse these ideological fantasies involves understanding that the sublime objects (*a*) of ideology comprise what? So many ways individuals misperceive *their own, non-substantial subjectivity or freedom*, seeing this lack of substantiality as if it were 'an inaccessible, reified Otherness'.
- The political corollary is that, when we do this, we are drawn to misperceive the inconsistencies, crises and injustices of our political regimes. In this manner, we avoid the potentially troubling insight that such problems indicate the possibility of political change, instead seeing them ideologically: as always the removable effects of the malign actions of Others supposed to enjoy (see Chapter 1).

Counting Ourselves in: Žižek's Hegel

Žižek's idea here, that ideologies are at base so many ways that subjects misrecognise their own active agency, reflects his reading of the idea of Marx's great predecessor, Hegel. In fact, we saw Žižek applying just these principles concerning subjectivity and its relation to ideologies when we introduced Hegel in Chapter 1. The point then was to show how Žižek applies Hegel's contextualist account of truth (the truth is the whole) to contemporary politics, with the 'speculative judgement' 'globalisation is fundamentalism'. The West wants to see fundamentalism as wholly, abstractly Evil: a sublime, horrifying Thing (*a*). In this way, the West 'counts itself out' when assessing the causes, meaning and drive behind contemporary fundamentalism.

To tie together the philosophical threads, Žižek sees the greatest merit and importance of Hegel's philosophy in opposing this ideological tendency to 'count ourselves out' of the world we would criticise and lament, as if we were powerless subjects before a wholly immutable set of sublime big Others. Such a position of 'counting oneself out' is what Hegel (1977: 383–401) pilloried as the 'beautiful soul'. Its opposite, as Žižek conceives things, is the infamous Hegelian formula 'the substance is subject' (Hegel 1977: 453–78). For him, this does not mean that any social substance (political regime or historical period) is an untroubled, undivided agent about which we could do nothing. No, for Žižek, 'substance is subject' *names* the internal division of all such substances: their minimal incompletion and openness to future change by us as subjects – the substance needs the subjects who misrecognise how they can also always reshape it.

Even Hegel's infamous method of 'dialectics' Žižek thinks can be understood only in the light of this ironic insight into our finitude. In order to criticise a position, Hegel effectively dramatically stages the attempts of subjects to live, enact or think it through fully – and shows how these attempts engender different outcomes from those they imagined (*FTKN* 142–6). The classic Hegelian example, which structures Marx's *Communist Manifesto*, is of how – in order to critique capitalism – we need to consider how, when the bourgeois *enact* capitalism, their *very attempt to do so* engenders economic crises and a unified working class, capable of running the vital machinery of state and industry without them. Hegel, 'the most sublime of the hysterics', is hence a deeply ironic thinker, in Žižek's reading. Almost all contemporary theoretical schools unite in declaiming his system as being the most disastrously inhumane attempt to rationalise away all chance or 'contingency', as well as individual difference and material suffering, in a grand philosophy of historical progress. For Žižek, Hegel is ever the contrarian, and his maligned 'absolute knowledge', with its dictum 'the substance is subject', actually gives the most sophisticated philosophical recognition to how humans 'do not know (the significance of) what they do', so that contingency and subjective agency must be 'counted in' to the historical process – if we are to do it, and progressive politics, justice (see especially *FTKN* 99–103).

Concluding: The Subject of Politics

The key terms and elements of Žižek's two major contributions to contemporary political theory have now been introduced. The first is Žižek's Lacanian theory of ideology based around the notion of ideological fantasies that renarrate the traumatic, usually violent

beginnings of political regimes (as heroic origin stories), and externalising any (causes of) internal division within the regime they
ideologically sustain by blaming Others (Jews, freemasons, terrorists,
petty bourgeois, Muslims) supposed to enjoy the difficulties and divisions 'we' suffer. The second, philosophical intervention is Žižek's
rehabilitation of the maligned modern subject through his Lacanian
rereading of Descartes, Kant and Hegel. Žižek's defence of the
modern subject is, politically, the defence of political agency, and the
possibilty of resisting and overthrowing avoidably unjust regimes.

Before we proceed to see how Žižek further applies and develops
these positions, however, let us consider the *prescriptive* possibilities
that Žižek's *descriptive* accounts of ideology and of the subject open
up. Žižek's own hesitations about what is to be done perhaps speak,
symptomatically, of the insufficiency of his critique of ideology and
theory of the subject – brilliant as both are – by themselves to make
up a political theory or orient an emancipitory politics.

For there are no less *than five* political possibilities Žižek has presented at different points in his *œuvre*, all of which can be inferred
from the premises we have now seen:

1. *A politics of permanent critique or analysis, grounded anthropo-
logically in a reading of the death drive.* In his critique of French
ultra-Leftist philosopher Alain Badiou's work in *The Ticklish
Subject*, Žižek brilliantly contests Badiou's apparently subversive theory of the (individual or collective) political subject who
declares and defends his faith in an indiscernible 'Truth Event' –
like Christ's resurrection as declared by St Paul. Žižek's argument
is that what Badiou sets up as a model of emancipitory politics in
fact gives a formal expression to the way subjects become interpellated into an ideology by identifying with an unquestionable
master signifier: whether 'the resurrection' or 'the German *Volk*'.
The question implied by this analysis and others, though, is how
does Žižek's prescriptive position differ, given particularly Žižek's
growing debt to Badiou in framing his own political prescriptions? Žižek's response is to emphasise that his politics depends
on his Lacanian, psychoanalytic premises. And psychoanalysis is
not called 'psychosynthesis' for a reason. The Lacanian–Hegelian
subject is 'the pure negativity of the death drive prior to its reversal
into the identification with some new master-signifier' (*TS* 160).
And the 'Act' involved in traversing the (ideological) fantasy (see
2) is also 'a purely negative category . . . the negative gesture of

suspension–withdrawal contraction . . .' (*TS* 160). The issue, which becomes more pressing as Žižek increasingly identifies subjectivity with this death drive (see 'Vanishing Mediations'), is whether such a 'purely negative' capacity can engender any political norms, lasting institutions or prescriptions.

2. *A politics of over-identification with the explicit symbolic terms of an ideology.* Žižek has at times proposed something like a Lacanian modulation of the old Hegelian–Marxian notion of 'immanent critique'. Immanent critique critically measures the actual conduct of political regimes against their own ideological standards. It does not critique capitalism for instance on the grounds of its irreligious amorality, but by saying to its representatives: 'you tell us this regime aims at liberty, equality, and fraternity, when what it actually produces is material inequalities which prevent the real liberty of large numbers of people, and turn people against their neighbours in a ruthless economic "survival of the fittest" struggle'. Žižek's notion of over-identification follows from his key distinction between the symbolic dimension of any regime's ideology – its elevation of a set of political ideals (justice, equality . . .), and the way regimes garner our support by tacitly providing for 'inherent transgressions': actions that subvert the explicit letter of the law (say the mistreatment of racial minorities) while being tacitly approved as a condition if a person is to belong in a given community. In response to this, Žižek's idea is that – sometimes at least, for the scope of the proposal here is unclear (cf. Parker 2006: 30–5) – the most effective action against a regime comes from 'over-identifying' with a regime's explicit ideals. In this way we 'show up' how the regime turns on inherent transgressions that remain effective only in so far as they are not publicly avowed (*CHU* 218–20; *DSST* 245).

3. *Most famously, a politics of the radical Act of traversing the fantasy, modelled on Lacan's notion of the cure in psychoanalysis.* For much of his career, Lacan argued that the end of psychoanalysis involves traversing individuals' fundamental fantasy, the last support of their neurosis or symbolic identity. The Act involves 'the fall of the object': in particular, the analysand cathartically passes through the transferential supposition that the analyst is or has the lost object-cause (a) of his desire. We have seen how Žižek uses the psychoanalytic categories Lacan developed for the psychoanalytic clinic, to understand political regimes' ideologies, and the way they interpellate subjects. The consequence of this

– which is not a necessary inference – is that Žižek equates political action in an unlikely way with the types of curative activities that transpire between analyst and analysand in the clinic. The result is that Žižek proposes that the model of efficacious political action is a political modulation of the psychoanalytic Act of traversing the individual fantasy. What is needed is a radical, revolutionary Act that traverses the elementary coordinates of the regimes' ideological fantasy as totally and cathartically as the end of an individual's Lacanian psychoanalysis. This radical Act necessarily has a messianic dimension, then, since it explicitly rejects or 'traverses' *all* the founding assumptions of the existing ideological regime, with its undergirding political fantasies. A psychoanalytically couched form of what Hegel called 'abstract negation', it cannot be justified in advance: it involves 'an ethics beyond the good' (*PF* 213–38). Rather, by engendering a new master signifier, it retrospectively creates the symbolic coordinates that might justify it: this is Žižek's primary proximity with Badiou. We will examine the limitations of this messianic decisionism, wherein Žižek also rejoins many of the post-structuralists he polemically opposes, in Chapter 5 (*PF* 223–4; *SO* 124–8; *TN* 251–7; *WDR* 152–4).

4. *Particularly in his post-1996 (Žižek₂) work, Žižek attaches the notion of a radical Act to the later Lacanian notion of 'identification with the* sinthome*'.* In Lacan's enigmatic later work, Lacan revised his notion of the end of the clinical cure. Just as the later Freud became increasingly pessimistic about the efficacy of the talking cure (which led him to posit the death drive as an immovable compulsion to repeat), so the later Lacan revised his notion of the symptom. The symptom, in his early work, was a linguistic (if embodied) symbolic phenomenon: an encoded message concerning repressed desire waiting to be interpreted by the Other/analyst (*SO* 73). In the later work, as we observed in the Introduction, Lacan coined the nearly homophonous notion of the *sinthome*, an irremovable 'stain' or 'knot' of 'idiotic' enjoyment that can be identified, but whose interpretation does not in any way move or dissolve it (*SO* 74–6). At most, a subject might 'identify' with this *sinthome* (*LA* 138). Žižek's political extrapolation of this difficult, seemingly highly pessimistic idea about the subject is to recall that ideologies operate by externalising (causes of) internal political dissensus. They do this by positing Others supposed to enjoy our sufferings, whose malignity has visited

84

our political problems upon us. For this reason, Žižek reasons, a truly radical Act that would traverse all the coordinates of the existing ideological regime must involve 'identification' with the scapegoated internal or external *'sinthome'* or 'Other supposed to cause our misfortunes' (CHU 126–7, 149–60; *PF* 30–4; *TN* 155, 220). For instance, since the Jews were posited by Nazi ideology as the cause of Germany's misfortunes, any progressive politics would have involved 'identification' with the Jews (*CHU* 126–7; *LA* 140). Žižek does not specify what 'identification' means here, but it seems to mean heroic symbolic and political advocacy of the minority cause. However, in some of the more bizarre passages in Žižek's *œuvre*, Žižek openly countenances an act of radical self-destruction – for instance, Medea's slaying of her own children, Sethe's comparable Act in Toni Morrison's *Beloved* or Edward Norton's character in *Fightclub* who beats himself up in front of his boss – as (it has to be said) the unlikely means of political empowerment in this vein. (*FA* 151–60).

5. *Political retreat, the attitudes of 'wait and see', what Žižek terms in* Parallax View *'Bartleby politics', and the denial of any attempt to propose a prescriptive politics.* Given the oscillation between positions, and the large problems a host of critics have repeated concerning prescriptions 1–4, Žižek has understandably become more politically circumspect, at least in moments of his recent texts. The bad news is that we live in a 'scoundrel time' wherein possibilities for immanent progressive change cannot be envisaged. At most we should model our political activity on the abstract 'I would prefer not to' of Herman Melville's Bartleby (celebrated by Deleuze, Derrida and Agamben – and, we note also, close to 1 above). In any case, theory can at most shape subjects' understanding of politics. The theorist cannot provide concrete political guidance (*PV* 385).

Chapter 3

Did Žižek Say Democracy?

Placing Žižek's Typology of Different Regimes

We have now seen the first two of Žižek's important contributions to contemporary theory and political philosophy: Žižek's theory of ideology, and his theory of the subject. In this chapter we will look at Žižek's third central contribution to political theory in his pre-1995 works: his Lacanian theorisation of the different types of political regimes. Žižek's radical-democratic political theory brings together his analysis of ideological cynicism (of enjoyment as a political factor) with his critique of post-structuralist theory in a powerful and coherent position.

One of political philosophy's tasks since Book VIII of Plato's *Republic* has been to generate typologies of the different types of political regimes. Philosophers have generally done this by recourse to two questions: how many people hold political power (one, a few, or many), and the purpose or end for which these rulers govern (for the genuine common good or out of self-interest). More empirically grounded thinkers such as Aristotle, Machiavelli and Montesquieu introduced further qualifications concerning the nature of claims to rule, the nature of the checks and balances on rulers, the political geography of the regime and the possibility of 'mixed' regimes incorporating elements from democracies, aristocracies and monarchical regimes. However, Plato's fundamental typology remained orthodox within the West until the modern period. Pre-modern thinkers assumed that good government was government that promoted a single vision of human flourishing – an ideal that it was the task of the political philosopher to discover and proselytise as best he might, if only by winning the ear of Princes.

With the advent of the Enlightenment and the remarkable technological changes of the Industrial Revolution, the way political agents and philosophers characterised regimes changed significantly. Political parties and regimes came to be classified primarily as either 'progressive' or 'reactionary', with primary reference to how they stood towards the Enlightenment claim to historical progress. They also came to be classified as 'conservative', 'liberal' or 'socialist', depending on their position on the freedom of the individual to hold their own personal conception of the highest good (that is, of human flourishing). Political liberalism, it is fair to say, is the hegemonic or predominant ideology in modernity. This is largely because it provides an excellent solution to the primary political problem that differentiates modernity from pre-modern society, highlighted painfully in the bloody religious wars of the sixteenth and seventeenth centuries. This is the emergence of political communities where a diversity of moral values and political ideals compete for popular allegiance: not everyone in any nation is Protestant, Catholic or of any other religious denomination. This 'value pluralism' is an irreducible but historically novel fact of modern political life. It raises the question of how liberal societies can be socially cohesive and make political decisions that do not boil down to what reactionaries declaim as the 'tyranny of the majority', which always means: the poor and poorly educated.

Political liberalism solves this question through its ideas about moral and political autonomy:

- individuals are free to select their own conception of the highest good, or human flourishing, from among the competing religious doctrines, political ideologies, moral ideals and so forth;
- individuals have the right to exercise their liberty to realise their own conception of human flourishing, except where the exercise of this liberty would infringe on the rights of others;
- the state guarantees the liberties of individuals by standing as a neutral umpire above the competing values, ideals and gods, merely enforcing the rule of law rather than demanding allegiance to a party ideology, state religion or official vision of human flourishing.

So compelling is the liberal position for modern societies that conservatives and socialists define themselves mainly in opposition to political liberalism. Conservatives propose that such political liberty underestimates the importance of 'blood, soil, tradition and god'. These are the real, non-rational roots of individual identity in ethnicity, nation and religion. In this light, liberalism stands accused of forcing individuals into an unnatural rootlessness that leads, ultimately, to postmodern nihilism. Socialists argue that political liberalism is suspiciously blind to those relations of power that lead to the inhumane treatment of individuals in market-based societies. They rebel against the way that liberalism's notion of liberty condones economic exploitation as a 'free contract' between autonomous individuals. The liberal reply to both sides of politics, against which Žižek rails again and again, is truly of this form: 'benevolent as this socialist or conservative communitarian vision seems, it will inevitably lead to the suppression of private liberty, or worse'. There are terrible historical experiences behind this accusation.

The other side to the development of liberal regimes is the technological progress of modern societies. This has enabled the emergence of regimes wholly beyond the imagination of older political philosophies, and totally opposed to liberalism. The first decades of the twentieth century saw the emergence of fascist regimes, which combined ruthless modern technological manipulation with the reactionary dream of pre-modern forms of organic community. These were opposed by new forms of communist regimes equally hostile to modern liberal-capitalism. The similarities manifest in the way the fascist and communist regimes governed (see below) led political theorists in the 1940s and 1950s to coin a new political category, 'totalitarianism', to name these horrifying regimes.

From the start, in its use by Hannah Arendt, Carl Friedrich and Zbigniew Brzezinski, 'totalitarianism' was a highly politicised category (e.g. Arendt 1966). Critics noted how readily it served the ideological purposes of America and the liberal-capitalist nations in the cold war with the Communist bloc after the Second World War. It did this by erasing the differences between Communism and the Nazis. We have seen in Chapter 1 how Žižek, too, has become very sceptical about the political use of this category in today's world. Academic debates concerning totalitarianism, and the features that make a regime 'totalitarian', are largely things of the past. Yet, perhaps for that reason, 'totalitarianism' has come to be bandied around by people of nearly every political stripe to enforce what Žižek calls today's liberal or postmodern *denkenverbot* about any political alternatives to today's globalising neoliberal capitalism. With typical precision, Žižek summarises in *Did Anybody Say Totalitarianism?* that, when people today use the term 'totalitarianism', they are taking one of five stances:

- "Totalitarianism' is modernism gone awry: it fills the gap opened up by the modernist dissolution of all traditional organic social links. Traditional conservatives and post-modernists share this notion: for some, 'totalitarianism' is the *necessary* outcome of the modernist Enlightenment, inscribed in its very notion; for others, it is more a threat that consummates itself when the Enlightenment does not fully recognise its potential.

- The Holocaust (or *shoah*) is the ultimate, absolute crime, which cannot be analysed in terms of concrete political analysis, since such an approach always trivialises it.
- The neoliberal claim that any radical emancipitory political project necessarily ends up in some version of totalitarian domination and control. Liberalism thus succeeds in bringing together new ethnic fundamentalisms *and* (whatever remains of) radical Left emancipatory projects, as if the two were somehow 'deeply related'.
- Today's postmodern claim (foreshadowed in Adorno and Horkheimer's *Dialectic of Enlightenment* 1986) that political totalitarianism is grounded in phallologocentric metaphysical closure: the only way to forestall totalitarian consequences is to insist on the radical gap, opening, displacement, that can never be contained within any ontological edifice.
- Finally, in a recent cognitivist backlash (also prominent in the Murdoch and similar right-wing media), 'postmodern Cultural Studies themselves are denounced as "totalitarian", the last island in which the Stalinist logic of unconditionally obeying the Party line has survived, impervious to any rational argumentation' (*DSST* 6–7).

In the light of Žižek's opposition to his perception of this anti-'totalitarian' *Denkenverbot*, we can frame Žižek's bold attempt to generate a new typology of the different modern regimes. Although Žižek uses the term 'totalitarianism' as a neutral term in his earlier works, Žižek's emphasis on the differences between fascist, Leninist and Stalinist regimes is a vital part of Žižek's political resistance of today's hegemonic 'liberalism or totalitarianism/fundamentalism' opposition. At the theoretical level, Žižek's understanding of the different logics in play in modern regimes is some of his most genuinely novel work.

Revolution, Quarter or Half Turn?

The basis of Žižek's distinctions between the different modern political regimes comes from Jacques Lacan's later work on what he termed the 'four discourses': where 'discourses' broadly means ways people can structure their social relations. Lacan developed his conception of the four discourses – the discourses of the master, hysteric, university and analyst – in his seventeenth seminar, *The Other Side of Psychoanalysis* (2006). The theory proposes that in all human relations there are four elementary or irreducible data, whose interrelations shape the possible ways people can interrelate. If this sounds terrifically abstract, in Chapters 1 and 2 we have encountered each of these four data. This puts us in a position to render Lacan's – and Žižek's – thought here more concretely:

- S_1, *the master signifiers* in any discourse, being the locus of subjects' primary political identifications: so key words such as 'the People', 'the Party', 'the Nation'.
- S_2, *'all the other signifiers' that the master signifiers (S_1) function to 'quilt' or stabilise.* Before this operation occurs, they remain 'floating signifiers', capable of being signified in more than one way – so, 'equality' means a different thing, depending on whether you identify yourself as a liberal or a socialist, for instance.
- *the object (a).* Psychoanalysis teaches that, in order to become civilised political subjects, we must all forgo immediate access to unadulterated enjoyment. The object (*a*) is the extraordinary-sublime or Real object of fantasy. As we saw in Chapter 2, Žižek's Lacanian claim is also that, for the S_1 to 'quilt' the S_2 in any ideology, the subjects must falsely suppose that these S_1 name sublime, Real objects (such as 'the popular', 'Australian-ness' and so on).
- *$, the divided or empty subject.* Nevertheless, as we saw in Chapter 2, what this ideological misrecognition conceals for Žižek is that the true support for the performative force of the S_1 lies in our subjectivity. Our capacity to give or withhold political assent reflects how subjectivity *per se* precedes and resists the ideological identities subjects take on.

In *The Other Side of Psychoanalysis*, Lacan generates the notion of four possible discourses shaping social relations by different arrangements of these four elements (S_1, S_2, (*a*), and $) on a grid. Every possible discourse involves:

(1) a 'place' of agency, from whence the defining message of the discourse is enunciated;
(2) an addressee, who or which receives or is affected by this message;

(3) some product or by-product, which is produced by the exchange;
     and
(4) most enigmatically, a 'place' of Truth, whereat what implicitly
     shapes the discourse is located, in a way often hidden to people
     involved in it.

The grid or schema involved in all of Lacan's four discourses is
then:

(1) place of agency	$\rightarrow$	(2) addressee
(4) The Truth underlying the discourse		(3) the (by-)product of the discourse

Žižek's bold wager is that he will be able to build a new, more
adequate basis for understanding and distinguishing the different
types of political regimes, on the basis of this formal account of the
four 'places', together with Lacan's four elements involved in any
discourse (S_1, S_2, (a), and $\$$). These shaping parameters, his argu-
ment suggests, are a more incisive basis for distinguishing between
the regimes than the traditional concerns with who and how many
rule, towards what end, together with the additional criteria listed
above concerning the complexities of place, time, history institutions
and culture that Aristotle, Machiavelli, Montesquieu and others
have used.

To illustrate how Žižek puts this theory to work, let us turn to one
of Žižek's examples: the Discourse of the Master, which Žižek argues
characterised pre-modern, monarchical societies and the absolute
monarchies of the sixteenth and seventeenth centuries. In Lacan's
terms, the Discourse of the Master looks like this:

Discourse of the Master (Absolute Monarchies)

$$\frac{S_1}{\$} \rightarrow \frac{S_2}{(a)}$$

Importing the historical data from the absolute monarchies, this
becomes:

S_1 (the King's/Master's words)	$\rightarrow$	S_2 (all the other subjects/signifiers)
$\$$ (the divided subject)		(a) (the sublime object: the King's 'second body')

To begin at the bottom right, the sustaining ideological fantasy produced by the Discourse of the Master in the addressee is that the King/Master (S₁) is the bearer of what political historian Ernst Kantorowitz called a 'second body'. Of course, the King is a mortal like all the other subjects (S₂) who are subject to his rule (the top-right position). However, as King, subjects believe that he is 'made of special stuff': in Žižek's terms, that he bears some sublime object of ideology (*a*) (*FTKN* 253–4). In hereditary monarchs, this special stuff is the royal blood that confers upon the first born of each generation the unique right to rule. The words (S₁) of the bearer of this sublime-ideological mandate in this discourse are accorded special, even absolute authority. They are recorded, doted and acted on, independently of whether the King is a genius of the public good, or a lecherous incompetent. One does not reason why, and nor is the Master obliged to give his reasons for one or other command (S₁):

> Traditional authority was based on what we could call the mystique of the institution. Authority based its charismatic power on symbolic ritual, on the form of the Institution as such. The king, the judge, the president, and so on, [might] be personally dishonest, rotten, but when they adopt the insignia of authority, the experience a kind of mystic transubstantiation . . . To ask if a King is a genius . . . is actually a *lese-majeste*, since the question contains the doubt in the sense [or legitimacy] of submission to his authority. (*FTKN* 249–50)

However, the usually concealed truth of this regime is different. Žižek cites Marx's astute *bon mot* that, while people believe that the king is king independently of their support, in political truth – as the case of Shakespeare's King Lear shows – the king remains king only so long as subjects *do* believe in his transcendent, unquestionable authority. This is why the $ appears in the bottom left, as the hidden truth of the discourse of the pre-modern masters. There is a 'politico-theological' wisdom in the biblical commandment 'thou shalt not put the Lord thy Father to the test'. For when we question the mystique of the institution, we come to understand – as another of Lacan's *bons mots* puts it – that, beneath the symbolic clothes of the king's institutionalised mystique, he is in fact naked.

As with other well-established academic debates, it is probably not possible to say that Slavoj Žižek has a 'theory of modernity'. Žižek has never written systematically on the long-debated sociological question of what makes modernity distinct from pre-modern societies. We have, however, seen already how Žižek situates his work in the heritage of the modern Enlightenment. What singles out the eighteenth-century Enlighteners, Lacan commented, was their belief that knowledge (S_2) might liberate rather than further subject individuals to power – or, in Lacanese jargon, allow new S_1 to be produced, enabling more rational and just social relations. Žižek's critique of ideological fantasy, and the heteronomy it enshrines, belong here. In terms of the four discourses, it represents a politicisation of the discourse of the analyst, the exact opposite or full 'half turn' of the Discourse of the Master:

The Discourse of the Enlighteners, the Discourse of the Analyst

$$\frac{(a)}{S_2} \rightarrow \frac{\$}{S_1}$$

As an example, we can sketch in some content for these terms, to illustrate how the Discourse of the Analyst works:

$$\frac{(a) \text{ (sublime object, critical questioning)}}{S_2 \text{ (scientific knowledge)}} \rightarrow \frac{\$ \text{ (subjects divided by encounter with a)}}{S_1 \text{ (new master signifiers)}}$$

The open question is whether this discourse can lead to any new, stable regime or order, or whether it must always represent a 'vanishing mediator' or moment of opening between two such stable orders. We have seen how Žižek challenges all pessimistic Heideggerian and later Frankfurt School-style accounts of modernity as enshrining the nightmare of a totally administered, scientised brave new world, when he defends the modern Cartesian subject. Nonetheless, Žižek has mostly argued that the predominant ideological logics of modern regimes have involved a mere 'quarter turn' in Lacan's schema of the four discourses, away from the pre-modern Discourse of the Master. Both Stalinism and modern consumerism evince the structure of the Discourse of the University, Žižek claims. The difference from what the enlighteners aspired to is that, in these still-heteronomous societies, knowledge has the place in the four discourses not truth, but agency. Indeed, far from questioning the bases of authority *per se*, the undergirding truth in these societies remains the 'S_1' of unquestionable master signifiers:

The Discourse of the University: Stalinism and Consumerism

$$\frac{S_2}{S_1} \rightarrow \frac{(a)}{\$}$$

As an example, we can sketch in some content for these terms, to illustrate how the Discourse of the University works:

S_2 (quasi-scientific knowledge/ ideology	(a) (objectified, known subjects
S_1 (unquestionable master signifiers)	$\$$ (hystericised, divided subjects)

$\rightarrow$

Let us see how.

Challenging 'Totalitarianism'

We have seen the ideological importance Žižek assigns to the way everyone from liberals to conservatives and post-structuralists today use the signifier 'totalitarianism'. Žižek believes that his Lacanian understanding of political regimes undermines the notion of a single 'totalitarian' form of government, wholly opposed to liberalism. It does this in two ways, which we will examine in turn:

- First, Žižek distinguishes between fascism, which he argues involves an attempt to reinstitute the Discourse of the Master in reaction to modern liberalism, and Stalinism, which represents a political instantiation of the Discourse of the University.
- Secondly, Žižek argues that consumerism, the predominant ideology in later capitalism, also represents an instantiation of the Discourse of the University, rather than the expression of a 'freedom' opposite to Stalinist totalitarianism.

FASCISM: THE REACTIONARY ATTEMPT TO REHABILITATE THE ABSOLUTE MASTER

Theorists and observers who defend the term 'totalitarianism' are struck by the commonalities between the fascist and Stalinist regimes. Friedrich and Brzezinksi's defining 1956 *Totalitarian Dictatorship and Autocracy*, for instance, identifies six features:

- an official ideology demanding general adherence, positing a 'perfect final stage of mankind' (Aryan domination or the dictatorship of the proletariat), which the regime devoted itself to achieving;

- a single mass party, hierarchically organised, closely interwoven with the state bureaucracy and typically led by one individual;
- monopolistic control of the armed forces;
- a similar monopoly of the means of effective mass communication;
- a system of terroristic police control;
- central control and direction of the entire economy (Friedrich and Brzezinksi 1956).

By contrast, Žižek does not specify the scope of his analyses of fascism and Stalinism. In contrast to other political-theoretic texts on these regimes, Žižek is largely silent about their economic and institutional elements, and the specific historical conditions to which they responded. Žižek's analysis focuses largely on the first of the six features, reflecting what we identified as Žižek's key contribution to political theory: his Lacanian understanding of ideology.

Probably the decisive sociological feature dividing the fascist regimes in Italy, Spain and Germany from the Communist regimes is that the fascist parties drew on support from elements within the established aristocratic and business classes. Fascist regimes have been termed 'reactionary-modernist' regimes. They ruthlessly manipulated the most developed modern media, industrial and military technology. However, fascism is predicated on a reactionary criticism of the decadence or 'nihilism' of liberal society, and the way that the intrinsic dynamism of capitalist economies breaks up traditional, organic, racially and culturally unified communities. Žižek indeed claims that fascism *per se* was a project in trying to reinstitute the Discourse of the (pre-modern) Master. We have seen that Žižek contends that the first task of regimes' ideological fantasies is to externalise any potential cause of political division, thus concealing internal divisions, or what Žižek calls the 'non-existence of the Other'. The Nazi's scapegoating of the 'Jewish conspiracy' often functions in his work as the example *par excellence* of this functioning of ideology.

The flipside of ideological externalisation of the cause of political conflict is the figure of the Leader. The Leader (Mussolini, Franco, Hitler) emerges as the one strong enough to do what is necessary to name and defeat these enemies. For these reasons, fascist rule is always in principle 'extra-legal', based on a 'state of exception' (Agamben 2001).

For this reason, Žižek comments, the image of totalitarian regimes as wholly 'repressive' is false. Rather, the message of the totalitarian ruler, and certainly the fascist ruler, is *if you obey, you can (and are encouraged to) violate the ordinary rules of law and morality, prosecuting your aggression against designated enemies.* Nowhere is Žižek's Lacanian emphasis on the political importance of *Jouissance,* enjoyment of what is usually prohibited, more apposite than in his comments on the fascist and Stalinist regimes. Žižek disputes Hannah Arendt's thesis of the banality or ordinariness of the evil perpetrated by figures such as Adolf Eichmann (a chief administrator in the Nazi's *Shoah*) (*PF 554–60*). As Žižek says, 'the execution of the Holocaust was treated *by the Nazi apparatus itself* as a kind of obscene dirty secret' (*PF 55*).

STALINISM: THE DISCOURSE OF THE UNIVERSITY GONE MAD

Žižek claims that the ideological universe of Stalinism was structured differently from that under Nazism. Without denying the horror that the Nazis visited upon the Jews and Gypsies of Europe, Stalinism, for ordinary Russians – as against the designated enemies of the fascist regimes – was a more brutally terrifying regime. If one was an 'Aryan' German, Žižek claims, some of the ordinary parameters of political life remained. The German secret police, so Žižek argues, continued to look for evidence to justify their actions against the German population (*PF 56–60*). Under Stalinism, the authorities would ruthlessly fabricate evidence of 'petty bourgeois' and other plots against them, in order to justify their terror. Subjects who protested their innocence of the charges against them, like Bukharin in the show trials, were declared 'objectively guilty'. By their very attestation of subjective innocence, the victims of Stalinist persecution showed that they put their own 'private' interests above that of the Party and the Revolution: a fact that, perversely, justified their persecution.

For Žižek, this flagrant Stalinist disregard for factual reality reflects the key ideological difference between Stalinism and the fascist regimes. Under fascism, the Leader's personality and authority were the decisive lynchpin (S_1) of the system: Nazism's classic text is Hitler's *Mein Kampf*, describing the personal struggle of the master-hero figure against the persecutors of Germany. Stalinism's classic text, by contrast, is Stalin's *History of the Communist Party* (*FTKN 234, 257*). The text, most famous for its writing-out of history of Trotsky, is written with the driest of would-be neutral objectivity. Similarly, where Hitler's speeches would be followed by the lengthy applause of his listeners, when Stalin finished speaking, he too would applaud. What this fact indicates is that, far from being an attempt to restore the pre-modern master, Stalinism instituted a regime where the quasi-scientific 'dialectical materialist' ideology (in Žižek's mathemes: S_2) occupied the position of agency. If Stalin the individual had any authority, it was because the 'Laws of History' happened to speak through him, and the other Party officials. It was not because of any heroic personal or struggle. As anticipated above, in Žižek's Lacanian terms, Stalinism was the most horrifying institutionalisation of the Discourse of the University:

The Ideological Discourse of Stalinism

$$\frac{S_2 \text{ 'dialectical materialism'}}{S_1 \text{ (extra-legal authority of the Party)}} \rightarrow \frac{(a) \text{ (objectified, known subjects)}}{\$ \text{ (terrorised ordinary subjects)}}$$

This greater importance Stalinism assigned to its scientific ideology is also evident in how the different regimes treated their victims. The paradigmatic victim of the Nazis is the horrifying figure of the silent, wholly crushed *Musilmann* in the camps, described harrowingly by Primo Levi. The paradigmatic victim of Stalinism is the 'traitor' who is asked to speak, to confess her 'objective guilt', and even call down her own punishment. Why is this?

> In fascism, the [properly] 'universal' medium is missing, the medium [of would-be universal scientific knowledge] that the accuser and the guilty would have in common and by which we could 'convince' the guilty of his or her fault . . . The victim is guilty and is at the same time capable of reaching the 'universal-objective' point of view, from which s/he can recognise his or her fault. This fundamental mechanism of 'self-criticism' is unthinkable in fascism . . This is the moment where Stalinist discourse is the heir of the *Lumieres* [enlighteners]. They share the same presupposition of a universal and uniform reason that even the most abject Trotskyist scrap has the capacity of 'comprehending' and from there confessing. (FP 16)

This is why the addressee in the Stalinist 'discourse' is for Žižek the object (a) – namely, a wholly objectified individual, who may not even be aware of the 'objective' significance of his own actions. This objective significance is decided by the Party, in the light of its privileged insight into the objective Laws of History.

The 'product' of this interpellation, on the bottom right of the schema, is that terror of the population, each of whom knows that he can at any moment be imprisoned extra-legally, and that any of his companions might be an informer for the state. The final truth of the regime, beneath the veneer of the objective and benevolent service to the people, is however S_1: the brutal reality that Stalin and the other leaders could arbitrarily decide at any moment who could be imprisoned, killed or deported to the gulags. This is the significance of the fact that the Discourse of the University characteristic of Stalinism (and as we are about to see, consumerism too) enacts only a 'quarter turn' from the Discourse of the Master. In Stalinism, the irrational ground of authority remains on the 'left' side of the schema. But it now appears in the bottom left, as the usually repressed truth of the system, saturated with enjoyment:

> The problem with the Stalinist communists was that they were not 'pure' enough, and got caught in the perverse economy of duty: 'I know this is heavy and can be painful, but what can I do, this is my duty . . .'. Of course, his excuse to himself (and to others) is: 'I myself find it hard to exert such pressure on the poor kids, but what can I do – it's my duty!'. . . [But] isn't it nice to be able to inflict pain on others with the full awareness that I am not responsible for it, that I merely fulfil the Other's will? . . . The position of the sadistic pervert provides the answer to the question: how can a subject be guilty when he merely realises an 'objective', externally imposed necessity: that is, [he can be guilty] by finding *enjoyment* in what is imposed upon him. (FP 36)

CONSUMERISM: THE DISCOURSE OF THE UNIVERSITY GETS HIP

Žižek's second move against today's political use of 'totalitarianism' is to challenge the presupposition of such use, that our political regimes in the West could have nothing in common with such regimes. He does this by way of his penetrating analysis of the logics of contemporary consumerism, the way individuals today are interpellated into the Western liberal 'way of life'. For Žižek, the superficial cyncism of Western individuals conceals subjects' unconscious, conformist identifications with the existing order, actually supported by the enjoyment we take in pointing out the corruption and incompetence of our leaders, bosses and bureaucrats. Žižek's deeper reading of consumerism however suggests that it, like Stalinism, involves the Discourse of the University.

It is in line with this analysis of consumerism that Žižek presents

Consumerism, Enjoy!

- Žižek again emphasises how ideologies work not by saying 'no', but by sanctioning modes of enjoyment. For him, the Coca-Cola advertising slogan 'Enjoy!' expresses perfectly how consumerism 'buys' our support – not by asking us to save and hold back from enjoying ourselves, but by stimulating our 'demand' by promising us Real enjoyment, in order to keep our national economies solvent.
- Advertisers have today become adept at selling us products by associating them with images of social and sexual success. As we shall see in Chapter 4, Žižek agrees with (neo)conservative sociology in arguing that consumerism has replaced the stern, self-denying 'paternal' superego characteristic of earlier societies (in the West, the Protestant ethic) with a 'maternal' superego, enjoining us to 'relax and enjoy ourselves'. The flipside of this paradoxical 'short-circuiting' of injunction with enjoyment (which usually requires us to feel as though we are *not* in any way being forced or enjoined) is depressive, self-punitive hatred, and the anxiety that we have not enjoyed enough, or that Others enjoy more than we do.
- Importantly, the position of agency in the consumerist 'ideology' – as in Stalinism – is, however, occupied by 'objective' knowledge. This is first of all the knowledge of the 'hip' advertisers, who claim psychological insight into what people Truly Want, in order to be happy, well-adjusted, successful individuals.
- Secondly, however, it is scientific knowledge – concerning our dietary, exercise, sexual and social needs – to which advertisements often appeal directly. Consumerism enshrines a mode of 'false' enlightenment, one that objectifies us (in the Lacanian mathemes, 'a') as what we might term 'enjoying animals', rather than encouraging the autonomous subjectivity enshrined in liberal philosophy (*TN* 216–19).

his most devastating political critique of post-structuralism, and of the philosophy of Gilles Deleuze in particular. The Deleuzian resistance to all fixed identities in the name of expressive individual 'lines of flight' is in fact a 'high theoretical' reflection of the consumerist injunction to enjoy ourselves by purchasing the latest wares (*OWB*).

Žižek, however, makes a deeper claim, which targets Deleuze's recourse to the philosophy of Baruch Spinoza. As Deleuze also does, Spinoza had claimed that the morality and religion of ordinary subjects, with their 'negative' prohibitions, were illusory: resting on individuals' ignorance concerning the objective truth revealed in his philosophy, and the emerging modern sciences. For Spinoza, for instance, God's Edenic prohibition against eating of the tree of knowledge can be restated philosophically as a point of prudential advice, based on objective knowledge concerning the harmful effects of this act of consumption. Thinking of consumerism, Žižek claims – despite Deleuze's suggestion that Spinozism is intrinsically radical – that 'it seems as if today we live in a period of Spinozism: the ideology of late capitalism is, at least in some of its fundamental features, Spinozist' (*TN* 218). Žižek is thinking here of the invariable 'small-print' warning on the packet about the deleterious effects on our health of everything we consume, bespeaking the neutral objectivity of modern science. As Žižek wryly comments:

> The contemporary version of Spinoza's reading of God's message [to Adam and Eve] would therefore run as follows: 'Warning! This apple can be harmful to your health, since the tree was sprinkled with pesticides . . .' (*TN* 217)

There is a kind of 'malevolent neutrality' at work in this Spinozist consumerism, one that conceals the continuing imposition of heteronomous authority on subjects: behind the replacement of direct injunction by allegedly neutral information stands the superego imperative to *Enjoy*! (*FTKN* 236–41; *TN* 216–19).

Whither Žižek₁, then? Is Žižek a Democratic Theorist?

With Žižek's Lacanian typology of the different regimes, and analytic unpacking of the predominant 'discursive' structures at play in them, we have examined Žižek's three key, pre-1996 contributions to political theory: his theory of ideology, his theory of the subject and his adaptation of Lacanian discourse theory. His accounts of discourses at work in Stalinism, fascism and consumerism are critical. They suppose, in order to garner our support, an appeal to the possibility of doing and seeing things differently. We commented above that Žižek in his early work sometimes associates his own position with the Enlightenment, as a kind of psychoanalysis of modern culture and its discontents. However, we have now seen that Žižek is also ambivalent or nuanced in his commitment to the Enlightenment's hopes. Žižek is highly critical of the way the Enlightenment's hopes for rational knowledge playing a greater role in societies has actually played out. This is one of the many points of proximity between his work and the many other contemporary theorists against whom he often polemicises. The question remains whether Žižek can point us towards any positive or constructive political project or ideal, which would have 'traversed' the ideological fantasies binding hetereonomous regimes, enabling a truly enlightened collective way of life?

The answer to this question in the radical-democratic Žižek, it has to be said, is a study in ambiguity. *The Sublime Object of Ideology*, published in a series edited by 'radical-democratic' theorist Ernesto Laclau, at least gestured at several points towards an affirmative answer (*SO* 6–7). What would be required, according to this strand in Žižek's thought, would be a regime that would, paradoxically, remain aware that 'the Other does not exist', and that social conflict between groups bearing different understandings of the good is inevitable. Indeed, it would embody a series of practical measures to try to institutionalise this theoretical, Lacanian truth.

The Empty Place of Power

For Žižek, in his radical democratic moments, the key to radical democratic politics is the 'empty place of power'. Žižek's ground for this political idea is the emptiness of the S_1 or master signifiers, which we examined in Chapter 1. In the pre- or early-modern Discourse of the Master, the fact that the truth of the Master's words is his empty assertion as a subject (the $\$$ on the bottom left of the diagram on p. 91) is concealed. One does not question why. For the radical democratic thinkers to whom Žižek_1 is sometimes indebted, principally Claude Lefort, Ernesto Laclau and Chantalle Mouffe, modernity is the age that does not just 'do and die' at the beck of the masters. It does ask why, and, as in Žižek's Lacanian theory of ideology, it discovers that, beneath the clothes of symbolic ritual, the place of power is, and ought to be, empty.

Modern democracy begins in the French Revolution with the literal and metaphorical killing of the king as unquestionable master. In pre-modern politics, as we have seen, subjects ideologically perceive the king as the direct incarnation of power. He is someone 'appointed by God', who provides a guarantee of social harmony. In striking off the king's head – and overthrowing monarchy *per se* as a type of government – what the French Revolution was more deeply doing was introducing a new prohibition into modern politics. This is the prohibition against any one person or in-group claiming to do anything more than *temporarily occupy* the place of executive power in a regime.

The idea is that, when the modern regimes displaced the king from absolute authority, what they were doing was also 'evacuating the place of power'. In pre-modern societies, as we have commented, there was generally held to be a single substantive vision of human flourishing uniting society: like Catholicism in feudal Europe. It was 'in the name of' this vision of the good life that the king could claim to legitimately rule. The place of power in pre-modern Europe was hence very much 'filled': by God's lieutenant, no less, the truest imaginable representative of what the people could want and stand for. There was hence no possibility, and no need, for a multitude of distinct groups with different conceptions of human flourishing to compete to hold political office. This all changed when, removing the office of an absolute sovereign, the modern liberal revolutions instead placed time limits and other checks and balances on society's rulers. In a republic, French revolutionary St Just famously argued, 'no one can rule innocently'. Indeed, all rulers must periodically expose themselves to election by consent of a majority of subjects, and hence the possibility of peacefully ceding office to political opponents. This is why Žižek₁ could argue in 1990 that:

> It is against this background of the emptying of the place of power that we can measure the break introduced by the 'democratic invention' (Lefort) in the history of [political] institutions: 'democratic society' could be determined as a society whose institutional structures includes, as a part of its 'normal', 'regular' reproduction, the moment of dissolution of the socio-symbolic bond, the moment of eruption of the Real: elections. Lefort interprets elections . . . as an act of symbolic dissolution of [the] social edifice . . . (SO 146–7)

In place of social harmony guaranteed by God's lieutenant, modern society must learn to cope with the anxiety that 'society does not exist' (as a monolithic closed community). In modernity, by contrast with the *Ancien Régime*, the imaginary unification of society is a function of the temporary, if democratically ratified, occupation of the locus of power by some particular group. Where the king was a sovereign, 'the people' shall be: power is now based in consent rather than in alleged wisdom or natural right, a stunning revolution in political history. The consequence is that any governing party necessarily speaks only temporarily 'in the name of the people'. It is, as Žižek says, at most 'a kind of surrogate, a substitute for the real-impossible sovereign' (*SO* 147).

This democratic theory present in Žižek$_1$ seems powerfully to bring together the several lines in his thought we have encountered so far. We have seen (Chapter 2) how for the early Žižek the subject is, at base, empty of or prior to all the symbolic and fantasmatic identifications it takes on. Žižek bases this account of the subject in Descartes's philosophy of the *cogito sum*, a single performatively self-guaranteeing certainty that escapes Descartes's characteristically modern attempt to doubt all his inherited ideas. There is, Žižek hence says, a 'structural homology' between this Cartesian subject and the Lefortian understanding of democracy, in which no one person can legitimately hold power by virtue of any inherited or natural traits:

> In other words, there is a structural homology between the Cartesian pro-cedure of radical doubt that produces the *cogito*, an empty point of reflec-tive self-reference as a remainder, and the preamble of every democratic proclamation: 'all people *without regard to* (race, sex, religion, wealth, social status). We should not fail to notice the violent act of abstraction at work in the 'without regard to': 'it is . . . a dissolution of all substantial, innate links, which produces an entity strictly correlative to the Caresian *cogito* as a point of non-substantial subjectivity . . .' (*LA* 163).

Indeed, Žižek characteristically works with, and occasionally explic-itly argues for, two other, interconnected 'structural homologies' at these points in his earlier texts when he poses as the radical democrat. The first is the homology between the democratic invention and his Lacanian account of how ideology might be traversed. The second is the homology of this same democratic invention with Kant's moral theory, for Žižek a further key philosophical touchstone.

DEMOCRATIC POLITICS

To see the homology between democracy and the Lacanian critique of ideology, we need to recall from Chapter 1 that Žižek argues that there is a permanent gap *within the Symbolic Order* of any political regime itself. There is the public side of ideology. This calls for the self-sacrificing identification with the regime: 'we are all Australians, so there are times when we have to put our differences aside . . .'.

Enunciation	SYMBOLIC ORDER 'Permitted'		REAL
Statement	Ego Ideal	Inherent transgressions. The superego: rooted in ideological fantasy	'Prohibited' by universal symbolic law – e.g. incest, murder, etc.
	'Prescribed' – e.g. prescriptive heterosexuality, faith in the law, willingness to accept outsiders as merely different	'Proscribed' – e.g. homosexuality, jingoism, killing and debasing enemies/outsiders.	
	(In Žižek's Lacanian mathemes, $S_1/\$$)	(In Žižek's Lacanian mathemes, S_2/a)	

Figure 3.1 *Žižek's psychoanalytic understanding of the Subject and Ideology*

Subjects' Ego Ideals are shaped by identification with such imperatives. However, Žižek also argues that each regime works, between the lines, by promoting forms of quasi-transgressive *Jouissance*. We can now put this more technically, by saying that there is a rupture between the statement or 'enunciation' of a rule or ideal, and the implied transgressions of that rule or ideal. We can see this immediately with reference to Žižek's Lacanian psychoanalysis, if we introduce the distinctions between permission (what we would be allowed to do according to a formally universal procedure), prescription (what we are in fact told to do by means of the stated ideal), proscription (the inherent transgressions of that ideal, that we are told not to do) and prohibition (what is under no circumstances permitted).

The 'democratic invention' at the political level, Žižek argues, aims at 'emptying out' all the 'proscribed' but secretly 'permitted' stuff of regimes' ideological fantasies (the middle-right column in Figure 3.1). The case *par excellence* for Žižek$_1$ is always his native Yugoslavia, riven after its post-1989 divide by the struggle of competing, ethnically based ideological fantasies: so the Serbs blamed the Croats and the Muslims for their misfortunes, who blamed the Serbs, and so on. In this vein, Žižek comments that what a peaceable solution would involve in Eastern Europe is not the 'empowerment of civil society', but 'more alienation: the establishment of an "alienated" State which would maintain its distance from the civil society which would be "formal", "empty", i.e. which would not embody any particular ethnic community's dream (and thus keep the space open for them all)' (*TN* 211–12).

MORAL UNIVERSALITY

The other homology at play in Žižek's early defence of modern democracy is between the democratic invention and Immanuel Kant's moral theory. We briefly encountered this theory in Chapter 2, in the context of discussing the significance Kant attributed to our encountering the 'dynamic sublime'. The key thing is that Kant's moral theory is famous for its rigor. At its heart is a call for subjects to do their moral duty (by following the 'categorical imperative' of the moral law), no matter how much it hurts them and everything they love. (So the parallel with Cartesian doubt is again clear: the modern subject in Kant as well can and should doubt all inherited conventions when faced with a moral choice. This is also why Kant, following his Rousseau, is among the first thinkers to justify civil disobedience to immoral laws.)

The moral law for Kant is also universal. It addresses each of us equally, again despite race, sex, gender, class and so on, just as in the modern democratic constitutional documents Žižek paraphrased above. The reason it can do this, however, is somewhat paradoxical. Kant argues that, for finite, limited human beings, there is no Sovereign Good: some particular thing or way of life that would reunite virtue and happiness, which are so often opposed in this life. Or at least, if there is such a thing, we cannot access it. (Žižek hence also follows Lacan here, in seeing a parallel between the Sovereign Good and the maternal Thing we have all lost access to as the price of civilisation.) More than this, the very possibility of trying directly to access such a Thing would be the worst evil of all, diabolical evil: the principled choice of a particular Thing with the same unyielding dutifulness that should characterise good moral action. The reason why Kant, dramatically, thinks we cannot attain to the Sovereign Good is the idea that humans are 'radically evil' (Kant's equivalent of original sin). This means that we have always, as particular, embodied beings, somehow 'chosen' our own interests and needs above the moral Law. Our radical evil nature Kant thinks is shown by how arduous it usually is for us to have to act morally, doing unto others as we would have done to ourselves.

So for Kant, the place held up in traditional religions and classical philosophy of a sovereign good (whether the life of contemplation of

POLITICS *Enunciation*	EMPTY PLACE OF POWER Democracy		TOTALITARIANISM
Statement	Hegemonic content of the universal, public law	Excluded particular contents, 'unwritten law': Others/ enemies supposed to enjoy	Social Harmony, The National Thing: 'Our society does Exist' (embodied in the Leader or Party)
ETHICS *Enunciation*	THE MORAL LAW		Diabolical evil = elevation of the (particular) Supreme Good *into the place of the universal Moral Law itself*
Statement	Public law as representation of the truly universal appeal of the categorical imperative: 'do you duty, no matter what!'	Radical evil in the form of a principled or consistent choice in favour of one's 'pathological' 'self-conceit' or particular interests	
SUBJECTIVITY *Enunciation*	SYMBOLIC LAW 'Permitted'		REAL
Statement	Ego Ideal 'Prescribed' – e.g., prescriptive heterosexuality (In Žižek's Lacanian mathemes, $S_1/\$$)	Inherent transgressions 'Proscribed' – e.g., proscribed homosexuality, adultery, masturbation, etc. (S_2/a)	'Prohibited' – e.g., incest, murder, etc.

Figure 3.2 The structural homologies between democracy, morality, subjectivity

God or of philosophy) is 'emptied' or 'evacuated'. And, here again, Žižek says that there is a parallel between this thought and Lefort's thought concerning the emptying of the political place of power in the modern democratic period, as opposed to 'totalitarian' attempts substantially and directly to achieve the Highest Good through politics.

Putting the three levels of Žižek's 'modern, democratic structural homology' together, we can schematise his political defence of democracy in Figure 3.2, drawing on Figure 3.1.

Radicalising Social Antagonism

So far, we have seen Žižek's debt to Claude Lefort's theory of democracy. We mentioned above, however, his second influence in this early line of political thought, Laclau and Mouffe. In Chapter 2, when we examined Žižek's idea that the master signifiers 'represent the subject for other signifiers', we saw the debt Žižek owes in his understanding of how political ideologies work to Laclau and Mouffe's great work, *Hegemony and Socialist Strategy*. Žižek for a long period endorses this theory that politics involves the struggle between relatively universal 'master signifiers': signifiers such as 'Democracy' or 'Socialism', which compete to represent the accepted common good, by 'requilting' all the other political signifiers. However, drawing on his Lacanian-psychoanalytic account of subjectivity and the unconscious, Žižek always refused to accept that political competition between master signifiers happens on a level playing field. The reason is social antagonism.

The theory of social antagonism is one of the most interesting aspects of Laclau's and Mouffe's position. It is based on a combination of the Lacanian category of the Real with the Derridean, deconstructive concept of *différance*. The social antagonism in play here involves the fact that, for engaged political agents, the other camp is not just the 'other team', a group of sterling chaps and lovely ladies whose ideas, unfortunately, are somewhat misguided. (Indeed, when, as is often the case in parliamentary party politics, the other side *is* just the 'other team', this often testifies to the concealment of social antagonism, to its displacement outside the field of mainstream politics.) No – in social antagonism, the other camp is an abominable stain on the political life of the nation, a blot on society, and it is so because it prevents the totality of national life from becoming socially harmonious under *our* master signifier. The politics of social antagonism are passionate and engaged. Žižek's understanding of subjectivity of course adds to Laclau and Mouffe that politics is such a passionate business because it very often rests upon unconscious fantasies about the opponent or antagonist, and their illegitimate 'theft of enjoyment'. It is *they* who spoil or have stolen the enjoyment of our way of life, and things would be better for *us* if they were ostracised from society altogether.

Laclau's and Mouffe's political stance is usually called that of 'radical-democratic' politics. It is *radical* because it proposes to learn to live with antagonism, to embrace the dimensions of democratic and popular oppositions. In Lacanian terms, as Yannis Stavrakakis (1999) has argued, this would mean refusing the ideological fantasy of social harmony and the drive to annihilate the other that arises from it. This perspective of democracy as an *agon* involves a spirited defence of social movements' challenging of the reigning ideology and political struggle in various arenas crucial to democratic politics

– under no circumstances can democratic politics be reduced to mainstream party processes and electoral campaigns.

What Žižek disputes about Laclau's and Mouffe's position, however, is their relativistic assumption that Left and Right are symmetrical antagonists, whose aims to achieve 'hegemony' are saliently the same. For Žižek, the 'Real of the antagonistic fight' beneath the surface of political competition emerges only from the Left. On the one hand, the Left – certainly today – is not hegemonic: the Right has control over the master signifiers and the way they are interpreted, limiting the accepted scope of what is politically legitimate to consider.

On the other hand, real social antagonism happens only when one of the antagonists locates its master signifier in the field of the proscribed transgressions ruled out by the reigning ideology. Of course, there are plenty of *inherent* transgressions of the reigning ideology that are merely morally abhorrent: neo-racism, ethnic nationalism, religious fundamentalism, and so on. But, in political terms, these are all radical particularisms and hence of the Right. They are not marginalised universals. A politics that appeals to these particular prejudices aims, in political terms, at the authoritarian effort to impose an authentic identity on everyone through enforced communal belonging.

But there is also a whole series of universal political positions that are marginalised by the reigning ideology, misrepresented as 'totalitarian' and treated as 'political Jews' (as it were), as a means to keep them on the sidelines. Some of these are positions that represent a *deepened and expanded form of universality* in contrast with the reigning master signifier – and these, especially socialism, are the ones that Žižek, at least in his early Leftist work, would seem to draw our attention to.

Consider, for instance, the politics of homosexuality. For the Right, homosexuality involves not just moral abomination and political violation of a legal ban on permanent unions between gay couples. The demand to recognise gay civil unions, for instance, also involves or invokes an obscene *Jouissance* that deprives the majority of moral citizens of justified enjoyment of their heterosexual marriages, by 'undermining the dignity of marriage' and 'marginalising the moral concerns of normal families', and so on. From Žižek's perspective, or at least one shaped by several of his premises, the only way to 'traverse the fantasy' that gay couples have 'stolen the enjoyment' of the mainstream way of life is through full identification with their struggle. This would involve the defiant affirmation that sexual liberation – the free right of people to choose their mode of sexual life – is an intrinsic part of the left-wing agenda – leading up to the installation of a deepened and expanded universal in the empty place of power.

But there is also a fantasy on the Left to be traversed: that, by legally criminalising movements like the Moral Majority, we could achieve socially harmonious sexual freedom, safe from moralising bigotry. The radical-democratic Left has to learn to live with the anxiety that the Right will always be with us, hostile to any deepened and expanded conception of the universality of sexual freedom, aiming to replace it with its more restricted notions in the name of Virtue. Žižek$_1$'s position is not utopian. Political antagonism is a universal part of political life, so the most we can do is try to institutionalise it in forms of radicalised democracy.

From Žižek$_1$ towards Žižek$_2$

The reader might have noted how much of the preceding section proceeded very largely without citation of Žižek's works. There is a reason for this. It is that part of what we have tried to do in this chapter is to draw out the progressive political arguments present in Žižek's work. But Žižek himself, it has to be said, was always hesitant and ambiguous when it came to travelling fully down a radically democratic path. Arguments that are clearly anti-democratic in force sit alongside these progressive moments even in his earliest texts. Understanding that the Left is in a subaltern position in the social antagonism produced by the Left–Right political struggle, Žižek is also keenly aware that it is all too easy for progressives to criticise neoliberal capitalism and liberal politics without taking responsibility for changing the world. The problem is that the Left is too fond of what Žižek's teacher Lacan called the 'narcissism of the Lost Cause' (*IDLC* 7): the self-sabotaging advocacy of impossible demands and defeated movements, as if the only way for the Left to believe in a political universal were to ensure that it could no longer be actualised in politics. What this reduces to, Žižek notes, is a hysterical demand for a new master. The Left bombards the master (political liberalism) with impossible demands, in the hope that the master will fix things up and prevent the hysteric (the Left) from having actually to take responsibility for implementing its proposed solutions to the mess we are in.

It has to be said that the moments where Žižek takes up the cause of radical democracy are matched from the very start by growing hesitations of this kind. In particular, Žižek wonders: what if radical democracy is just a radicalised liberalism, which leaves the economic exploitation intrinsic to modern capitalism in place? One reason for Žižek's ambivalence surely has to be because, in all of his voluminous *oeuvre* to date, Žižek has never produced a sustained *analysis* of even a single liberal political philosophy. Indeed, Žižek's thinking on parliamentary democracy remains strictly within the coordinates of the Marxist doctrines of the former second world. This is expressed most graphically in Žižek's unthinking repetition of the condensation 'liberal democracy' when he means representative government with a relatively liberal economy. 'Formal', 'bourgeois' or 'liberal' democracy is, of course, opposed to 'real democracy' or the 'dictatorship of the proletariat', something that for Žižek initially meant: totalitarianism. But, as his suspicions that radical democracy involved a renaturalisation of capitalism increased, his position on totalitarianism reversed. By 2001, Laclau was able to note that in Žižek's recent 'R-R-Revolutionary' turn, he advocates not only the overthrow of capitalism in the name of 'class struggle' (see Chapter 5), but also the abolition of liberal democratic regimes and their replacement with 'proletarian dictatorship' (*CHU* 289). As we will see in Part II, this is exactly what Žižek has come vehemently to advocate.

In his excellent book *The Real World of Democracy*, the socialist philosopher C. B. Macpherson elaborated on an argument originally made by the great revolutionary Rosa Luxemburg. If we look at the actual history of 'liberal democracy', what we see is the Right fighting tooth and nail to prevent each and every expansion and deepening of political universality, from the popular franchise, through female suffrage, civil liberties and social rights, down to the extension of the vote to indigenous people. At the same time, the vast majority of working people passionately support parliamentary democracy and organise their everyday struggles, from trade unionism through to civic activism, through democratic institutions and civil society. The democratic process is the only form of democratic training the immense majority knows. Certainly, supplements can be imagined that would improve the depth of civic participation in democratic politics, ranging from workers' councils on the soviet model through to the trade associations of guild socialism. Those who wish to throw away parliamentary democracy, however, seek to dispense with something that many of the oppressed and exploited have fought and died for. Such people may say they are on the Left. But they may not say that they are part of the self-emancipation of the majority of people (Macpherson 1972, 1973, 1977).

'Žižek's political thought', Laclau (2000b: 204) writes, 'suffers from a certain combined and uneven development', where a sophisticated theoretical apparatus is juxtaposed to political immaturity. 'And this is because Žižek's thought is not organized around a truly political reflection, but is rather a psychoanalytic discourse which takes its series of examples from the politico-ideological field' (Laclau 2000a: 289). Perhaps that is why it is through the category of ethics that Žižek organises his turn from radical democracy to messianic Marxism. *For They Know Not What They Do*, arguably his most radical-democratic book, nonetheless closes on an ominous note: 'The ethics which we have in mind here, apropos of this duty, is the ethics of Cause qua Thing, the ethics of the Real' (*FTKN* 271). After *The Metasases of Enjoyment* (1994), in any case, Žižek shut himself up in his study with the Romantic philosophy of Schelling, and uncharacteristically wrote almost nothing for two years. When he emerged, with *The Indivisible Remainder* (1996) and *The Abyss of Freedom* (1997) in his hands, he was a changed man.

Inter-chapter

Žižek's Vanishing Mediation

The Turn to Schelling: Žižek's Vanishing Mediations

Probably the deepest theoretical change in Žižek's work so far is his turn to the Romantic philosopher Gottfried Schelling in 1996–7. Up to this point, Žižek had seen in Kant and Hegel the philosophical origins of his own Lacanian theories of ideology and the subject. Yet, in two works, *The Indivisible Remainder* (1996) and *The Abyss of Freedom* (1997), Schelling's thought suddenly takes pride of place. Žižek claims to see in Schelling's rare work, the incomplete manuscript of *The Ages of the World*, nothing less than the fundamental matrix of German idealism, as well as the most telling anticipation of his own position (*IR* 1–3).

There are several surprises that meet the reader of Žižek's *Indivisible Remainder* and *Abyss of Freedom*. Abruptly dropping analyses of popular culture and theoretical interventions into contemporary ideology, Žižek engages directly with Schelling's speculative theology (his vision of God), or, more accurately, Schelling's theogony (his metaphysical account of how God came to be). Plunging into this esoteric field fearlessly, Žižek claims to uncover several deep truths there that became vital for his thinking. These are first of all a metaphysical account of how God, in a moment of 'madness', gave birth to the Symbolic Order of the world before the beginning of time as we know it. But Žižek finds, at the same time, an account of how every individual must emerge from the 'rotary vortex of the drives' in the Real of the body into the shared social space of the Symbolic Order. Lacanians have insisted that the Symbolic Order is not spawned from inside the individual – human beings are profoundly social and the individual enters social space by accepting those pre-existing rules that govern a network between individuals. But Žižek, following Schelling, disagrees. If we understand correctly the metaphysical truth, Žižek claims, we will see how Schelling's thought is not after all an irrationalist regression from the Enlightenment's critical philosophy of Kant and Hegel (*AF* 4).

112

On the contrary, it anticipates many insights of post-structuralism and indeed contains the germ of what Žižek, from here on, begins to provocatively call 'dialectical materialism'.

Dialectical materialism is a famous term used by Friedrich Engels to describe Marxist theory, but which Stalin transformed with his distinction between 'historical materialism' and 'dialectical materialism'. Žižek is evoking the Marxist legacy with his 'dialectical materialism', but he is also refusing to rule out the reference to Stalin's *Dialectical and Historical Materialism* (1938) as a provocation.

- In Engel's usage, 'dialectical materialism' refers to Marx's famous claim to have turned Hegel's dialectics on its head. The laws of dialectics discovered by Hegel (the unity of opposites, the transformation of quantity into quality and the negation of the negation) turn out, according to Engels, to be the reflection in ideas of material and historical processes. Stalin tried to codify this into a 'proletarian world view,' maintaining that 'diamat' (dialectical materialism) was the philosophy of Marxism based in the discovery that everything is ultimately 'matter in motion', while 'histomat' (historical materialism) is the application of this philosophy to human history, resulting in the conception of the historical process as a sequence of stages leading to communism.

- Žižek's 'dialectical materialism' has an ambiguous relationship to Engels and Stalin. On the one hand, the birth of the Symbolic from the Real without the intermediary of a socially shared space bears a strong resemblance to the emergence of universal human history from matter in motion, histomat from diamat. On the other hand, Žižek's twist on the whole topic of the relationship between matter and society and history, the Real and the Symbolic, denies a key tenet of Stalinist dialectics. For Stalin, history and society are totalities – that is, unified wholes. For Žižek, by contrast, what is *materialist* about his 'dialectical materialism' is the denial of totality.

- For Žižek, 'the Other' (whether the Symbolic Order, or a political regime) never 'exists' as the fully consistent whole that subjects imagine, as they shape their identities in relation to it. This means that society, history and culture ultimately always depend for their illusory 'existence' as apparent wholes on the (unconscious) beliefs of subjects in them. This truth is registered in a series of 'material' inconsistencies: the way ideologies have to posit enemies 'supposed to enjoy' our difficulties, and to rest at their heart on sublime Ideas like 'the Nation', which no one can directly say what their content is. Thus, Žižek's 'dialectical materialism' is ultimately the doctrine that 'the Other does not exist'.

In this 'mediating' section of *Žižek and Politics*, beginning from Žižek's pivotal encounter with Schelling's *Ages of the World*, we are going to lay out the key parameters of the changes between the two Žižeks we identified in the Introduction: the radical-democratic Žižek who is an Enlightenment Lacanian–Hegelian critic of ideology; and the revolutionary-vanguardist Žižek, who embraces a Romantic and pessimistic Freudian–Hobbesian philosophy of culture and of total political revolution. We commented in the Introduction that Žižek's 'break' between these two positions is not clean or absolute. Anticipations of Žižek's later pessimistic positions are evident from the beginning. The revolutionary-vanguardist Žižek still recurs to motifs from his earlier texts, if only politically to 'soften' the radical impact of his later, more radical or reactionary positions.

Nevertheless, the sudden turn to Schelling in 1996–7 stands as something of a 'vanishing mediator' between the early and later Žižeks (Gigante 1998; Hamilton-Grant 2007; Johnston 2008). Žižek, following Fredric Jameson, has argued that often decisive conceptual or historical changes cannot occur all at once, as clean breaks. The change from feudal-religious (Catholic) to capitalist property relations at the end of the medieval period, for example, had to pass by way of Protestantism (and the absolute monarchies of the sixteenth through eighteenth centuries). This is because Protestantism was a religion (which meant it could emerge within the old order), but it is also a highly individualistic religion (which means it could and did give birth to modern, secular capitalism). In the same way, Žižek's turn to Schelling plays a key role in his philosophy of the subject, his understanding of moral philosophy and ultimately his politics. The two books that he devotes to Schelling have not been followed by any studies on Schelling of comparable length. Yet, in the second half of the 1990s, Žižek's thought takes all the turns we listed in the Introduction, and which we can now summarise.

The radical-democratic Žižek is concerned to link the moral philosophy of human freedom, in the form of moral autonomy, to a fully democratic politics that takes into account social antagonism.

Žižek's early work shows how our implied commitments to the unity of the social order – our unconscious belief in the 'existence of the Other' – lead us to internalise forms of socio-symbolic authority that prevent us from determining progressive new symbolic identifications and lock us into exclusionary politics, through the unconscious mechanism of the 'theft of enjoyment'. By grasping that 'the Other does not exist', that is, by 'traversing the social fantasy', the subject can propose forms of symbolic authority that refuse the superego's command to exclude certain marginalised others.

As we saw in Chapter 3, at this stage, for Žižek, democratic politics and moral autonomy have the same psychological structure. This depends on rejecting the allure of a forbidden 'supreme crime' (and the despised others supposed to enjoy this ultimate transgression) by realising that this fantasy actually only props up an unjust social order as necessary and inevitable. Although the death drive – the 'kernel of the real', disclosed in social antagonism – is a permanent feature of the human condition, such that social conflict will always exist, the crucial thing for human freedom and a politics of liberation is to get beyond the fantasy that annihilation of our political adversaries will finally make the social order harmonious and whole. This is the political equivalent to the Freudian 'talking cure': by understanding the unconscious roots of our desires, we progressively 'drain the Zuider Zee' of the death drive, and arrive at a mode of social cooperation that depends less and less on aggression and repression. We have to find a *modus vivendi* with the death drive that drains it off into the ongoing expansion of moral universality, through the extension and deepening of democracy. Of course, we cannot hope just to get rid of it – but at the same time, we must avoid rushing into the void of its seductive aggression.

Writing in *The Plague of Fantasies* about the death drive in relation to the psychoanalytic theory of morality and politics, Žižek asks: 'Is not Lacan's entire theoretical edifice torn between . . . two options: between the ethics of desire/Law, of maintaining the gap, and the lethal/suicidal immersion in the Thing?' (*PF* 239).

Whatever the case for Lacan, this is certainly the dilemma central to Žižek's politics. But if the radical-democratic Žižek is all about 'maintaining the gap' and expanding democracy through refusing the revolutionary Romanticism of the death's drive's promise of a clean slate and a new order, then the revolutionary-vanguardist Žižek is all about the lethal plunge into the Real. For the recent Žižek, acknowledgement that 'the Other does not exist' does not mean recognition that society is an open framework within which morally autonomous subjects can propose social alternatives. It means the moment when the subject turns its back on society altogether and discovers, in the death drive that inhabits the core of the individual, the resources for a truly radical politics. Instead of autonomy, this is a moral theory of authenticity – being true to oneself, that is, true to the 'real kernel of human existence' in the death drive. The desire of the subject, the expansion of democracy and the struggle for autonomy become, through this lens, part of the problem. On the one hand, the revolutionary-vanguardist Žižek is convinced that an obscene enjoyment is the underside of every commitment that falls short of total revolution. On the other hand, instead of draining off the drives into socially constructive desires, and thereby liberating the subject from their subjection to repressive authorities, the aim of this strategy is to mobilise the destructive force of the drives for a politics that seeks to achieve a clean sweep of the political field. Žižek has moved increasingly towards speaking of this politics as 'the Good Terror' (*IDLC* 7, 164, 174, 417–19, 442, 462). To some extent (but only some), that is a Žižekian provocation. We can certainly say that the revolutionary-vanguardist Žižek mobilises the death drive in support of moral authenticity and political authoritarianism, rejecting democratic politics and the effort to socialise desire.

Žižek's passionate encounter with Schelling in 1996–7, then, clearly served to consolidate certain, more theoretically radical – if politically regressive, even openly anti-Enlightenment – tendencies present in his earlier texts. These have now supplanted the Enlightenment commitments of Žižek's earlier critique of ideology and his defence of the divided, but potentially autonomous, subject, with telling political results.

So in this 'mediating' section in the middle of *Žižek and Politics*, we will begin by looking at what Žižek claimed to find in Schelling's obscure *Ages of the World*. Some of this material, as in Chapter 2, is highly abstract, philosophical and inevitably difficult. Ironically, what Žižek claims he can see in Schelling is a theory that effectively 'vanishes' Žižek's earlier commitment to the idea that human identity is always shaped or 'mediated' by the symbolic, political worlds into which we are socialised. It replaces these critical ideas with a metaphysical or speculative account of how the subject allegedly can give birth to its own symbolic identity in a world-creating Real Act. Having then reflected philosophically on the stakes of this move, and the confusions that it consummates, we will be in a position in Part II of the book to examine Žižek's own recreated, revolutionary-vanguardist, post-1997 self.

God as Subject; the Subject as a God: Žižek's Schelling

Gottfried Schelling is certainly one of the most unusual modern philosophers. In Schelling's 'middle' period, the one that intrigues Žižek and that spanned roughly the two decades from 1801 to 1820, Schelling produced a series of incomplete, often mutually contradictory works (Bowie 1993; Dudley 2007). His lasting concern was to try to overcome the division of the subject introduced by Kant's critical philosophy. Kant had sharply divided the world up into free, moral subjects, who determine their actions through their own desire, and wholly determined objects, shaped by the causal laws of nature. Like Hegel and Fichte, the two other great idealist successors to Kant, Schelling wished to provide an account that would 'synthesise' freedom and necessity, human subjectivity and the natural world. His first attempts saw him try to come up with an account of how free subjectivity might emerge from out of nature. In his middle works, however, like those to which Žižek refers, Schelling undertakes an 'unheard-of reversal'. In Žižek's approving words, in *The Ages of the World* Schelling began to ask:

> what if the thing to be explained is not freedom, but the emergence of the chains of reason, of the causal network [of nature] – or to quote Schelling himself: 'The whole world is thoroughly caught in reason, but the question is: how did it get caught up in it in the first place?' (AF 3)

This is a question not just about the relationship between matter and ideas, nature and freedom, the real and the symbolic. It is the question of the origins of everything. So we have to stress: Žižek thinks that Schelling can provide us with an account of the 'problem of [the] Beginning' of reason and nature as we know it, which he tells us is 'the crucial problem of German idealism' (AF 14). This is the type of problem that Kant argued philosophy could not resolve, since it would take a God to know what was happening 'before' the world, as we finite humans know it, began. It is beyond the scope of possible human experience. Schelling, however, tells us that 'there is something that precedes the beginning itself'. Schelling claims metaphysical knowledge about this 'something', which, if it can bear the name, concerns the pre-history of God Himself.

Žižek's retelling of Schelling's tale has several stages and is very nearly as convoluted as the original. In brief, though, before the beginning, God was mad. Trapped within the nothingness of the 'abyss of freedom' prior to the existence of anything but Himself, God then 'contracts' the two drives, of unrestricted expansion and unlimited contraction. This engenders a 'vortex of 'divine madness' that threatens to swallow everything' (AF 16) in the 'rotary motion of the drives', so that God is like an animal caught in a cage, which repeatedly dashes itself against the bars that contain it. God engenders the ordered World from the *Logos* or Word, according to Žižek, as the only way of breaking out of this (self-)destructive rotary motion. Breathlessly summarising Schelling, Žižek reports:

> the Absolute 'opens up time', it 'represses' the rotary motion into the past, in order to get rid of the antagonism at its heart that threatens to drag it into the abyss of madness . . . eternity itself begets time in order to resolve the deadlock it became entangled in. (AF 29, 30)

So, concludes Žižek, in complete agreement with Schelling, creating the world was for God an 'unconscious Act', not the intelligent reflective design of an omniscient, omnipotent, let alone omnibenevolent agent. It was as a 'passage through madness' for God: the only way for him to escape from this tortured rotary motion of the expansionary and contractionary drives (cf. *TS* 34–41).

That all this borders on the mystical or unintelligible is of the essence here. But what interests us most is the political implications of Žižek's speculations, rather than his heterodox theology. For the truth is that for Žižek, the Lacanian theoretical relation between the subject and the Other is anticipated by Schelling's speculations concerning the relationship between God and the world. In other words, the Lacanian subject is a world-generating entity with godlike powers, and the socio-cultural system, the Other, is nothing more than the expression of the subject's constitutive act. This will be decisive for us in all sorts of ways. Let us list them straight away.

- First, what is at stake in Schelling's theogony is a founding, Radical Act. Because this decision comes before the Symbolic Order, it cannot be rational (because it cannot be signified). 'The abyss of an act of decision breaks up the causal chain, since it is grounded only in itself' (AF 32). It suspends the principle of sufficient reason, which means that all events have a preceding cause or reason that explains how it came to be. It is completely groundless, utterly arbitrary. And its result is to create a (new) world. This sort of a decision 'taken in the Real' will become the model for Žižek's Political Act.

- Secondly, the Symbolic Order is not something that this subject, God, finds external to himself: it is projected out of God himself. In psychoanalytic terms, primary repression of the 'rotary motion of the drives' happens not through the entry of the infant into the Symbolic Order under the sign of the paternal 'no!' to incest, but, instead, through a radical decision taken by the subject to project a Symbolic Order as the solution to its libidinal deadlock. In Žižek's Hegelian language, the symbolic Other is God himself externalised, in the form of the Other (AF 42).

- Thirdly, in this way, this primordial Act involves 'the principle of identity'. God is not, in this moment of decision and Act, a 'split' subject. It is true that, after the Act is accomplished, He has a 'contracted Substance' – namely the World – that is Other to Himself. But the God 'posits Itself as grounded in and simultane-ously different from its [own] contracted Substance', the Wor(l)d, in His creative Act (AF 33). By implication, what Žižek is claim-ing is that, in the authentic political Act, the political subject is no longer a divided subject. It is an 'acephalous saint', a subject of the drives – a full subject 'in the Real'.

The Paratactic View: What's God to Žižek's Political Philosophy?

So the question is: why in heaven or on earth does Žižek think that Schelling's mythology concerning God is essential for political philosophy, and his own Leftist thought? One of our arguments is that Žižek$_2$ consolidates some of the metaphysical gestures present in Žižek's work from the start. The most striking tendency of all is Žižek's paratactic style, which can make him so difficult to read. As we have said, by parataxis we mean the way that Žižek jumps between radically different fields in the space of a paragraph or page. Why does Žižek think that using psychoanalysis to analyse cinema, then philosophy and then politics is justified intellectually, when these are such apparently different social practices, each with its own specific logics and modes of operation?

The answer, we would contend, is as ultimately unavoidable as it is deeply telling. For Žižek, his Lacanian psychoanalysis is what phi-losophers used to call a *mathesis universalis*: a universal method. But to suggest we can use one method to fit all topics is to (pre)suppose that all the different fields Žižek examines must in the crucial respects all be 'the same'. The objects in these structures might appear to be very different – individual psychology in the case of psychoanalysis, collective organisation in the case of politics, cultural mythologies in the case of popular culture, and so on – but somehow the underlying structure must be the same structure in all cases. In other words, Žižek must be arguing that one logic, or what we are about to call a single 'subject–object', is at play in all these fields, unfolding or expressing itself in them. The idea that the true object of Žižek's analysis is such a single 'subject–object' – the 'big Other' as the projection/expression of an undivided subject 'in the Real' – is what philosophically licenses Žižek's characteristic sideways rhetorical jumping between fields. All fields are ultimately the same field, the expression/projection of the one world-constituting subject.

So, when Žižek turns to Schelling in 1996–7, we think that Žižek finds a metaphysical and theological confirmation of his own supposition concerning the world as subject–object. In Schelling, he sees himself, or a theological account for what he has been doing all along. We have just seen how, explicitly, Žižek is fascinated by how Schelling argues that the Other (the world, the word, the Symbolic Order) is God himself, or his 'contractionary' drive, externalised. It is He, God, a subject, before it is Other, an object. This God is not divided first of all because he enters into a Symbolic Order, or Other, not of his own creation. On the contrary, the division of the subject is a solution to the problem of the 'rotary motion of the drives' and the 'vortex of madness' involved in God's own, internal, absolute solipsism.

So we should not be surprised that in *The Indivisible Remainder* and *The Abyss of Freedom* Žižek, in typical clip, interweaves his story about how God engendered the world with psychoanalytic categories there to explain the subjectivity of individuals. That vanishing mediation, the rotary motion of the divine drives, gives Žižek occasion to raise the controversial topic – which becomes increasingly central in Žižek$_2$, as we shall see – of the death drive. We then discover that the description of God as a 'subject' licenses Žižek to apply lessons from the Schellingerian Creation narrative to the psycho-biography of individual children. He simply cuts straight from the theogony to a section on Melanie Klein's child psychology, and Lacan's account of symbolic castration, as if the two objects were the same (AF 20–1, 43–4). Faced with this characteristic textual pastiche, we could say Žižek is 'psychoanalysing God', already a fairly difficult endeavour.

Unfortunately, it is more accurate to say that Žižek is in the process of 'theologising' the individual subject (equating subjects with God), with potentially disastrous consequences for his theories of ideology and politics.

Žižek draws the following analogies or 'structural homologies' (see Chapter 3) from his narrative of God's passage from infinite-expansionary freedom, via his 'capture' in the repetitive cycle of expansionary–contractionary drives, to creating the symbolic Other. These analogies structure Žižek's politics after 1997, and force him into increasingly pessimistic positions:

1. In terms of individual development, Žižek is suggesting that the Symbolic Order is the paranoid projection of a meaningful universe around the lonely subject. It just so happens that most individuals in a society share the same delusion (the same Symbolic Order). The implication is that a new subject can project a new Symbolic Order that would be inhabited by those individuals who reject the old Symbolic Order (and who shed their former subjectivity in the process). But, in psychoanalytic terms, the Symbolic Order of the psychotic is not centred on the 'signification of the phallus' – that is, on a master signifier. This signifier is what the psychotic subject lacks. Instead, the psychotic compensates by building an *imaginary* replacement for the missing master signifier – some image of God or a Master supposedly filled with Meaning and capable of directly manipulating the Real. Žižek's revolutionary conception of subjectivity can look, then, from a Lacanian perspective, suspiciously like collective psychosis, and the new worlds that he proposes, as we will see, are centred on curiously 'full' signifiers that somehow operate 'in the Real'. Indicatively, Žižek often endows these 'master' signifiers with capital letters, implying both their undivided unity and their potent ability to tap into subjects' drives.

2. In terms of philosophical anthropology, Žižek has always maintained that human beings are neither wholly cultural, nor able to 'get back to nature'. There is a 'vanishing mediator' between culture and nature. This 'imp of perversity' – or, as Kant says, a kind of ineducability in the human being – is the Freudian death drive. But Žižek has also insisted that the death drive cannot be directly accessed – it is like a black hole in the psyche, a distortion of our cultural and social lives whose source cannot be inspected, only known through its disruptive effects on our sociable existences. Post-1997,

however, once the death drive is made to correspond to God's rotary drives, the clear implication is that it *can* be directly accessed in moments of the 'madness of decision' and political Acts.

3. In terms of moral philosophy, human beings' deepest, most revealing capacity is the capacity for diabolical *evil*, an act whose intransigence has the same 'form' as a perfectly moral act (because both involve rigorously putting aside all our usual, particular, affective and personal concerns for the sake of the action). However, unlike the Moral Law, diabolical evil overthrows the existing Symbolic Order, giving birth to a new order as God gives birth to creation. (We will expand on this below.)

4. In terms of the ethics of psychoanalysis, the traversal of the fantasy after 1997 does not involve the subject coming to terms in a new way with the Symbolic Order, into which he has been born. The end of analysis is no longer the acknowledgement of castration (that is, recognition of how human beings are finite, mortal and sexed beings, who do not possess the symbol of potency that would enable us to transcend this condition). The traversal of the fantasy now involves confronting the 'vanishing mediation' of the drives and 'identifying with the *sinthome*'. This effectively means acknowledging our potential for diabolical evil. Consequently, instead of acknowledgement of castration, the end of analysis is the projection of a new master signifier (and a new world).

5. In politics, we need courageously to confront our capacity to engender wholly new political orders, completely overthrowing the old regimes. This will involve re-enacting collectively God's abyssal Act of decision, which saw him give birth to the world as his own self-externalisation. Total revolution becomes a permanent possibility, and this allows Žižek to sidestep a lot of the work of empirical sociological analysis of what is possible, and patient political advocacy of change as desirable. The reason is ultimately that we can as bearers of death drive engender a new political regime or Other as God engendered the world.

In our view, these ideas are a 'tissue of errors', theoretically erroneous and politically problematic. Their consequence is that Žižek's Enlightenment critique of ideology passes directly into a pessimistic theory of culture (Chapter 4), that his theory of politics passes from a democratic one, towards regressive authoritarian vanguardism (Chapter 5), and that, in the end, Žižek turns to religion or 'political theology' to try to bring coherence to his position (Chapter 6).

But, in order to demonstrate our point, let us go to the heart of things: the 'absent centre' of Žižek's theoretical edifice, his later notion of the subject.

Žižek's Embrace of Schelling's Identical Subject–Object

In Chapter 2, we saw how Žižek argues for a remarkable synthesis between Lacan's 'subject of the enunciation' and Kant's subject as 'unity of apperception'. Both are purely empty and completely 'formal' subjects – not substantial objects, like the empirical things we encounter in the world, or the types of metaphysical substances (the soul or God) posited by theologians. Kant's subject is permanently divided. It cannot know what it is, at the point where it thinks, just as Lacan tells us that, as social substances, we have always already lost access to that maternal Thing (*Das Ding*) that would secure our substantial identity and final bliss.

The radical-democratic Žižek's subject is a clearing or opening wherein things can be perceived, and spoken about as having meanings – not a Thing in the Real. Consequently, his political model is that of 'traversing of the fantasy' at the end of the Lacanian cure. This is a politics of social transformation based on 'acceptance of castration', where this is both a surrender of fantasy and a liberation from self-imposed limitations. It is a surrender of the fantasy that the socio-symbolic order can be made whole and therefore an acceptance of human finitude and social conflict. Democracy becomes a *modus vivendi* with our divided condition and with the social antagonisms that arise because of it. But it is also a liberation from the subject's own unconscious supposition that, if only the 'lost object' formerly possessed by the Other could be restored, then the subject would be unambiguously allocated a social role and a political mandate. By losing the guarantee of this sort of full identity, the subject also loses the restrictive assumption that the socio-symbolic order is ultimately closed. In an open order, the decisions and actions of the (finite, divided) subject *matter* to the shape that society takes – hence 'acceptance of castration' means, finally, a liberating embrace of moral autonomy and political agency.

After 1996 and the encounter with Schelling, however, Žižek's claims about the aims of analysis and his ethico-political recommendations flowing from this undergo a significant change. Let us now see how this is so, by looking first at Žižek's ontology of the subject, then at his remarkable reading of Kant's moral philosophy.

TOWARDS THE SUBJECT AS DEATH DRIVE

The implications of Schelling's theology for Žižek's recent notion of the subject are most fully developed in the opening chapter of *The Ticklish Subject*. There, Žižek focuses on one of the most famous episodes in twentieth-century European philosophy, Martin Heidegger's reading of Kant in his 1929 lectures *Kant and the Problems of Metaphysics* (1990). In this work, Heidegger famously argued that Kant's obscure notion of a 'transcendental imagination' is the hidden key to Kant's philosophy. What is in question is Kant's idea that human imagination is capable not only of rearranging objects or 'representations' into new configurations, as in fictions – the way we can, for example, imagine beasts like centaurs that combine a human torso with the body of a horse. The imagination, Kant argues, also has a 'transcendental' role in bringing together particular sensations into the ordered, intelligible objects of our experience (a horse or a person) in the first place. If it did not do this, we would have no such experiences, which our 'empirical' imagination can then rearrange so creatively into centaurs and other such follies.

Žižek's later notion of the subject draws heavily on, and radicalises, the Heideggerian reading of Kant's transcendental imagination. In *The Ticklish Subject*, Žižek proposes that the transcendental imagination, at its most basic, is not a force of synthesis at all, bringing together divided sensations into coherent representations of the objects of our experience. At its most basic, the transcendental imagination for Žižek$_2$ is an elemental force of 'analysis', which separates things out from their natural contexts before they are then reassembled in our empirical experiences. 'Imagination *qua* the activity of dissolution" . . . treats as a separate entity what has effective existence only as a part of some organic Whole' (*TS* 29).

How can Žižek 'know' that the world is an 'organic whole', before any possible experience of the objects in this world? The answer is: through an unacknowledged metaphysical speculation. Žižek's new conception of the transcendental imagination, as elementary 'negativity' that tears apart all unified wholes and his often-repeated citation of Hegel on the understanding as the 'night of the world' of the imagined body in fragments, is part of this metaphysical speculation based on Schelling. As Robert Sinnerbrink has observed, it is Schelling's Romantic attempt to think how freedom could give birth to an ordered world that is the final arbiter of Žižek₂'s position:

> Žižek goes on to link the Hegelian 'night of the world' with Schelling's conception of the subject as 'pure night of the Self', 'infinite lack of Being'; the 'violent gesture of contraction' that also forms the basis of Hegel's account of madness as the cutting of all links with external reality . . . (Sinnerink 2008: 6; see *IR* 8; *TS* 34–5)

The implication of this speculative claim is that, in Žižek's later conception of the subject, the subject is no longer the empty, formal presupposition or place that must be there in order for there to be an ordered experience of the world. For Kant, the subject cannot know what it is, as a thing-in-itself – that is, 'in the real'. But, as Žižek has been moved to speculate concerning this subject 'in its becoming', the subject has increasingly become a substantial thing. Žižek insists that we can not only pose, but also answer, the metaphysical question of how subjectivity could have emerged out of the natural world 'in the beginning'. For Žižek, the truth of subjectivity is a 'passage through madness', a 'violent' Schellingian 'gesture of contraction' – that is, the work of the Freudian death drive. So the Žižek₂ position is that we *can* know what Thing or object the subject is in the Real. Žižek₂'s subject is the bearer of this Real death drive, capable of breaking down and reassembling all the representations the subject encounters. The human being is the bearer of what Žižek specifies as an 'infinite' death drive, and this is now something like a secularised, 'undead' Freudian successor to the theologians' immortal soul. In the language of German philosophy, this later Žižekian subject is actually a metaphysically endowed identity of subject and object, an identical subject–object.

THE SUBJECT–OBJECT, THE DEATH DRIVE AND DIABOLICAL EVIL

Romanticism has long had a not-so-secret sympathy for the Devil. It is a mark of Žižek's philosophical Romanticism that, in his work since 1997, he has increasingly associated the subject as bearer of the death drive with the capacity for what he terms 'diabolical evil'. There is a dimension of provocation in this position, since Žižek does not by this move necessarily mean to praise terrible criminals such as Josef Stalin or Adolf Hitler. Instead, the concept of diabolical evil comes out of Žižek's reading of Immanuel Kant's philosophy by way of Hegel and Lacan, but after his turn to Schelling.

Now, despite its name, Žižek argues that in talking of diabolical evil he means nothing more than the *form* of the Moral Law as Kant conceived it, as any act motivated solely by a sense of duty alone, despite all the individual's pre-existing 'pathological' feelings and attachments (*PF* 227, 229). To give up all pathological motives and to nominate something – even some supposedly 'good' content like not lying – as a worthwhile 'end in itself', Žižek is suggesting, is necessarily to appear to other, more 'rational' individuals as inhumane, inexplicable, incomprehensibly intransigent: in short, diabolically evil. So the idea is that, in holding uncompromisingly to a set of principles without any consideration for self-interest or the communal good, we perform a supposedly superhuman act of 'angelic good' – which from the purely formal perspective is equivalent to its opposite in content, an act of 'diabolical evil' (that is, evil for its own sake). Žižek's controversial claim is that Kant himself at several points approached recognition of this 'speculative identity' between the angelic good and diabolical evil, before piously denying its unbearable truth (Zupančič 2000: 79–82).

Now, there is in fact much more at stake in the concept of diabolical evil than Žižek openly acknowledges. Since 'angelic good' and 'diabolical evil' are in the first place purely formal concepts, the commission of evil for its own sake must mean taking the opposite of the moral law as the guideline for action. But the moral law is only the imperative always to act in formally universal ways. Therefore, diabolical evil must mean always acting in radically particular ways, ways that are nevertheless irreducible to mere self-interest or the holding of a specific set of values. It must mean always acting in ways that are radically anti-universal and exclusive – for instance, being *always* prejudiced, simply for the sake of prejudice and irrespective of the specific prejudice in question, and of what personal or other gain one would achieve by it.

Is this, then, what Žižek means when he advocates diabolical evil? Fortunately not. For Žižek, diabolical evil is somehow beyond – or, strictly speaking, before – good and evil in any moral sense. It underlies our very capacity to imagine forms of good and evil as the consequence of our projection of (ethico-political and socio-cultural) worlds. Diabolical evil is the transcendental imagination in action, after Žižek's Romantic twist on this idea. As early as *Tarrying with the Negative*, Žižek speculates that diabolical evil – wholly hateful, irrational, motivated by no explicable good – is in truth 'Good itself "in the mode of becoming" ' – namely, the precondition for founding any social or political order wherein people can then judge actions at all (*TN* 97). So, for Žižek, diabolical evil (hence transcendental imagination, hence the leap into madness of God's world creation) is the arbitrary and groundless 'act of decision' that founds a Symbolic Order, and thereby also standards of right and wrong, good and evil. Žižek maintains that examples of this are the political revolutions of modernity – the French Revolution of 1789 and the Russian Revolution of 1917.

The implications of this are unmistakably relativist. Just as Žižek's later ontology sees death drive, radical negativity and the analytic imagination as the 'truth' beneath our subjective capacity to understand the world, he insists that diabolical evil is the transcendental and *political* precondition for morally good or dutiful actions. Rather than using the Moral Law (a standard of universality) to assess social and political orders, these are supposed to result from an act of diabolical evil that generates the standards of assessment in the first place. Further, if we accept Žižek's reading of Kant on diabolical evil, there is really no way to differentiate the moral law from its opposite in Žižek's perspective. What this ultimately means is that there is no means available to us to judge other social and political totalities. We simply have to make a groundless decision to act and 'courageously [to] accept the full actualization of a Cause, including the inevitable risk of a catastrophic disaster' (*IDLC* 7). Žižek's advocacy of figures such as Heidegger, Mao, Stalin and Robespierre in *In Defence of Lost Causes* implies just such a suspension of moral judgement in the name of a Romantic valorisation of the revolutionary act that is supposedly 'beyond good and evil'.

Political Theology and the Subject–Object

Of course, Žižek is far from the only theorist to return to such theologically loaded notions as the diabolical, after 1989. 'Political theology', a term coined by reactionary thinker Carl Schmitt (1985), has recently been dusted off as a new master signifier in academic theory. Although it seems that many people who use it today do not understand this, 'political theology' after Schmitt involves the view that no enlightened, secular society can stand, because at the basis of all authority there is a groundless abyss – the abyss of the sovereign's decision – that should preferably be theologically justified or ideologically obscured. The other key thing for political theology in the Schmittian inheritance is that the social order can be thought of in theological terms, since all modern ideas (like the state, the sovereign, human rights) are 'secularisations' of old theological ideas anyway. In particular, the modern executive or 'sovereign state', with its capacity to make the final decisions on how a society is run, is a 'secularisation' of the idea that God absolutely governs all His Creation. Despite an excellent critique of Schmitt (see CS), the revolutionary-vanguardist Žižek duly arrives at these anti-Enlightenment ideas, one after another. This is because Žižek's argument that we can use Schelling's theology as the key to thinking about subjectivity and politics is its own, idiosyncratic species of political theology.

So what is the problem with this? We would assert that the idea that the Other, the Symbolic Order, is the expression/projection of the Subject in its momentary, world-constituting political Act, inescapably denies two important things about psychological and social reality. The first problem is that the Symbolic Order both precedes and post-dates the subject. The linguistically mediated socio-cultural rules of communal life are something that individuals are born into and die within. Of course these change. But the big Other or Symbolic Order, as an intersubjective space, transcends the individuals operating within it. Žižek's political theology instead involves effectively denying the Otherness, the materiality and independence of the Other into which the child is educated. Indeed, in the psychoanalytic clinic, the type of subject who thinks that he can project his own private social reality is the psychotic. But perhaps Žižek is thinking of the political Act of a subject incarnated, not in an individual, but in a collectivity such as the nation or the party?

The second problem is that the idea that the national socio-cultural institutions are the expression of a collective act of political creation, or 'inauguration', represents a sociologically primitive flattening of society. Favourite examples of thinkers who reason in this reductive way are the American Constitution and the French Declaration of the Rights of Man. Another sort of example often used in the same way is the socialist revolutions of Russia in 1917 and China in 1949. These are held to be 'inaugural declarations' of new societies – with new socio-cultural rules and institutional embodiments of these rules – that happened because collective subjects made political decisions. We have already stated that Žižek thinks that the French and Russian examples are evidence for exactly this sort of view.

To hypostasise such exceptional moments is something of an occupational hazard for philosophers, who tend to think that political ideas determine social reality. But no major sociological theory of the last two hundred years has accepted that societies are created by virtue of political decisions – no matter how stirring these inaugural declarations might be. For Marx, for instance, societies are complex totalities involving economic, political and ideological relations, and these societies undergo uneven forms of development as a result of material factors. Ultimately, it is the historically developing relationship between humanity and nature that decides what happens – not the ideological statements of collective political subjects. That is why Marx calls himself a 'historical materialist' and not a political idealist.

One consequence of the Marxist position on society is that social revolutions do not, in fact, wipe the slate clean. Instead, as Marx explained in the *Critique of the Gotha Programme*, the political decision to stage a socialist revolution merely opens up a long historical period of partial and uneven transformations (Marx 1986: 319–21). These transformations, strictly speaking, do not instantly abolish capitalism but rather modify its rules, during the entire historical epoch that Marx calls socialism. Based on the experience of the Russian Revolution, the Marxists such as Lenin and Trotsky concurred with Marx's view: the revolutionary insurrection merely opened up a heightened period of social struggles, and of confused and partial experimentation with modifications to the old rules. The fantasy of the instant transformation, of the clean slate and the new beginning, is the idealistic hope of those who do not actually participate in social revolutions. It is the dream of the disenfranchised and politically disempowered, not the means of their empowerment.

Sociology from Weber onwards has insisted that modern society is not the closed totality of the pre-modern community. Instead, modern societies are complex open structures with extensive functional differentiation, and where the value spheres of science, morality and art have separated off into distinct realms of action. Whether we are talking about the functionalism of Talcott Parsons or Nikolaus Luhmann, the post-structuralism of Foucault, the structural Marxism of Althusser, the neo-Weberian analysis of Habermas or the neo-Durkheimian perspective of Bourdieu, there is a solid consensus despite other major differences. The idea that society is the simple and undifferentiated expression/projection of a collective subject, 'identical subject–object' or 'historical meta-subject' went out of the window with Hegel. Of course, Žižek's project is to revive

Hegel, and his instinct is polemically to oppose any present consensus in 'Western academia'. But it is worth asking what the costs of these moves might be – because Žižek is not the first to claim to revive Hegel for the Marxist lineage in exactly this way. The tragic precursor to Žižek's current position is the revolutionary Romanticism of György Lukács, where commitment to the total revolution staged by the proletariat as an 'identical subject–object of history' saw him become first a revolutionary Romantic, then a reluctant Stalinist (Arato and Brienes 1979).

We believe that there are two key consequences of Žižek's conception of society as a subject–object, which will structure and inform our criticisms of Žižek$_2$ in Part II of this book.

1. The first, decisive for Chapter 4, is that Žižek collapses the distinction between the Ego Ideal and the Symbolic Order. We examined the Ego Ideal in the context of examining Žižek's theory of ideology in Chapter 1. For the subject, the Ego Ideal is the locus of symbolic identification. It is the master signifier that 'sews' the subject into the social totality. In Lacan's early seminars, the Ego Ideal is referred to as the 'Name of the Father', the idea being that symbolic identification with parental ideals is reflected in the subject's patronymic, or surname. Just as there is a huge number of surnames in the Symbolic Order, so too the Symbolic Order holds many social ideals. But Žižek's notion that the subject and the Other are somehow 'the same' leads inevitably to him talking as if the Ego Ideal and the Symbolic Order were somehow identical – as if there were room for only a single, social ideal or highest good in any society, and cultural pluralisation were somehow equivalent to the undermining of social cohesion.

2. The second, decisive for Chapter 5, is that Žižek cannot conduct a critical analysis of economic processes. Yet he himself argues that this is decisive for an understanding of contemporary capitalism. The consequence is that his Marxism is mostly rhetorical, a provocation to the hated 'PC multiculturalists' but not grounded in any adequate social theory (Laclau 2000: 289–90). Elsewhere, for instance in *In Defence of Lost Causes*, Žižek simply tells us that the relations between economics and politics are logically the same as those between the latent and manifest content of dreams in Freud's *Interpretation of Dreams*. There could hardly be a more direct statement of Žižek's thinking of political societies as 'subject–objects' than this (*IDLC* 285–93).

Since this second conflation is such a fundamental problem, before we proceed let us look at some concrete results of this sort of monological psychoanalytic social Theory.

What is Capitalism? Žižek's Evasion of Economics

In his defence, Žižek is one of the few celebrated Theorists today who talks about 'capitalism', which is an inescapably economic notion, rather than attacking 'liberalism', 'biopower', 'the society of the spectacle', or, recently, 'democracy'. We can list at least five attempts Žižek has made to discuss capitalism as his theoretical object, and thereby to theorise the differences, and inter-relations, between the economic, political, cultural and ideological social structures.

1. First, Žižek takes Marx's notion of the 'commodity fetish' as something like an elementary cell to think through the paradoxical logics of ideological interpellation. Here, he follows Lukács directly. Commodity fetishism is for Marx the most basic way subjects 'buy into' the economic system, or accept its elementary subjective assumptions – through a fundamental *misunderstanding* of how capitalism works. But this in no way speaks to the logics of the economic system, which requires a scientific analysis that *breaks* with commodity fetishism. The chapter of commodity fetishism in Marx's *Capital* is for this reason only the first chapter in a multi-volume work, which then proceeds to analyse the accumulation dynamics and crisis tendencies of capitalism, including proposing mathematical formulations of its laws of motion. Žižek simply stops at commodity fetishism and goes no further.
2. Secondly, Žižek has argued that capitalism is 'the discourse of the hysteric'. Just as capitalism produces surplus value through the exploitation of labour, so too, it is claimed, the hysteric produces 'surplus enjoyment' from her symptom. It is difficult to know what to make of this argument from analogy, except to note that it gets no closer than the 'commodity-fetishism' approach to actually specifying how capitalism operates, what sorts of crises are likely and where social agents might appear who are capable of challenging the logic of the market. The mere fact that Lacan is the origin of this particular theoretical figure does not, by itself, make it accurate – or helpful.
3. Thirdly, targeting the culturalism of Butler, Laclau et al., Žižek suggests that the untouchability of the economy is the 'fundamental

fantasy' of the present global order that needs to be traversed. This idea aligns with Žižek's propensity to talk in a populist manner about how today 'the experts' run a type of administrative biopolitics (or 'post-politics') immune to politicisation (*TS* 198). To denounce the supposed untouchability of the economy in contemporary politics, however, is again not to say anything concerning its workings, or how its untouchable system dynamics impact very tangibly upon the lived experiences of subjects.

4. Fourthly, in *The Parallax View* and *In Defence of Lost Causes*, Žižek has argued that one cannot look at the economy and politics in a single theoretical or analytic perspective at all! Alongside a series of oppositions from other theoretical fields, like the mind versus the body, the material versus the ideal, and so on, Žižek proposes a 'parallax view' of the relations between the economy and society. This parallax view turns out to be a rewriting of Žižek's Lacanian concept of anamorphosis. Apparently, the reason why one cannot adopt such a meta-linguistic, external perception on such anamorphotic objects as the relation between economy and politics is because of the Lacanian Real. The Real distortion of the theoretical field reflects, in this objective field, our own subjective implication, and the implication of our biases and desires, in what we perceive. The issue is whether, as a 'solution' to this issue, it is anything more than a restatement of the problem (*PV* 54–61).

5. Last and not least, since 1999 Žižek has sometimes proposed that the capitalist economy is Real in the Lacanian sense: ' "reality" is the social reality of the actual people involved in interaction, and in the productive process; the Real is the inexorable "abstract" spectral logic of Capital which determines what goes on in social reality' (*FA* 15–16).

It is clear that what unites these different approaches is Žižek's tendency to transpose categories that deal with subjectivity onto the objective mechanisms of the economy. But, since the fifth proposition is so revealing, let us focus on it. Ernesto Laclau has rightly questioned whether Lacan would recognise himself in this idea that an entire economic system could be 'Real', rather than Symbolic. To assert that capital is Real is to assign an inexplicable, fateful significance to it. Its movements are, *ex hypothesi*, beyond human comprehension, or 'spectral', as Žižek says. As in the quotation above, the capitalist economy's edicts are for modern subject what the edicts of the gods were for pre-modern subjects. We note how closely Žižek's position here ironically approaches the worst fetishisations of the market that emerged in the neoliberal management literature of the soaring 1990s and early years of this century.

So the point is that, far from resolving the problem, there could hardly be a clearer statement of Žižek's failure to provide the political economy for which he has called than his own repetition of the 'Capital is the Real today' theme. It is less a statement of theoretical understanding or insight than a confession of the inability of his theoretical categories to gain analytic purchase on economic concerns.

But more can and should be said about this telling mystification. Consider the way Žižek explains the distinction between 'reality' and 'the Real' in making his case. To cite again: ' "reality" is the social reality of the actual people involved in interaction, and in the productive process; while the Real is the inexorable "abstract" spectral logic of Capital that determines what goes on in social reality.' Notice how Žižek's distinction between experiential social reality and something else, which operates anonymously 'behind the backs' of agents and that cannot directly be an object of possible experience, corresponds to the central socio-theoretical distinction in Jürgen Habermas's *Theory of Communicative Action* (Habermas 1984, 1987a).

For Habermas, the lifeworld (Žižek's 'social reality') is something inhabited by subjects and experienced as a meaningful world. By contrast, the system (Žižek's 'Capital as Real') is a network of processes that function independently of the intentions of the agents who operate these processes. The actions of agents in the economy and the administration are integrated, meshed, through anonymous 'steering media' such as money and power, and not through the intended meaningfulness of subjects' actions. Thus, for instance, subjects go to work in a workplace – an experiential arena full of meaningful (for example, just and unjust) relationships. But the actions performed in this workplace, which require subjective motivation and social ideals to perform, are integrated into the economic system through the movement of prices, in ways that have nothing to do with the employees' motivations and ideals. The systematic regularities of the economy and administration can be detected only from the perspective of an observer – participants cannot experience this directly. Yet the workings of the system have very concrete effects in the lifeworlds of subjects, including the devastating consequences of economic dislocation and political turmoil.

Getting Real with the Economy

- Žižek's reversion to the reality/Real distinction to describe the distinction between the lived experience of subjects and the economic system attests to the precise boundaries of Žižek's psychoanalytic reason. Psychoanalysis remains a theory of the lived, first-person 'lifeworld' experiences of subjects. It is only from this perspective that capitalism's functioning can appear as Real – that is, as traumatic and senseless.

- The theoretical object of psychoanalysis is the way people (mis) perceive the lifeworld in which they live, because of the distorting effects of the drives, and competing identifications. The contribution of psychoanalysis to political theory, then, is in its uncovering of unconscious motives and mechanisms that support and shape identifications that are decisive for social participation.

- These motives, as 'unconscious', share the feature in common with the media-steered economic subsystem that they produce effects 'behind the backs' of subjects' conscious intentionality. However, individuals' unconscious symptoms and commitments remain a psychological datum, a truth shown by the psychological efficacy of psychoanalytic interpretations, which directly change what they interpret.

- But this is not so with the effects visited upon individuals by media-steered subsystems involving millions of agents and transactions, even though the market seems, like the unconscious, to be a sort of 'fate' in ideological (mis)recognition. The limits to effective political intervention in the economy and administration are objective and can be disclosed only through social science.

The big difference between Habermas and Žižek is that Habermas recognises that he needs a functional systems theory to map the 'system', and an action theory informed by psychoanalysis to understand the lifeworld. Žižek, by contrast, thinks that psychoanalysis can do both – by silencing the insights of systems theories under the sign of 'Capital as the Real today'. Beyond this, a whole series of other differences open up that have to do with the way that Habermas continues to defend the Enlightenment legacy, while Žižek has progressively abandoned it.

But does not Žižek have a reply to all these problems – that he has a Romanticist theory of society as the expression/projection of an identical subject–object and that as a consequence he refuses to accept the theoretical limitations of psychoanalysis? Žižek would probably reply that his claim is not the identity of subject and object, but that 'the Other does not exist'. In closing this chapter, let us examine this rejoinder.

Žižek maintains that the analysis of the big Other is the link between individual and society. For Žižek, the seeming focus of psychoanalysis on the individual must also take in a theory of the social Law of the big Other: 'the Social, the field of social practice and socially held beliefs is not simply a different level from the individual experience, but something to which the individual has to relate . . .' (RL 16). Ultimately, 'the unconscious is structured like a language', and what this means is that the unconscious is actually 'out there' in social space, rather than something private, locked away in the individual. Specifically, the Symbolic Law that inserts the big Other into the psychic economy of the individual is borne by public, social ideals, images of symbolic authority that represent, for the subject, the threat of castration. But, in the final analysis, the subject must realise that 'the Other does not exist', that the subject is already castrated, finite, and that therefore the Other does not possess an ultimate signifier that would make it into a whole, undivided Self. One of the things that this means in modernity is that the subject must realise that his lifeworld is penetrated from the outside by system imperatives that cannot be dealt with through interpretation or Theory alone, but also should not be misrecognised through ideology as 'inevitable and natural'.

The problem is that Žižek's analysis, when it gets this far, stops right here. He cannot go on from this point to an analysis of these system imperatives themselves, as we have seen. Instead, he turns back towards another possible meaning of 'the Other does not exist', the idea that the 'Other does not exist' because it is only the expression/projection of the subject. From here, it is a short step to placing society on the couch: why does the historical subject misrecognise its world-constituting power, why does the social subject think that the big Other exists, when in fact, 'the Other does not exist'?

In the next three chapters we will see Žižek again and again ascribing categories of psychoanalytic diagnosis to social structures themselves – the 'society of generalised perversion' and 'capitalism as hysteria' are examples. We would ask: if a theorist proposes a metaphysical theory of subjectivity in which the undivided subject constitutes the world in an act of inaugural decision; and that theorist models political action on this theory, going on to propose a psychoanalysis of social forms that treats them as if they could be diagnosed, just as the subject can; and that theorist comprehensively fails to describe any reality outside the sphere of subjectivity, despite strident claims to be a dialectical and historical materialist, then does that theorist not have a Romantic theory of the identical subject–object?

The key idea that we have argued for is that no theorist can psychoanalyse society without first reductively positing it to as a single 'metasubject' or 'subject–object'. Once Žižek, albeit never explicitly, had arrived at the idea that society is a single metasubject or subject–object, a certain style of social analysis and political strategy came to recommend itself more and more strongly. As categories of subjectivity usurp the place of an analysis of objective structures, Žižek's politics become increasingly voluntaristic – that is, he tends to substitute injunctions to have political willpower for analyses of the dynamics of society.

Part Two

$\check{Z}i\check{z}ek_2$

Chapter 4

Postmodernity and the Society of Generalised Perversion

Introduction

Žižek regards the supposed consumer paradise at the 'end of history' more as a bleak dystopia. With Marxists such as Fredric Jameson, Žižek describes postmodern culture as the cultural logic of global capitalism. But Žižek adds that this culture is characterised by 'generalised perversion' (e.g. *OB* 20). The cultural liberation of 'new individualists', which is supposed to go with economic globalisation, is really a new domination of the individual by capitalism.

Žižek's description, to be examined now, of the contemporary situation as 'generalised perversion' needs to be read in conjunction with his basic assessment of the period in terms of the 'end of history'. The 'triumph of capitalism' means a society ruled by what Marx called 'commodity fetishism', wherein the dominance of capitalism seems natural and inevitable. Although Marx based his idea of commodity fetishism on anthropology, Žižek adds to it a psychological aspect, not just in individuals' perverse fetishisation of consumer items, but, more fundamentally, in individuals' disavowal of the way that capitalism now rules their lives. Individuals today, in the industrialised world, celebrate a cultural liberation that for Žižek has a darker underside – where their celebration of cultural struggles for recognition, new identity possibilities and market-driven cultural differences conceals the radical depoliticisation of the capitalist economy.

For Žižek, this depoliticisation prevents us from confronting global injustice head on. As he shows in works like *Iraq: The Borrowed Kettle* (2004), with its recognition of human-rights violations committed by imperialism, and in books like *On Violence* (2008), with its critique of the structural violence of global capitalism, world capitalism involves manifold suffering. Mindlessly to celebrate consumerism, or even to engage in cultural politics in the privileged centres of the industrialised world without making any contribution to wider struggles, is, for Žižek, morally abominable. Žižek cites a great deal of evidence to support his perspective on late capitalism, and descriptions of the social problems created by unregulated markets are harrowing. A society that turns everything over to the free market courts moral free-fall, and Žižek insists that, when politics is closed to social justice and culture lacks social ideals, then the result is heightening aggression. Yet it is not just a case of a moral reminder about global poverty and international inequality. Žižek warns that universal commodity fetishism fundamentally means an alienated society. The flipside to the consumer paradise full of supposedly liberated individuals is a dark need for both domination and submission, while resentments simmer just below the surface. Accordingly, the society of generalised perversion is characterised by the breakdown of civility, rising belligerence, paranoid delusions, social fragmentation, widespread anomie and outbreaks of irrational violence. It is here, in describing the momentous psychological consequences of the 'triumph of capitalism', that Žižek is at his most interesting, provocative and controversial.

According to Žižek, postmodern culture not only conceals the injustices of world capitalism. What he calls the 'permissive society' also blocks political resistance from emerging, because it also represents something approaching a catastrophe for socio-political subjectivity. The story that Žižek tells goes like this. In pre-modern societies, the cultural totality was unified by the reigning master signifier (the official religion, in societies with no separation between Church and State), and subjects shared a single Ego Ideal, generally personified in the figure of the monarch (the king as the lieutenant of God). By contrast, our postmodern societies lack any such unifying symbol or point of identification. Optimistically, the modern democratic revolution had attempted to generate a rational society by getting rid of the arbitrary power of the ruler. It dispensed with the Discourse of the Master as the primary organising principle in society. The Enlightenment hoped thereby to liberate human beings from the dark side of human nature, the drive to annihilate the other that appears in envy, warfare and prejudice. Thinkers such as Rousseau and Voltaire, Locke and Paine, had associated aggression and violence with the blind acceptance of irrational authority, material scarcity and religious superstitions. Modernity would remove these factors by eliminating the master (the monarch) and his signifier of authority (religion), thereby improving and ennobling the human animal. But, the story goes, what modernity got was a nasty surprise. The attempt to dispense with the Ego Ideal, or master signifier, failed to consider the possibility that aggression was in fact the result, not of the Ego Ideal, but of the superego, and that, actually, the master signifier *pacifies* the superego by regulating it through a symbolic contract. Žižek maintains that dethroning the Ego Ideal meant liberation of the superego and that postmodernism begins when this process is complete (*IDLC* 30; *PV* 303–4; *TS* 313). By the time of our late capitalist consumerism, what has emerged is a society without any reigning social ideals, where subjects are delivered over to the brutal injunctions of an unrestrained superego.

Far from expressing a new freedom, then, the constant pressure to consume today represents a punishing injunction. It is as if an inverted moral conscience operated in all of us, forcing us to do our 'duty' of consumption. This breaks up social bonds and isolates the individual. As Žižek says, 'from all sides, Right and Left, complaints abound today about how, in our postmodern societies composed of hedonistic solipsists, social bonds are progressively disintegrating; we are increasingly reduced to social atoms' (*IDLC* 34). What is missing, then, is the figure who embodies the social bond, the master (*IDLC* 35) – and what is wanted, Žižek's analysis seems to suggest, is an alternative to the Enlightenment: instead of the superego without the master, the master without the superego.

In this chapter we are going to discuss Žižek's diagnosis of the 'spirit of the times' as the 'reign of the superego' and 'generalised perversion'. We need to know not only whether this is a credible description of contemporary social reality, but also what the fault lines in the situation are that make an escape possible, and whether Žižek has overlooked anything of importance that qualifies his particular vision.

Reflexive Modernity

To understand why Žižek thinks that the new era is a wasteland for political resistance, we need to look at how he sets up his analysis of the latest stage of capitalism via a critique of celebrations of the new epoch as 'reflexive modernity'. According to sociologists Ulrich Beck and Anthony Giddens, we are in the midst of the unfolding of a major new epoch in Western history, a 'second Enlightenment' bringing 'reflexive modernity', whose cultural implications will be as dislocating as was the advent of modernity in the Renaissance. For them, modernity was characterised by the use of radical doubt as a method to break up traditional authority as well as the basis for the scientific investigation of nature. But they also acknowledge that many islands of nature and tradition survived in modernity, especially in the form of the traditional family, regarded ideologically as the natural basis for human community, and that this provided the bedrock of certainty within a modern age otherwise characterised by uncertainty. According to Beck and Giddens, the 'risk society' of the 'second Enlightenment' involves the final dissolution of all natural and traditional grounds for cultural formations (Beck et al. 1994). A new epoch of freedom beckons.

But, for Žižek, the major characteristic of this new epoch is not mainly accelerated scientific discovery, political democracy or economic prosperity. Nor is it primarily a higher level of social complexity combined with radical doubt, as proposed by the theorists of the 'risk society'. Rather, the massive shift registered by terms such as 'second Enlightenment' and 'reflexive modernity' is a mutation in subjectivity to a post-Oedipal order:

> today we are witnessing a shift no less radical than the shift from the pre-modern patriarchal order directly legitimized by the sexualized cosmology (Masculine and Feminine as the two cosmic principles) to the modern patriarchal order that introduced the abstract-universal notion of Man. (TS 360)

In other words, Žižek's analysis of global capitalism today is nested within a historical narrative where pre-modern, modern and post-modern societies are lined up with pre-Oedipal, Oedipal and post-Oedipal subjectivities. Aware that many feminist and postmodern theorists have proposed that a post-Oedipal subjectivity would be a deliverance from patriarchy, however, Žižek warns darkly about the 'obscene need for domination and subjection engendered by the new "post-Oedipal" forms of subjectivity themselves' (TS 360).

For the enthusiasts of the second modernity, the dawning era is marked by a tremendous new freedom characterised by individual self-fashioning, in which people are released from natural and traditional constraints to choose from a multiplicity of identities, as they make themselves whatever they wish to be. Advocates of the New Individualism, Anthony Elliott and Charles Lemert (2006: 13), for instance, celebrate the new freedom, but add revealingly that 'the designing of life as a self-project is deeply rooted as both a social norm and cultural obligation'. Apropos precisely of this element of compulsion at the heart of a supposed liberation, Žižek asks:

With regard to the postmodern constellation . . . in which patriarchy is fatally undermined, so that the subject experiences himself as freed from any traditional constraints, lacking any internalized symbolic Prohibition, bent on experimenting with his life and pursuing his life project, and so on, we have to raise the momentous question of the disavowed 'passionate attachments' which support the new reflexive freedom of the subject delivered from the constraints of Nature and/or Tradition. (*TS* 344).

Žižek's explanation for this is that the invasion of radical doubt – that is, reflexivity – into the habitual routines of the lifeworld (of everyday life and 'non-political' social conventions) generates tremendous anxiety. The subject is called upon to decide, without complete information, upon alternatives, and accept the consequences of his actions. Instead of a liberating experience, then, the 'second modernity' generates a return to pathological defences against anxiety that take the form of an anti-Enlightenment reaction (religious fundamentalism, ethnic nationalism, gender essentialism). By concentrating on the discontents of the risk society – the emergence of new fundamentalisms and obscurantisms – Žižek hopes to illuminate the connection between the new subjectivity and its perverse discontents.

> The fundamental lesson of *Dialectic of Enlightenment* is, therefore, still relevant today: it bears directly on what theorists of the risk society and reflexive modernisation praise as the advent of the 'second Enlightenment'. Apropos of this second Enlightenment, with subjects delivered form the weight of Nature and/or Tradition, the question of their unconscious 'passionate attachments' must be raised again – the so-called dark phenomena (burgeoning fundamentalisms, neo-racisms, etc.) which accompany this second modernity can in no way be dismissed as simple regressive phenomena, as remainders of the past that will simply vanish when individuals assume the full freedom and responsibility imposed on them by the second modernity. (*TS* 359)

Žižek's 'momentous question', then, is about whether it is possible to have a new society that leaves intact the old reflexive subject of modernity. It is an excellent question. But Žižek frames the answer in extremely negative terms: 'what psychoanalysis enables us to do is to focus on [the] obscene, disavowed supplement of the reflexive subject freed from the constraints of Nature and Tradition' (*TS* 360). So, why is Žižek so confident that the other side of reflexive freedom is an 'obscene, disavowed supplement'? The reason for this goes right to the heart of Žižek's cultural diagnosis, and this chapter.

Ultimately, behind the global spread of free-market capitalism

and liberal democracy, beyond even the momentous cultural consequences of this in the advent of reflexive modernity, stands, for Žižek,
the relation of the subject to the Symbolic Order. In the final analysis,
for the subject to become morally free and politically liberated, a
'cut' must be introduced between the Symbolic Order and incestuous
enjoyment. And that is precisely what Žižek believes today is lacking.
The reason is that what he calls 'paternal authority' in postmodernity
has begun to disintegrate:

> when one today speaks of the decline of paternal authority, it is *this*
> father, the father of the uncompromising 'No!' who is effectively in
> retreat; in the absence of this prohibitory 'No!' new forms of phantas-
> matic harmony between the symbolic order and incestuous enjoyment
> can thrive. (*TS* 322)

In other words, although Žižek cogently identifies a problem with
the assumptions of the theorists of reflexive modernity, it appears
that he has an assumption of his own that, at a minimum, needs some
explanation. That is that questioning the traditional authority of the
father in the household is uncomfortably close to undermining symbolic authority *per se* in society. Žižek's conceptual bridge between
the domestic situation (of patriarchal power in the household in
retreat) and the political space (of a breakdown in the effectiveness
of social ideals and therefore of the authority of public figures) is the
notion of 'paternal authority'. For Žižek, the problem today is, in
the final analysis, that the Strict Father lacks the authority to enforce
moral limits, just to say 'No!'

Pathological Narcissism

The roots of Žižek's concerns about the decline in paternal authority run deep – all the way back to his early, enthusiastic embrace of
the neoconservative, psychoanalytically influenced social theory of
Christopher Lasch, in Žižek's *Looking Awry* (1991). According to
Lasch, the 'permissive society' of late capitalism has turned decisively
aside from the work ethic to adopt consumerist hedonism. Catalysed
by the youth rebellions of the 1960s, the new anti-authoritarian attitude of the late capitalist individual has become the norm in a society
that can no longer tolerate delayed gratification, and that actually
requires the desire for instant satisfaction as the driving mechanism of
consumer culture. These individuals – themselves deeply ambivalent
in their attitudes to authority – although they lack the internalised

discipline to enforce rules anyway, congratulate themselves on their libertarian revolt against the generation that taught self-sacrifice and social ideals, especially the idea that nobody is above the law. The focal point for Lasch is feminism, which combines youth movement anti-authoritarianism with an attack on the commanding heights of the work ethic, the father who lays down the rules in the private households.

Lasch (1979) maintains that, instead of liberation, these individuals find themselves enslaved to a new and infinitely more demanding authority, one that refuses to acknowledge the binding character of rules and reigns by coercive force: the maternal superego. Žižek summarises his agreement with this proposition superbly: when the family is fatherless, Žižek suggests, when 'the father is absent, the paternal function . . . is suspended and that vacuum is filled by the "irrational" maternal superego':

> The dead end [Hitchcock's film] *The Birds* is really about is, of course, that of the modern American family: the deficient paternal Ego-Ideal makes the law 'regress' towards a ferocious maternal superego, affecting sexual enjoyment – the decisive trait of the libidinal structure of 'pathological narcissism'. (*LA* 99)

But after *Looking Awry*, the term 'maternal superego', with its connotations of strident anti-feminism and cultural conservatism, disappears from Žižek's theoretical lexicon. In its place, a whole series of substitute expressions make their appearance: the decline of paternal authority, the decline of symbolic authority, the ferocious God, superego enjoyment and, most exotically of all, 'the phallophany of the anal father' (*ES* 124–46). What remains the same is the diagnosis that there is a fundamental disturbance in subjects' relation to the father and that this potently distorts the Symbolic Order *per se*.

Initially, the name for this disturbance is 'pathological narcissism', as relayed through Lasch's appropriation of the clinical category. In the psychological work of Otto Kernberg, pathological narcissism is a diagnostic category located in the borderline conditions that surround fully blown psychosis. Because of a deficient internalisation of the Ego Ideal, the pathological narcissist displays low anxiety tolerance, a narcissistic inability to love others and high levels of promiscuity combined with rage.

Lasch (and Žižek) incorporate this category into a historical narrative about the passage from the autonomous individual of liberal capitalism, through the 'organisational man' of monopoly capitalism, to the pathological narcissist of post-war capitalism (*LA* 102). But, for Žižek, the first two moments in this history involve a change only to the contents of the Ego Ideal: 'the Ego Ideal becomes "external-ised" as the expectations of the social group to which the individual belongs' (*LA* 102). With the onset of late capitalism and consumer society, instead of a symbolic prohibition (that is, castration), we get the injunction to enjoy through the elevation of transgression to the norm. So, for Žižek, 'the third stage, the arrival of the "pathological narcissist", breaks precisely with [the] underlying frame of the Ego Ideal common to the first two forms' (*LA* 102). The pathological narcissist, then, represents a radical mutation in subjectivity.

Žižek is devastating in his analyses of the pathological narcissist as the late capitalist individual, especially in the form of the marketing executive or cultural analyst who is convinced that they are a rebel, but is in actuality deeply conformist.

> The narcissistic subject knows only the 'rules of the (social) game', enabling him to manipulate others; social relations constitute for him a playing field in which he assumes 'roles', not proper symbolic mandates; he stays clear of any binding commitment that would imply a proper sym-bolic identification. He is a radical *conformist* who paradoxically experi-ences himself as an outlaw. . . . this disintegration of the Ego Ideal entails the installation of a 'maternal superego' that does not prohibit enjoyment but, on the contrary, imposes it and punishes 'social failure' in a far more cruel and severe way, through an unbearable and self-destructive anxiety. All the babble about the 'decline of paternal authority' merely conceals the resurgence of this incomparably more oppressive agency. (*LA* 102–3)

For the pathological narcissist, socio-cultural rules are simply external regulations to be broken whenever possible. In this situation, the Ego Ideal becomes something from which the subject measures a cynical detachment: they can stand on the sidelines and manipulate the guidelines, because belief in the Ideal is something for everyone else – the pathological narcissist merely plays along to gain personal advantage. Žižek's argument is that this apparent liberation from the master signifier only instates the injunctions of the superego as a more brutal and exigent authority in the place where the Ego Ideal was.

Ambivalent Diagnosis

Now we have a fairly good idea of what Žižek is driving at with the idea of the 'decline of paternal authority'. But what are the politics of this position?

146

What makes Lasch's position so conservative is its combination of the anti-feminist insistence that the crisis is caused by questioning the traditional authority of the father with the sociological assumption that society needs a single set of binding representations for social cohesion. This (Durkheimian) assumption is common to both neoconservative sociologists like Daniel Bell and radical theorists like Fredric Jameson – both major sources for Žižek's ideas about postmodern culture (e.g. *LA* 112). For the sociologist Emil Durkheim, the 'collective conscience' of society takes the form of a binding doctrine or shared set of ideals, whose roots are ultimately religious. In the hands of neoconservative sociologists, this assumption is expressed through their anxiety that the decline of the Protestant ethic might mean the breakup of Western society. When Lasch lends this a psychoanalytic twist, it becomes the idea that, in the absence of the paternal authority of a unifying Ego Ideal, we will get the 'permissive society' of pathological narcissists – that is, cultural fragmentation, social disintegration and, ultimately, the war of each against all.

Although Žižek adapts this idea, and eventually recasts the 'maternal superego' as the 'anal father', he does so without breaking fully from the assumption that the Ego Ideal supplies the social bond. Indeed, Žižek accepts the idea that the Ego Ideal is *the same as* the Symbolic Order, that the symbolic authority of the master signifier is *the same as* the existence of the big Other. The idea here is not just that the master signifier 'holds the place' of the big Other, and, ultimately, of the subject. The idea is that every Symbolic Order, hence political regime, requires one master signifier or Ego Ideal, a 'highest good' or shared moral value, in order to exist *at all*. Without a shared value, societies lack social cohesion. Stated differently, this thesis means that the existence of multiple (non-shared) values in a society equals social breakdown.

Žižek states this assumption through his heterodox interpretation of the Hegelian idea of the 'concrete universal'. If the universal is the empty place ultimately occupied by the subject – the empty place of power, the empty imperative of the moral law and, finally, the empty differential Law of the Symbolic Order – then the 'concrete' universal is the shared social Ideal that 'represents the subject for another signifier'—that is, that represents the subject of this society to another society. The Hegelian thesis that the abstract Idea of universality – the Symbolic Order – must appear in the form of a concrete universal Ideal – an Ego Ideal, or master signifier

– becomes, on Žižek's treatment, the notion that the binding representation supplied by a shared Ego Ideal is *coextensive* with the Symbolic Order. So, when Žižek says that 'the Hegelian "concrete universality" is uncannily close to what Althusser called the articulation of an overdetermined totality' (*CHU* 235), what this means is that the concrete universal is the underlying principle lying behind the rules and regulations of the entire society. But he also makes it clear (*CHU* 235–41) that the concrete universal is the 'phallic' master signifier, the universal that is an exception to its own universal rule (because, as a master signifier, it is ultimately meaningless). No wonder, then, that the link between the two roles that the concrete universal plays, in its suture of Ego Ideal and Symbolic Order, is theorised as 'the structurally necessary short circuit between levels' (*CHU* 235).

The problem is that, confronted with the logic of a position that implies that the multiplication of Ego Ideals in a value-plural society means the disintegration of social cohesion through the break-up of the Symbolic Order, Žižek does not quite know what to do.

- On the one hand, the absence of the supposedly necessary shared Ego Ideal might mean that the 'pathological narcissist' has radically foreclosed paternal authority and the Symbolic Order has disintegrated, with the consequence that the postmodern individual is actually proto-psychotic.
- On the other hand, the fact that today's hedonistic consumers are manifestly non-psychotic, combined with evidence that the social bond is more immovable now than ever before, might imply that there really is a Symbolic Order, only that it is hidden, so that the 'pathological narcissists' are really engaged in perverse disavowal of it.

Whatever the case – and Žižek will ultimately plump for Option Two, under the topic of the 'society of generalised perversion' and the 'fetishistic disavowal of the global capitalist economy' – he is convinced that the individual of late capitalism is definitely not 'normal' because today any commonly shared, singular Ego Ideal is in abeyance.

For Žižek, then, the universalised reflexivity of the second modernity has two consequences – the collapse of the big Other and the uncontested hegemony of global capitalism. But, in truth, these supposed correlates represent, in Žižek's actual analyses, mutually exclusive diagnoses of the 'spirit of the times'.

Option One: The Proto-Psychotic Narcissist

On this analysis, the generalisation of reflexivity means that the Symbolic Order (the underlying socio-cultural rules) is disintegrating because it lacks a metaphysical guarantee in the 'Other of the Other' (such as Nature, Tradition or God). Instead of the big Other, or Symbolic Order, what we get is a multiplicity of localised fragments of the big Other with a merely regional application, together with a proliferation of 'little brothers' and 'obscene neighbours', sinister others who – in the absence of a communal Symbolic Order that might constrain their action – confront the subject as bearers of a threatening enjoyment. In the place where the Symbolic Order was, there is only the competing confusion of a multiplicity of incommensurable language games, heterogeneous discursive universes whose coexistence depends upon the suspension of warfare rather than a social pact. This situation is exemplified, for Žižek, in the proliferation of specialised committees called upon to deliberate on ethical dilemmas: the lack of a Symbolic Order means that moral questions cannot be referred to a social consensus, but become the province of fragmentary and transient 'little big Others'. For Žižek, the non-existence of the big Other means the dissolution of the communal network of customary norms and social institutions that regulate the everyday lives of all members of a society. The consequence is that many people adopt the desperate solution of paranoid fantasies about a Real 'Other of the Other', a world conspiracy, new messiah or alien invasion, as a compensatory delusion. This is an analysis that, in psychoanalytic terms, indicates a diagnosis of postmodern culture as a psychotic condition.

Are we All Psychotics Now?

- Žižek argues that contemporary conspiracy theories and religious fanaticisms represent efforts to locate the vanished Other 'in the Real'. According to Lacanian psychoanalysis, psychotics' paranoid, persecutory delusion is their best effort to heal the wound of the lack of the Symbolic Law in their psychological structure – this lack means that the master signifier has been 'foreclosed', because of the failure of the father to live up to his symbolic mandate as the bearer of the Law. The foreclosed Symbolic Law has been replaced by an imaginary representation of a completely external authority. In the delusions of Judge Schreber – the subject of Freud's most extended case study on psychosis – the paternal imago or Ego Ideal 'returns in the Real' in the form of a punitive deity who demands that Schreber renounce masculinity and become feminine. Meanwhile, so the delusion goes, God enjoys Schreber's feminised body, and (analogously) his doctor commits 'soul murder' upon Schreber, probably through sodomy.

- Žižek proposes that the typical postmodern subject is a pathological narcissist, whose cynical detachment from symbolic authority is counterbalanced by the delusional belief that there is an 'Other of the Other', a big Other in the Real, directing a sinister global conspiracy against the subject themselves:

> The paradoxical result of the mutation in the non-existence of the big Other – of the growing collapse of symbolic efficiency – is thus the proliferation of different versions of *a big Other that actually exists, in the Real*, not merely as a symbolic fiction. The typical subject today is the one who, while displaying cynical distrust of any public ideology, indulges without restraint in paranoiac fantasies about conspiracies, threats and excessive forms of enjoyment of the Other. (*TS* 362)

OPTION TWO: THE SOCIETY OF GENERALISED PERVERSION

At the same time, Žižek insists that reflexive modernity, the second Enlightenment, maintains a structure of disavowal, a non-reflexive ballast of dark matter, at its core. This is its acceptance of global capitalism as 'the only game in town', which leads Žižek to relate the reflexivity of the second modernity to a renaturalisation of the commodity form. For Žižek, this situation involves 'commodity fetishism' in both the anthropological (Marxist) sense and the psychoanalytic sense (perversion). Here, the emphasis is on the disavowal of the real big Other of the risk society, the world economy as a form of global Symbolic Order supported by the fantasy narratives of the 'victory of capitalism', the 'triumph of liberal democracy' and the 'end of history'. According to this diagnosis, the new epoch is characterised by 'generalised perversion', by the elevation of transgression into the norm, within which individuals seek to make themselves into instruments of the universal superego imperative to 'Enjoy!' consumerism.

The Lacanian Conception of Perversion in General and Fetishism in Particular

- Perversion is the technical term psychoanalysts use to describe people who lack the usual sense of social Law (norms and limits) that represses direct *Jouissance*. So, paradoxically, perverse subjects actively seek out forms of repression or Law in their sexual lives: paradigmatically, in sadism, by inflicting 'punishments' on their partner, or, in masochism, by 'contracting' to be whipped and so on by their partner.
- Importantly for Žižek's diagnosis of today's culture, the fetishistic pervert consciously 'disavows' something he knows or has experienced, which is too traumatic consciously to assimilate or symbolise. In Freud's famous analysis of fetishism, this is the knowledge that the mother does not have a phallus. The fetish objects that then become necessary for the subject to experience sexul enjoyment are so many substitutes for the 'maternal phallus', whose absence has been disavowed by the fetishist.

The advantage of this description is that it also applies to the apparent opposite of hedonistic consumerism, religious fundamentalism, ethnic nationalism, neo-racism and so forth. Here, the imperative to 'Enjoy!' is translated as 'punish!' – the fanatic makes himself into the instrument of God's vengeance against the immoral normalisation of transgression, a tool in the Nation's cleansing of the perverted filth who have ruined our way of life, and so on. Žižek insists on the underlying link between liberal democracy and fundamentalist terrorism on just these lines (*IDLC* 11–51).

Basically, Žižek hesitates between the following two, contradictory, diagnoses. He is on the horns of a dilemma.

- The diagnosis of reflexive modernity as psychotic is theoretically consistent. The foreclosure, in the individual, of the Ego Ideal would indeed mean that the subject was not properly inserted into the Symbolic Order – that is, that the fundamental Symbolic Law was lacking in that person. This would lead to the 'return in the Real' of the foreclosed Symbolic Law as an external persecutory agency commanding enjoyment, a 'big Other in the Real' or 'Other of the Other', together with a collapse of the symbolic elements of interpersonal relations, so that others would confront the subject as narcissistic rivals or as the bearers of an obscene and threatening drive to annihilate or dominate the subject. Unfortunately, this diagnosis is descriptively implausible – although it is certainly colourful, as we will see in a moment.

- The alternative is a position that is theoretically inconsistent but descriptively plausible. The idea of generalised perversion seems to capture beautifully a whole series of contemporary phenomena, from the dark underside to reflexive subjectivity through to the way in which ideological cynicism and political apathy today are in fundamental collusion with global injustice. But it rests on the theoretically problematic proposition that there can be a Symbolic Order operative in the lives of individuals without the Ego Ideal to 'quilt' the subjects into it. A superego without the Ego Ideal does not really make theoretical sense within a Lacanian framework. Žižek is, therefore, forced by the logic of his position to assert that the superego is the underside, not of the Ego Ideal, but of the Symbolic Order and its Law of Prohibition.

But, to see how Žižek arrives at this sort of conclusion, we need to clarify his analysis of the superego further.

Superego Enjoyment and Generalised Psychosis?

For Freud, the superego was the same as the moral conscience and was therefore an aspect of the Ego Ideal. Yet Freud (1984: 374–9) also noted that often it is the most moral people who are most tortured by the unconscious sense of guilt the superego visits upon us. It is as if the superego tended to punish the ego according to a 'sadistic' logic where efforts to conform to the superego's commands were greeted not with rewards, but with further punishments (Freud 1984: 389–401). For this reason, Freud had called the superego in *Civilization and its Discontents* a 'pure culture of the death drive' (Freud 1985: 315–32). Lacan picks up on this darker conception of the superego, noting how it undermines Freud's 'official' position that the superego is the individual's conscience. If the superego is the conscience, it is a perverted one.

Lacan analytically separates the Ego Ideal from the superego, proposing that the superego is the dark underside to the pacifying Ego

Ideal. In Lacan's terms, the conscience is closer to the Ego Ideal of an individual, enjoining her to live up to her ideals, defer satisfaction and avoid illicit enjoyment. The superego, by contrast, is for Lacan a perverse injunction to 'enjoy' – that is, to engage in the illicit transgressions that bring this forbidden enjoyment. In the most straightforward terms, the Ego Ideal is created through a desexualisation and idealisation of the parental image – that is, through identification with the noble social ideals promoted by the parents, and repression of the Oedipal desires the individual experienced during infancy. The superego is where the sexuality went, when the Ego Ideal was, well, idealised. It is the repressed component of the Ego Ideal, and it functions to remind the subject – through a guilt whose origins are unconscious because repressed – that their shining ideals have something disturbing attached to them after all.

In psychosis, the pre-Oedipal father appears to the child as something like a superegoic figure – what Žižek calls, drawing on the work of Eric Santner on psychosis, a *Luder* or 'obscene *jouisseur*'. So it makes sense that Žižek begins the major essay 'Whither Oedipus?' in *The Ticklish Subject* with Option One: superego enjoyment as theoretical shorthand for a psychotic form of social disintegration. Žižek's explanation of how this came about is unorthodox. Pre-modern societies distribute the Symbolic Ego Ideal to the king, while the superego role is reserved for the patriarch of the extended family. What happens in the modern world, Žižek argues, is that, 'in the modern bourgeois nuclear family, the two functions of the father which were previously separated, that is, embodied in different people (the pacifying ego-ideal and the ferocious superego), *are united in one and the same person*' (*TS* 313). But this coincidence of superego and Ego Ideal in the figure of the father of the bourgeois nuclear family means that 'symbolic authority was more and more smeared by the mark of obscenity and thus, as it were, undermined from within' (*TS* 313). Modernity drags to the surface the hidden link between Ego Ideal and superego, with the result that 'the figure of paternal authority turns into an obscene *jouisseur*' (*TS* 313). With the end of modernity and the beginning of postmodernity, or reflexive modernity, this process is completed:

What happens in today's much-decried 'decline of Oedipus' (decline of paternal symbolic authority) is precisely the return of figures which function according to the logic of the 'primordial father', from 'totalitarian' political Leaders to the paternal sexual harasser – why? When the 'pacifying' symbolic authority is suspended, the only way to avoid the debilitating deadlock of desire, its inherent impossibility, is . . . a despotic figure which stands for the primordial *jouisseur*: we cannot enjoy because *he* appropriates all enjoyment. (*TS* 315)

Notice, though, that the culprit here is not so much global capitalism as the culture of modernity itself. According to Žižek, with the decline of the Ego Ideal, the superego's policing of transgressions through guilt turns into the elevation of transgression into the norm – a consequence of the way that, for Lacan, the superego is the malevolent gaze of the Ego Ideal 'in the Real', as an agency that makes the subject guilty through its simultaneous *instigation* and *punishment* of transgressions. Lacking the symbolic identification that would define a limit beyond which transgressions are punished, the superego simply enjoins transgression.

There is a certain resonance between Žižek's claim and a commonplace of neoconservative social commentary, the depiction of late capitalism as the 'fun society,' where the provocations of the artistic avant-garde become the logic of advertising-driven consumption. Consumerism's constant demand for novelty, combined with capitalism's recuperation of every form of cultural rebellion as a commodified stylistic innovation, mean that the norm of transgression is driven by an uncanny repetition compulsion that has a 'daemonic' quality to it. But, according to Žižek, the superego injunction to enjoy (and the consequent guilt in failing to comply with this demand for pleasure) is an effective prohibition against enjoyment – once everything is permitted, nothing is desired. The subject experiences an abstract guilt and tremendous anxiety, without the bonus of pleasure associated with a real transgression, because there are no longer any clearly symbolised limits. In Father's absence, in other words, instead of fun, we get a sort of gothic inversion of the consumer funhouse: 'the lack of symbolic prohibition is supplemented by the re-emergence of ferocious superego figures . . . [and] so-called postmodern subjectivity thus involves a kind of *direct "superegoisation" of the imaginary Ideal*, caused by the lack of a proper symbolic Prohibition' (*TS* 353).

Žižek argues that this 'direct "superegoisation" of the imaginary Ideal' cashes out at two levels: that of the big Other (the Symbolic Order) and the little other (the other person). The Symbolic Order, he proposes, disintegrates into an archipelago of 'small big Others', islands of regulation in a sea of transgression, generating a multiplicity of inconsistent rules or heterogeneous language games. Ethics committees with the mandate to regulate a localised area of social life, for instance, represent a desperate replacement for the missing social consensus (*TS* 334).

At the same time, cynical detachment from official institutions and symbolic authority is counterbalanced by the delusional belief that there is an 'Other of the Other', or big Other in the Real, an invisible master who supplies an ultimate guarantee and manipulates the world, directing a sinister global conspiracy against the subject themselves. Likewise, the little other undergoes a mutation best expressed through the figures of the totalitarian leader and the corporate executive. Žižek proposes that Bill Gates, for instance, is the exemplary figure of corporate capital today – not the corporate master, but 'little brother', an ordinary person who is elevated to an uncanny (monstrous) position. Where the authority of the traditional master is anchored in the symbolic, the postmodern 'lesser master' depends upon the Real, upon the superego. Bill Gates, then, is 'the superego figure of the omnipotent Evil Genius' of the post-Oedipal society (*TS* 349).

Here, Žižek's heroic attempt to remain theoretically consistent runs up against the descriptive problem that, whatever wild fantasies some people have about Microsoft Corporation and its 'postmodern Evil Genius', the term 'psychotic society' is an oxymoron. As Santner (1996) suggests, the psychotic lives in a private universe. This is because they are never integrated into the shared basis of society, the Symbolic Order. A 'collectivity' of psychotics means a cluster of individuals each existing in their 'own private Germany', their own personal Symbolic Order. Lacking the medium of social cooperation, for the psychotic, their encounter with others is fraught with potential violence because – as Žižek concedes – 'imaginary (semblance) and the real (of paranoia) overlap' (*TS* 349).

The Decline of Symbolic Authority and Generalised Perversion

Not surprisingly, then, Žižek turns from the proto-psychotic Option One to Option Two, the society of generalised perversion, within the space of the same chapter of *The Ticklish Subject*. Option Two suggests that the superego has removed the Ego Ideal but left the Symbolic Order in place – indeed, that superego enjoyment is the hidden obverse of the Symbolic Law. In the society of generalised perversion, the Symbolic Order operates under the superego's direction, without the pacifying screen of the Ego Ideal. For Žižek, this has the general ramification that there is a 'decline of symbolic authority', by which he means the 'dissolution of the performative efficiency' of the assumption of social mandates. Žižek has several other designations for this as well: the 'crisis of symbolic investure' and the prevalence of cynical ideology and political apathy are included under the heading. What does it mean?

In psychoanalysis, perversion differs from hysteria. In hysteria, there is a performative contradiction between the enunciation and the statement of which the hysteric is unaware. The hysteric does not know that his bombardment of the authorities with impossible demands at the level of the statement ('more democracy!') is actually a hysterical demand for a new master at the level of the enunciation ('prove your authority to me!'). The pervert, by contrast, is highly self-reflexive. This does not mean she escapes from performative contradiction, though. It means she tries to make use of it. She knows all very well that the authorities are opposed to more democracy . . . but she is still protesting anyway, in a spirit of cynical resignation. The aim of this manipulative attitude is to stay in control of the enjoyment that a relationship to authority brings, to make sure that it is the figure of authority and not the pervert who gets hystericised. To do this, the pervert makes himself into an instrument of the will of the authorities, pushing the logic of authority right to its final limits. This is all done in the hope that the authorities will step in and say 'stop', finally laying down the law. So the pervert defines himself in terms of a conscious acceptance of the performative contradiction between the enunciation and the statement. 'I know all very well that . . . but nonetheless, I am doing it' is the 'formula' for the pervert, and his secret aim is to discover the limits to his provocative transgressions.

In a more sinister vein, the pervert is the Stalinist or the Nazi who knew all too well that he was committing terrible crimes against innocent people . . . but still did it anyway. Žižek brilliantly brings out how the perverse attitude in totalitarian politics – from fascism through fundamentalism to Stalinist authoritarianism – involves the subject making himself into an instrument for the achievement of some impersonal, totalising force: the Nation, God, the Historical Process.

What this implies is a disturbance in the functioning of what Žižek calls symbolic authority. Where the hysteric thinks (unconsciously) that she is addressing, at the level of the enunciation, a benevolent Master who needs to lift his game, the pervert thinks (unconsciously) that he is addressing a malevolent Leader or dark God of sacrifice. To protect himself from the disgusting enjoyment compelled by this malevolent Leader or dark god, the pervert engages in a game of cynical resignation and ironic deflation. The power of perversion as a social-theoretical category is that it seeks to unmask contemporary cynical culture and postmodern politics as deeply complicit with the practice of not challenging global capitalism and political oppression. But it also seeks to describe the way that religious fundamentalists and ethnic nationalists perversely make themselves into instruments for the dark enjoyment of their God or Leader, through acts like suicide bombing and ethnic cleansing. Unlike the hysteric, who unconsciously believes in the benevolent Master, the pervert believes that the apparently benevolent authority is in actuality a malevolent Leader, demanding something truly atrocious. Accordingly, every symbolic authority figure in contemporary society – politicians, judges, teachers, parents and so forth – become, in the eyes of today's perverse subjects, 'smeared with an obscene enjoyment'.

Žižek's analysis of the decline of symbolic authority is extremely important. It is theoretically subtle, highly descriptively plausible, and it makes substantive connection with broader social-theoretical claims about reflexive modernity. It does not necessarily have to involve the diagnosis that everyone in reflexive modernity is a pervert in the clinical sense, because it can simply claim that the sort of radical doubt operative in reflexive modernity fosters a perverse attitude towards symbolic authorities.

The potential problem is that it is nested within Žižek's assumption about society, that society needs a unifying Ego Ideal. How can this be, if the Ego Ideal is precisely what is lacking today, but society (as society) is not totally fragmentated – that is, psychotic? In other words, Žižek is compelled to explain the decline of symbolic authority in terms of the *presence* of the Symbolic Order but the *lack* of a socially cohesive Ego Ideal. His strategy goes as follows:

- Global capitalism operates as the new Symbolic Order coordinating a worldwide society of generalised perversion. This can happen because commodity fetishism has the double meaning of reification (the naturalisation of capitalism) and also clinical perversion.

157

- Multicultural societies and liberal pluralism, the decline of symbolic authority and the rise of fundamentalist violence, the decline of paternal authority and numerous social pathologies, all evidence the resulting lack of a social ideal.

We can see how these two moves connect in *The Ticklish Subject*. First, Žižek directly claims that capitalism is the contemporary replacement for the symbolic big Other:

> The spectral presence of Capital is the figure of the big Other which not only remains operative when all the traditional embodiments of the symbolic big Other disintegrate, but even directly causes this disintegration: far from being confronted with the abyss of their freedom – that is, laden with the burden of responsibility that cannot be alleviated by the helping hand of Tradition or Nature – today's subject is perhaps more than ever caught in an inexorable compulsion that effectively runs his life. (*TS* 354)

Then, secondly, Žižek links the idea that the 'spectral big Other' of capitalism is disavowed to the idea that, with the lack of an Ego Ideal, the 'basic error' of postmodern politics is not to generate this unifying ideal, but to play with the resulting fragments. For Žižek, that is, the contemporary left-wing strategy of multiple struggles for cultural recognition, alliance politics across broad Left concerns and the underlying ideal of radical democracy rather than socialist revolution, are all part of the problem.

> Because the *depoliticised economy is the disavowed 'fundamental fantasy' of postmodern politics* – a properly political act would necessarily entail the repoliticisation of the economy: within a given situation, a gesture counts as an act only in so far as it disturbs ('traverses') its fundamental fantasy. (*TS* 355)

For these reasons, new Left identity politics does not count as a political Act – it is part of the society of generalised perversion and not an effective opposition to it.

Ideological Disavowal and 'Disidentification'

Žižek, following Octave Mannoni, formulates this contemporary ideological perversity according to the formula: 'I know well, but nevertheless . . .'.

- Today's subject's 'know well' that global capitalism governs their lived experiences, how and whether they work, what parameters limit in advance any 'feasible' political proposal – 'but nevertheless' they act as if they did not recognise this. Instead, today's typical subject considers himself a rebel, different from all the others, nobody's fool, and so forth.
- Žižek thinks this 'I know well, but nevertheless . . .' formula holds across different ideological regimes, at least within modernity. It is connected to his notion of ideological disidentification (Chapter 1). The Stalinist subject, for example, 'knew well' that the Party was corrupt and riven by chaotic in-fighting, 'but nevertheless' continued to support the regime; the typical subject 'knows well' that the judge might be a philandering cheat in his private life, a normal man like us, 'but nevertheless' quakes to hear his judgment in a court of law, since he bears the phallic insignia of public-symbolic authority.

So readers can also see that Žižek's connection between the disappearance of a cohesive ideal and the triumph of capitalism has some concerning implications. For one thing, the insistence on a single Ego Ideal as the bond of social cohesion for all citizens in a society implies that multicultural society and political pluralism are a problem. For another thing, it means that the radical-democratic political strategy of supporting multiple struggles for cultural recognition and different sorts of political demands (ecological, feminist, and so on), actually makes things worse.

Generalised Perversion and Commodity Fetishism

Perhaps because the stakes in Žižek's position are really about the politics of contemporary theory, Žižek is rather cavalier about the theoretical coordinates of the Marxist analysis of commodity fetishism. The Marxist claim involves the idea of ideological inversion: the worker becomes an object and the commodity takes on the properties of the subject. But this inversion is based on projecting mysterious properties onto things (commodities). Specifically, Marx's analysis of commodity fetishism had sought to undermine the confidence of liberal subjects in their modern Enlightenment by pointing out how capitalism involves treating all objects, and other people, as if they were the bearers of an invisible, metaphysical substance called 'exchange value'. This substance, Marx delighted in observing, was every bit as mysterious as the divine substance pre-modern subjects had seen in their totems and Gods. The result is pseudo-ideas such as that the 'world market *decides* the best allocation of goods and services', while 'labour must *respond* to global conditions of cheap materials and services'. As Marx (1962b: 830) says, commodity fetishism 'is an enchanted, perverted, topsy-turvy world, in which Monsieur le Capital and Madame la Terre do their ghost-walking as social characters and at the same time directly as things'.

Marx is using 'perverted' as a *normative* term to express the immorality and inhumanity of capitalism. Likewise, his use of the term 'fetishism' is anthropological, drawing on the nineteenth-century idea that so-called primitive cultures project their own humanity (their capacities and properties) onto the fetish object (for example, a totemic figure) that stands in for their gods. It does not have the psychoanalytic meaning of a self-objectification in which the subject forces the Other to lay down the law through a masochistic 'contract' or sadistic 'punishments,' unless:

1. the 'surplus enjoyment' of the pervert is held to be somehow the same as the surplus value extracted through capitalist profit, because
2. the commodity form is ultimately the structuring principle for modern subjectivity. In other words, commodity fetishism *really is* a clinical perversion.

Now, Žižek has been convinced that these two propositions are true, probably from the very beginning.

1. Lacan (2007) says in Seminar XVII that surplus enjoyment and surplus value use the same theoretical model (a hydraulic model) for conceptualising different processes. Žižek takes this to mean that 'there is a fundamental homology between the interpretive procedure of Marx and Freud' (*SO* 11), so that it can seriously be claimed that Marx 'invented the symptom' (*SO* 11–53). But he also accepts that part of this apparently surprising theoretical convergence is actually because Lacan consciously modelled surplus enjoyment on Marxian surplus value (*SO* 50). Nonetheless, Žižek believes that, despite the potential vicious circle involved in arguing from the (artificially created) homology

between the two surpluses to the supposed identity of the two different things the models apply to, there is a deeper reason why this can be done.

2. In the chapter on how Marx invented the symptom, Žižek turns to the work of Hegelian Marxist Alfred Sohn-Rethel to propose that the 'real abstraction' of commodity exchange 'is the unconscious of the transcendental subject' (*SO* 18). What this means is that the commodity form fundamentally structures the psyche of the subject. Sohn-Rethel radically extended the arguments of György Lukács (1971: 122), who supposed, as part of his argument for the identical subject–object of history, that the commodity form was the structuring principle of both social objectivity and psychological subjectivity in the modern world. For Sohn-Rethel, what this meant was that the categories of rationality proposed by Descartes, Kant and Hegel could be deciphered in terms of commodity exchange (Sohn-Rethel 1978). Žižek agrees, but suggests that a Lacanian framework is best suited for incorporating these insights (*SO* 19–21).

Žižek brings these two propositions together through the idea that fetishistic disavowal (in the clinical context) has the same form as commodity fetishism (in market exchanges). In both cases, the subjects 'know all very well', but nonetheless 'they are still doing it' (*SO* 23–6). But it is at this point in the original argument that Žižek inserts one of those surprising turns whose reversal is so characteristic of what we are calling the shift from the radical-democratic to the revolutionary-vanguardist Žižek. For Žižek maintained in 1989 that:

in societies in which commodity fetishism reigns, the 'relations between men' are totally de-fetishised, while in societies in which there is fetishism in 'relations between men' – in pre-capitalist societies – commodity fetishism is not yet developed . . . This fetishism in relations between men has to be called by its proper name: what we have here are, as Marx points out, 'relations of domination and servitude' – that is to say, precisely the relation of Lordship and Bondage in the Hegelian sense. With the establishment of bourgeois society, the relations of domination and servitude are *repressed*: formally, we are apparently concerned with free subjects whose interpersonal relations are discharged of all fetishism; the repressed truth – that of the persistence of domination and servitude – emerges in a symptom which subverts the ideological appearance of equality, freedom and so on. (*SO* 26)

Accordingly, Žižek aligns commodity fetishism with the 'conversion hysteria proper to capitalism' (*TS* 26) and *not* with 'generalised perversion'. Until 1996, Žižek concentrates on analysing the symptoms of liberal democracy and late capitalism – 'the repressed authoritarian-patriarchal logic that continues to dominate our attitudes' (*ME* 56) – as evidence of the continued relevance of a struggle against domination and servitude. It was this indirect approach, rather than placing liberal democracy and late capitalism directly on the couch, that prevented Žižek, until after 1997, from bringing out into the open the identical subject–object that all this supposes. After the encounter with Schelling, however, Žižek's diagnosis changes from 'hysteria' to 'perversion', and the task he proposes is no longer to interpret symptoms but directly to analyse the society. What this analysis reveals is that the superego imperatives of capitalist consumerism and fundamentalist reaction are just the flipside to how global capitalism is the new world Symbolic Order.

Some Theoretical and Cultural Concerns

Circularity is not the only worrying problem with Žižek's new raft of positions on the 'atonal worlds' of late capitalism. There is something fundamentally nostalgic about Žižek's analysis of the 'spirit of the times'. It mimics an elegy for the authority of the Father, conducted in terms that uncannily echo the cultural diagnoses of the neoconservative Right. Disquietingly, there is also significant agreement on some political topics, such as the undesirability of multicultural societies (*TS* 215–21), liberal tolerance (*PD* 7), sexual harassment regulations and racial vilification laws, the importance of the strict father, the misguided nature of feminism, the religious roots of Western culture, the idea that the old Left was authoritarian and that the new Left consists mainly of 'politically correct multicultural liberals' (e.g. *IDLC* 1, 333). Many of Žižek's stances are provocations, of course, so that his 'plea for intolerance', for instance, turns out not to be an embrace of ethnic particularity, but the idea that only a post-capitalist world could *truly* include the other. But the reader might wonder whether blocking liberal cultural reforms in the name of a utopia that is declared, from the outset, to be politically both 'impossible' (e.g. *CHU* 121) and 'terroristic' (*TS* 377) might not just effectively line up Žižek with the neoconservative Right *in practice*, if not in theory. And some of the provocations generate real concern, such as, for instance, when Žižek announces that a certain minimum of sexual harassment is necessary to every romantic overture, or that we need to junk the term 'totalitarian' in order to 'reinvent emancipatory terror' (*IDLC* 174).

Beyond these moments of the 'coincidence of opposites' between Left and Right in Žižek's cultural politics, there are some substantive positions that are also somewhat controversial. Foremost of these is the idea that social cohesion depends upon a unifying Ego Ideal held in common by the entire society. This characterises a pre-modern closed community, but, as readers of Durkheim will know, modern societies can be socially integrated through the division of labour and so exist as value-plural open cultures. Subsequent critical theorists from the Frankfurt School, such as Jürgen Habermas and Axel Honneth, have managed to combine Marxist sociology with post-Marxist political and social ideas, to explain how value-plural societies can have social solidarity – and they have managed to do this without surrendering to political liberalism and renouncing the critique of capitalism (see Habermas 1984, 1987a; Honneth 1995). It is an *assumption*, grounded in the idea that truly cohesive societies must be organic communities, rather than an obvious fact, that society 'needs' a unifying Ego Ideal.

Indeed, the idea is foreign to Lacan. For Lacan, one description of the Ego Ideal is the Name-of-the-Father – that is, the subject's surname (or patronymic, strictly speaking) as the locus of his symbolic identification with the parental imago. Is it a trivial observation that, in *any* society, there is a vast multitude of such names of the father, or Ego Ideals, doing the rounds? Even if the Ego Ideal is formed less around the father as a person than around some social ideal, it is still not obvious that there can be only one of these. This is because, as Lacan (2006: 197–268) explains in his seminal 'Rome Discourse', it is the Symbolic Order – speech in a common language – that represents the social pact, not sharing a social ideal.

But the way Žižek has set the problem up precludes this solution, because he associates the Symbolic Order with global capitalism and the ferocious superego. Consequently, Žižek's call for a renewal of the Symbolic Order must necessarily lead to the call for a new Ego Ideal, and for this Ego Ideal to be universally shared. This is a substantive point of agreement, or coincidence of opposites, between the neoconservative Right and Žižek's Leftism: the Durkheimian assumption that 'society needs a unifying Ego Ideal' means that Žižek's solution to the decline of symbolic authority leads towards a reinstatement of *paternal* authority combined with a rejection of multicultural society and value pluralism. It seeks an organic (post-capitalist) community, but, because the Ego Ideal or master signifier is in Lacanian theory *arbitrary*, Žižek also thinks that there is no way to say, before the revolution, which Ego Ideal is the best (*IDLC* 7). This means that Žižek's position has major potential to be at once restrictively monocultural and decisionist – that is, grounded in an arbitrary assertion of political willpower.

We began this chapter by probing the credibility of Žižek's diagnosis of the present conjuncture. We can now reach some conclusions. Although the notion of a decline in symbolic authority is descriptively rich, and Žižek's resistance to postmodern culture as the cultural logic of late capitalism is something to celebrate, there are several points in his analysis that are disturbing. The insistence on a new social Ego Ideal, in combination with worrying implicit assumptions about social cohesion, makes Žižek's overall diagnosis less helpful than his many local insights. There are political reasons to be concerned about the provenance and the destination of important elements of Žižek's framework, and theoretical reservations need to be voiced about his hesitations and reversals. Indeed, without these qualifications, Žižek's cultural diagnosis has the potential to set up answers to the questions – how to escape this situation and how to have the social ideal without the punitive superego – that are very one-sided. The assumption that the solution to the 'generalised perversion' of the capitalist Symbolic Order is a new, unifying Ego Ideal, sets up the politically problematic idea of a total revolution on the basis of an arbitrary decision (Chapter 5). And it licenses the notion that the basic blueprint for the post-capitalist, non-superegoic society is one that, like a pre-modern society, has a state religion or official ideology (Chapter 6).

Chapter 5

Žižek's Vanguard Politics

A Paradoxical View

We saw in the Introduction how political philosophy addresses the questions of what is desirable (the best form(s) of regime) and what is possible. We also saw that the politics of different philosophers rests on competing visions of the human condition. Yet if people can remake the world, they never do so under conditions wholly of their own choosing. Theorists' prescriptions concerning what is possible – with a view to the highest possible good political subjects can pursue – will be determined by their descriptive estimation of the present world. As Žižek's thought has developed, he has turned from the advocacy of an extension and deepening of democracy to an entire change of political regime. So what does Žižek end by proposing as possible or desirable, given his estimation of the present 'scoundrel time'? How can we interpret Žižek's politics, and how does his political philosophy measure up?

In this chapter, focusing on Žižek's two recent long books, *The Parallax View* and *In Defence of Lost Causes*, we are going to show how Žižek, since 1997, has increasingly come to embrace a position calling for a total revolution against global capitalism. This is not a simple position to interpet, because Žižek frames it as a reaction against what he calls the 'liberal blackmail' that, as soon as people criticise the existing status quo, they become 'terrorists' or 'totalitarians' or 'fascists'. Is Žižek's position a provocation designed to open up debate again by refusing this blackmail, or is it what he now believes is necessary and desirable?

Part of the difficulty may be that Žižek himself does not really escape the logic of this blackmail, although his merit is to call it what it is. Žižek's rebellion against the hidden violence of today's liberal democracies (*OV* 9–29), together with his recent philosophical Romanticism, seem to drive him fatefully towards a reactionary, merely adversarial stance. In *In Defence of Lost Causes*, Žižek defiantly announces that the work is something like every liberal's worst

165

nightmare (*IDLC* 4–7). Perhaps so – but, instead of generating a new politics capable of animating or guiding progressive political movements, this accepts the antagonist's framework of debate. It risks merely reversing the value judgement on the opposed terms, 'liberalism versus terrorism'. The cost is to equate 'real' politics with the sort of pre-political violence that happens when people, in the *absence* of a viable non-liberal political option, strike out in despair.

In order to show how this occurs, let us begin from Žižek's most extended post-1999 political diagnosis of the times, in *The Ticklish Subject.*

Post-Politics in the Age of Generalised Perversion

Recall that, in Chapter 1, we saw Žižek's assessment of our political situation as the 'end of history' in liberal democracy and global capitalism. Additionally, as we saw in Chapter 4, the late capitalist society of Nietzschean 'Last Men' is composed of individuals who lack a higher purpose or ideals, because of the 'decline of paternal authority' generated by consumer society. The global dominion of liberal capitalism, meanwhile, is maintained by a prohibition against thinking about political alternatives, or ideals for which a person might live and be willing to die (e.g. *OV* 29). This bleak dystopian vision – a sort of theoretical variant of the fictional universe presented in the film *Fight Club* (1999) – places Žižek uncomfortably close to the motif developed by reactionary-cum-authoritarian thinker Carl Schmitt (1996), that liberal societies 'threaten the concept of the political'. For Žižek, answering to a nostalgia Fukuyama identified in the despairing later part of *The End of History and the Last Man*, the task of committed intellectuals and political activists is to *re*-start history by breaking radically with liberal democracy (Fukuyama 1992: 330; cf. Strauss 2000: 210–11).

Nevertheless, Žižek believes, as Schmitt also did, that, 'in human society, the political is the englobing structuring principle, so that every neutralization [a key Schmittian term] of some partial content as "non-political" is a political gesture *par excellence*' (*TS* 191; Schmitt 1998). Just so, in what is probably his most sustained assessment of the global political field today, Žižek argues that there are four or five models of politics out there. In line with his analysis of generalised perversion, however, Žižek argues that each of these involves a fetishistic 'disavowal' of political conflict in the sense Žižek understands it. For Žižek, most of what is called politics today simply avoids 'politics proper'. Adapting categories from French thinker Jacques Rancière, Žižek calls today's predominant political options *arche-*, *para-*, *meta-*, *ultra-* and *post-*politics – the last of which is Žižek's most lasting assessment of the whole field today.

- *Arche-politics* names forms of political communitarianism. Communitarians argue that humans' higher capacities can flourish only in close-knit communities, because self-identity depends upon internalisation of the particular moral values of the community. Individuals therefore always engage in 'strong evaluations' of moral debates that are framed by the way that their self-identity depends upon what the individual holds to be the highest good. Citizens, in other words, are completely embedded in their political community, and no moral debate *between* frameworks is possible – communitarianism is a radical particularism and a form of moral relativism, although right-wing communitarians tend to forget this as they lacerate the postmodern Left for relativism. Often, organic metaphors will be used to describe society as like a natural being, each of whose parts should work in unison if the whole is to flourish. The flipside is that political dissent or cultural differences tend to be thought of as being like diseases contaminating the organism, which need to be excised, by force if need be. Neoconservatism, for instance, with its opposition to liberal multiculturalism and universal rights, and hostility to political dialogue and social protest, is a right-wing form of communitarianism. As the name implies, *arche*-politics is a politics of nostalgia for an archaic, prelapsarian form of community.
- *Parapolitics* is Žižek's neologism for forms of radical democratic politics. In democratic polities, the contest of political opinions and groups is not denied. But it is regulated by the rule of law, so direct violence is prohibited. Parties and groups with a differing view of the community's good compete in elections and the court of public opinion for people's support. Unlike liberalism, however, *para-politics* does not reduce political competition to the contest of interest groups in a system of lobbying and compromise. *Para-politics* insists that political competition is generated through wider social antagonisms and that therefore politics is the way social conflict is democratically resolved, preferably through sweeping social reforms. In the world of Theory, Laclau and Mouffe are the spokespersons of *para-politics*, which, as we saw in Chapter 3, Žižek also embraced early in his career.

- *Metapolitics* is, interestingly, the word Žižek coins in 1999 for forms of Marxism. It is something of the joker in this taxonomical pack. It is 'meta' (beyond or before) 'politics proper', because, like *para-politics*, it looks at the official contest of differing political opinions and groups as secondary. But, unlike *para-politics*, *meta-politics* does not regard political institutions as capable of providing a fundamental resolution of social antagonism. Instead, what is decisive is the 'other scene' of the economy, which has the primary role in shaping people's lives. The aim of *meta-politics* is to generate scientific knowledge of this other scene, to allow enlightened intervention in the economy and the real reshaping of people's lives. Now, Žižek aligns *meta-politics* with his analysis of Stalinism as the institution of a 'Discourse of the University' based on the pseudo-scientific ideology of dialectical materialism. The Leader, unlike the traditional Master, positions himself as the mere instrument of the supposed objective laws of history. *Meta-politics* hence justifies political violence by recourse to its 'grand narrative' about the meaning of politics and history, as in the Stalinist case. *Meta-politics* is the joker in Žižek's pack, however, because he seems at times himself to embrace positions that look very like those he describes as '*meta-political*'.
- *Ultra-politics* is Žižek's name for forms of right-wing populist, or openly fascist, political regimes. The pre-eminent theoretical spokesperson of *ultra-politics* (who has, significantly, undergone a recent rehabilitation after his post-war disgrace as a leading Nazi intellectual) is Carl Schmitt. For Schmitt, the concept of the political involves war between friends and enemies, including the physical destruction of political adversaries, rather than the politically regulated opposition between social antagonists. The enemy is whoever the sovereign Leader (the S_1 of the 'Discourse of the Master') decides 'threatens our way of life' (Schmitt 1996). This decision ideally should be extra-rational, not open to citizens' assessment or debate. The *ultra-political* Leader is charged as the commander-in-chief to destroy the enemy, a military task that forms the basis of his legitimacy. *Ultra-politics* is, therefore, always authoritarian: Schmitt argues that the Leader is or ought to be considered, 'theologically', as unchecked in his political power as God is over his creation (Schmitt 1985). There is more than an echo of *ultra-politics* in the way that the Western neoliberal governments responded to the terrorist attacks on 11 September 2001 with a 'War on Terror'. For Žižek, however, what is at stake in *ultra-politics* is:

the attempt to depoliticize the [political] conflict by bringing it to an extreme, via the direct militarization of politics. [This happens] by reformulating it as the *war* between 'Us' and 'Them', our Enemy, where there is no common ground for symbolic conflict – it is deeply symptomatic that, rather than class *struggle*, the radical Right speaks of class (or sexual) *warfare*. (TS 190)

- *Post-politics* is the neutralisation of political struggle through the transformation of politics into the technological management of society. Yet Žižek's account of *post-politics* reflects his oscillation, examined in Chapter 4, between saying we live in a society of generalised perversion and claiming that today's world is psychotic. Today, the 'denegation of the political' predominantly involves not simply the 'disavowal' of the political – as with the first four types of politics. Rather, 'politics proper' in Žižek's sense is 'foreclosed' by the predominant post-political consensus today, in terms that again closely reflect the populist neoconservative diagnoses in the culture wars:

> In *post-politics*, the conflict of global ideological visions embodied in different parties which compete for power is replaced by the collaboration of enlightened technocrats (economists, public opinion specialists . . .) and liberal multiculturalists: via the process of negotiation of interests, a compromise is reached in the guise of a more or less universal consensus. *Post-politics* . . . emphasizes the need to leave old ideological divisions behind and confront new issues, armed with the necessary expert knowledge and free deliberation that takes people's concrete needs and demands into account. (TS 198)

The clearest example of such 'post-politics' is the Third Way accommodation of old Labour parties to the 'small-government' premises of neoliberalism, justified by the argument that the New Labour is interested only in 'ideas that work'. As Žižek observes:

> To say that good ideas are 'ideas that work' means that one accepts in advance the (global capitalist) constellation that determines what works (if, for example, one spends too much money education or healthcare, that 'doesn't work', since it infringes too much on the conditions of capitalist profitability). (*TS* 199)

The logic of Žižek's argument, which claims that all these forms of politics represent so many 'neutralisations and depoliticisations' of politics, means that we should not be surprised that the last, 'take-all' category Žižek introduces in *The Ticklish Subject* is 'post-politics'.

But the real question, given Žižek's criticisms of arche-, para-, meta- and ultra-politics, is what is *his* alternative, and why does it open the dimension of 'politics proper', or 'the Political,' when the others do not?

As we shall see, many critics have argued that Žižek, rather than providing an alternative, merely combines the main features of meta- and ultra-politics (e.g. Parker 2004: 85–104). He thereby generates a form of Schmittian, decisionistic ultra-politics that adopts a super- ficial meta-political coloration as 'messianic Marxism' in order to position its hostility to global capitalism and liberal democracy as on the Left.

So What was Politics Proper?

Now, to answer this question – and reply, if possible, to objections – Žižek needs to explain what 'the Political' *is*. He needs to specify his Truth of politics or concept of 'politics proper', which Žižek thinks everybody else in the theoretical and practical universe is frantically avoiding.

What is 'Politics Proper'? Žižek's Founding Act

In fact, Žižek is clear:

- As for many other contemporary Theorists, for him politics proper in the last instance involves or invokes the arbitrary decision that founds a political community upon a social ideal or form of the highest good, but that also represses into the political uncon- scious the fundamental social fantasy of that political community.
- Thus, given Žižek's framing parataxis (or system of homologies), the reigning universal social ideal has the same status, in political life, as the prohibition of incest in psychic development. Equally, the ideological fantasy that supports a political community leads the same sort of subterranean existence in public life that the repressed incestuous wish leads in private life.
- It follows that 'the Political' or 'politics proper' is the political Act by which this ideological fantasy of a political regime is inaugurated. The 'political Act' is a total revolution that replaces the old social fantasy with a new social fantasy.

According to Žižek's psychoanalytic 'homology' with political life, we could expect the 'repressed' Real of the founding Act of 'politics proper' to return symbolically in political 'symptoms' – that is, in political life, through social antagonism, as we saw in Chapter 3. But, according to Žižek, in today's technocratic post-political universe, the foreclosed political dimension returns 'in the Real'. It does so in the series of disturbingly politico-psychotic 'symptoms' that rock the post-political world today, and about which we have often now remarked: the outbreaks of ultra-political racism and neo-nationalism, religious fundamentalism and political terrorism, and apparently senseless acts of cruelty and violence.

According to Jacques Rancière's differing, radical democratic conception of 'politics proper', the dimension of politics proper emerges only momentarily. This happens when a particular political demand (say, about the mistreatment of a minority) is 'sublimated' or elevated to a universal claim – that is, one that appeals to universal ideals such as justice and equality (Rancière 1999). A truly *political* claim emerges when an individual, or group, maintains that the particular injustice under which he is suffering is not completely distinct from all other forms of injustice – it is just one example of the violation of the universal norm of justice.

At moments of his texts, Žižek proposes that the problem with post-political 'tolerance' is that it forecloses exactly this possibility. A black lesbian single mother who raises a claim about rights or injustice, which are universal notions, is immediately treated by one or several administrative agencies, who respond to her as only a member of a specific group whose specific needs can readily be administratively addressed by more government money or schools in the area, and so on:

> What such a tolerant approach precludes is the gesture of politicization proper: although the difficulties of being an African-American unemployed lesbian mother are adequately catalogued right down to their most specific features, the concerned subject none the less somehow 'feels' that there is something 'wrong' in this very effort to mete out justice to her specific predicament – what she is deprived of is the possibility of the 'metaphoric' elevation of her specific 'wrong' into a stand-in for the universal 'wrong'. (*TS* 204–5)

It is such frustration at having one's differences so thoroughly respected in their particularity that leads contemporary subjects and theorists into performing or advocating acts of apparently senseless political violence, what used to be called 'active nihilism': 'The only way to articulate the universality – the fact that I, precisely, am not merely the specific individual exposed to a set of specific injustices – consists then in its apparent opposite, in the thoroughly "irrational" excessive outbursts of violence' (TS 204).

Žižek's is an interesting position, which closely approaches the observation of Herbert Marcuse (1969: 95–137) concerning repressive tolerance. It also evokes the Enlightenment's language of universal political claims. We certainly agree with Žižek's judgement that recent left-wing Theory has fetishised immediacy and particularity, whereas no emancipatory politics can be sustained by positions that 'renounce the discourse of the universal' (Laclau and Mouffe 1985: 3–4). But what does Žižek argue concerning other contemporary political theory? In particular, does any such theory show us how we might reopen this dimension of 'politics proper', and so provide a way out of the postmodern dilemma of desublimating multicultural tolerance and equally empty, violent reactions against it?

The Theoretical Left and its Disavowals

The reader will not be surprised that the answer Žižek gives is finally, 'No!'. With typical acuity, Žižek diagnoses that the academic Left, and the wider Left today, is facing a 'crisis of determinate negation' (IDLC 3379). Recall that determinate negation was Hegel's term, taken on by Marx, for the way something (say, a political regime) can be 'negated' or overcome when it contains some 'immanent' potential (like an organised but exploited working class) whose realisation would mean that the entire substance would have to change (say, by a revolution wherein the workers take control of the state, factories and corporations). Determinate negation is different from merely 'abstract negation'. This is what is involved when we deny or 'negate' something from the outside, or with reference to a wholly different set of ideals – as in the Iranian revolution briefly embraced by Michel Foucault, for instance, which 'negated' that nation's Westernised regime in the name of a highly regressive form of Islamic religion (IDLC 107–17). Determinate negation mediates between a theoretical account of the political world and practical conclusions, for it theoretically identifies points in the political world where political change and new forces can reasonably be identified, and identified with.

To believe in the possibility of a determinate negation of today's globalising regime would be to identify potentials within it whose realisation would justify and involve changing the entire system. However, Žižek says, today's Left can generally not see any such potentials. Žižek's key, typically acute criticism of Laclau, Balibar, Badiou and Rancière in *The Ticklish Subject*, is to note how their thought is structured around an abstract opposition between the existing regime (the order of Being in Badiou, or of 'the police' in Rancière) and some event or possibility that would wholly overturn the existing situation from the outside (*TS* 171–244).

So, here again reflecting his 'generalised perversion' hypothesis, Žižek alleges that contemporary Theory involves a series of *disavowals*, less of some 'true' radical position than of 'the lack of such a position' involving any determinate negation of today's order. Let us quote at length Žižek's devastating assessment of these disavowals. Today's 'radical' theorists in fact oscillate between:

> (1) Full acceptance of this framework [of neoliberal capitalism]: continuing to fight for emancipation within its rules (Third Way social democracy). (2) Acceptance of this framework as something that is here to stay, but which one should nevertheless resist . . . (3) Acceptance of the futility of all struggle, since the framework is today all-encompassing, coinciding with its opposite (the logic of concentration camps, the permanent state of emergency) so nothing can really be done . . . (4) Acceptance of the temporary futility of struggle . . . '[un]til the renewal of the revolutionary spirit in the global working class . . . withdraw into cultural studies, where one can silently pursue critical work'. (5) Emphasis on the fact that the problem is a more fundamental one: that global capitalism is ultimately an ontic effect of the underlying ontological principle of technology or 'instrumental reason' . . . (6) Belief that one can undermine global capitalism and state power . . . not by directly attacking them but by reformulating the field of struggle on everyday practices . . . (7) A 'postmodern' shift of the accent from anti-capitalist struggle to the multiple forms of the politico-ideological struggle for hegemony . . . (8) A wager that one can repeat at the postmodern level the classical Marxist gesture and enact the 'determinate negation' of capitalism . . . (*IDLC* 337–8)

Žižek's challenge to contemporary theory is that, politically speaking, much of it amounts to a reactive culture of complaint and bad faith. The appearance of 'radical' intellectual activity is really a disguise for its opposite: a complete lack of connection with any real social or political movements; a complete lack of vision for a renewed society; and the secret desire for nothing to change. Theory with a capital 'T' is one more 'inherent transgression' in our society of generalised perversion that sustains ideological disidentification, and postmodern cynical conformism.

We can isolate four specific, powerful criticisms Žižek makes of the existing neo-Leftist theoretical authorities with whom he engages (Badiou, Butler, Laclau and Mouffe, Critchley, Stavrakakis, Rancière, Balibar): *forgetting the universal, forgetting the economy, wishful thinking, and forgetting the state.*

FORGETTING THE UNIVERSAL

We have seen how Žižek argues that multiculturalism, despite first appearances, leads to what Žižek calls a 'foreclosure' of the dimension of universality, in the case of the single black mother whose grievance is immediately treated as the specific demand of a specific subgroup. The language of universality also speaks to the claim to be continuing the Enlightenment project, by rehabilitating Lacanian psychoanalysis and German Idealism. However, in his recent work, Žižek's earlier commitment to 'democracy' – so often associated with Enlightenment thinking – as a desirable or defensible political position disappears. Žižek comes very close to the old Leninist position that the liberal-democratic political 'superstructure' is wholly illegitimate, a mere front for economic and other forms of domination.

This move undoubtedly reflects Žižek's observations concerning the real problems facing contemporary society. These include the calculated disempowerment of ordinary voters and nation states by neoliberalism and the global plutocracy of multinational corporations. They also include the Western government's late-found willingness to roll back civil liberties in the name of national security. But criticisms of 'actually existing democracy' as falling short of the democratic ideal are not what Žižek has in mind. To see why, we need to look at Žižek's more recent criticisms of his former radical-democratic allies, Laclau and Mouffe.

According to Žižek, the problem with radical democracy is that it falls prey to a version of the old liberal paradox – that just as a tolerant liberal must be intolerant towards all intolerant – that is, non-liberal – positions, so, too, a radical democrat must be anti-democratic towards all anti-democratic positions. The implication is that neither tolerance nor democracy can be basic political values. The Laclavo-Mouffian 'para-political' notion of a hegemonic politics envisages different particular groups competing to have their view of the 'universal' accepted as the general will. But according to

Žižek this is impossible. Radical democracy demands of citizens that they regard every political universal as merely a particular value that might temporarily occupy the 'empty place of power'. But no political group believes that its view of the common good is just one of many different, equally (in)adequate attempts to represent this good. And no democrat thinks that the empty place of power is a neutral locus that can be filled out with just any content – they think that democratic institutions are politically universal and therefore that anti-democratic forces, such as fascist parties and military dictatorships, should be prevented from taking over.

The question is whether what Žižek is denying, in maintaining that political passion springs from pre-reflexive commitments to exclusivist forms of the common good, is the very possibility of an enlightened, reflexive political community. For Žižek's refusal of radical democracy has strong overtones of communitarian 'arche-politics'. Žižek has always maintained that loyalty to the national Thing, supported by the founding ideological fantasy, has been the Archimedean point around which most modern regimes have turned, beneath their symbolic commitments. The question is whether his ultimate point is that any commitment to democratic politics must turn on just this sort of hidden passionate attachment to the national Thing (*LA* 165–9). The inference is that, to found any new political community, we need to traverse the *existing* fantasy of national origins – not fantasy *per se* – so as to replace this foundation with another fantasmatic regime, built around the former regime's exception or *sinthome*. Instead of this more radical pose, however, the 'radical democrats' are stuck insisting naively that civic loyalty to democratic institutions might be sufficient, when the formalism of these institutions actually prevents subjects' decisive, unconscious attachment to them.

To specify Žižek's rejection of radical democracy in psychoanalytic terms, Žižek turns to the opposition between desire and drive. The politics of competition for (temporary) hegemony represents the attempt to institutionalise recognition of something like the Lacanian notion of desire (Stavrakakis 1999). By contrast, as we commented in 'Vanishing Mediations', Žižek now endorses a politics of the (death) drive, an 'active will to disrupt' (*TS* 184), to take sides, even 'fanatically' (*IDLC* 345), rather than to accept the neutral rules of the liberal contest of political opinions. For Žižek$_2$, more and more stridently, Laclau's or Stavrakakis's hope that we should aim for a society not held together by a particularistic tie to one or other sublime-ideological Thing (like 'the Nation') and ideological fantasy is itself fantasmatic. The reason is that, when Žižek talks in Hegelian terms about the need for a 'concrete' political Universality, it is clear that what (heterodoxically) he means is that there is no abstract or 'neutral' universal field or perspective that could (or *should*) adjudicate between different views of the good in a society. Rather, each particular perspective on the political good involves its own, equally particular or 'singular', incommensurable view of the 'universal' topic of what politics is all about. The Left and the Right on this view do not really contest for power within a shared or agreed-upon field of struggle. Rather, each contests to have its own 'universal' view of the entire political struggle become the dominant one (e.g. *CHU* 215–16; *TS* 215).

Politics is hence all about the struggle – which can reach no reasoned reconciliation – between irreconcilable and incommensurable 'concrete universalities'. Theory at most can endorse a 'parallax view' that accepts this fundamental incommensurability. Žižek's recurrent example is how the supposed creation of neutral, universalist civil societies in modern Western democracies, wherein the different perspectives can peacefully compete for power, is itself historically predicated on people's continuing attachment to particularistic National Things (*CHU* 106–7, 399; *LA* 164, 166). We are only a hair's breadth – or the breadth of Žižek's Hegelo-Lacanian terminology – away from the views of reactionary political theologians from de Maistre to contemporary neoconservatism: the old wisdom that people's political attachments must always rest on an irrational, untraversable core of particularistic beliefs. As Žižek writes, sharply dismissing Stavrakakis's advocacy of a Lacanian democratic theory:

> Because he ignores this excess of the drive, Stavrakakis also operates with a simplified notion of 'traversing the fantasy' . . . the common sense idea of what psychoanalysis should do: of course it should liberate us from the hold of idiosyncratic fantasies . . . but this, precisely, is what Lacan does not have in mind . . . To 'traverse the fantasy' paradoxically means fully identifying oneself with the fantasy – namely with the fantasy that structures the excess resisting our immersion into daily reality. (*IDLC* 329)

Forgetting the Economy

As we saw in Chapter 4, Žižek argues that subjects today perversely disavow their conformist acceptance of the global capitalist regime.

Indeed, we have been living – between 1989 and 2008 – through two decades in which capitalism has had an unprecedented dominance around the globe. Economics now has an unprecedented centrality in public discourse. It is the key component of the post-political consensus, with which even moderate progressive ideas are quickly walloped over the metaphorical head – 'as good as that sounds, it will lead to increased spending, hence higher taxes, more bureaucracy, crowding out of capital markets, disincentives for investment . . .'. It is these observations that underlie Žižek's untenable attempt to identify Capital today with the Lacanian Real (*FA* 15; *OV* 13).

Yet contemporary 'radical' theory in this very period – everyone from the democrat Laclau to the ultra-Leftist Alain Badiou – has been overwhelmingly *silent* in this period concerning economics, and its key role in shaping people's lived experiences. This is a remarkable observation, confirming that something like Žižek's notion of a disavowal of economics must be true:

> as long as the fundamental depoliticisation of the economic sphere is accepted, all the talk about . . . public discussion leading to responsible collective decisions . . . will remain limited to the 'cultural' issues of religious, sexual, ethnic . . . differences, without actually encroaching upon the level at which long-term decisions that affect us all are made. (*TS* 353)

As we have already seen, however, the key problem with Žižek's calls for a return to political economy is that they have remained just that: calls. They have not led to his own engagement with the extensive literature on political economy that continues to be generated around the world. Yet this point is not just of descriptive importance. Marxian political economy was a key component of Leftist immanent critique, and the search for a determinate negation of capitalism. If we accept that humans' economic 'metabolism with nature' – our continuing need to work to generate materially necessary goods for our survival – has a large role to play in the structure of society; and if we can understand how goods are presently generated and circulated; *then* we can give efficacious, enlightened, concrete form to our abstract desire to reshape the way people live and behave politically. What is needed is to focus our energies on what our analysis shows are the decisive moments (crises), elements and emerging points of solidarity within the existing political and economic system whence real change might be generated.

In this vein, flying the flag for 'determinate negation', Žižek has at several points insisted that he continues to think that the existing globalising capitalism is generating such potential sites of immanent transformation and political forces capable of carrying it out. *In Defence of Lost Causes* ends by listing five such potential 'eventual sites' in the new global order. These include the new 'technoscientific' developments, like the genome project, that now challenge long-standing understandings of the human condition; the 'new forms of apartheid', walls and barriers, associated with nation state's attempts to control immigration and prevent terrorist strikes; and the growing importance of intellectual property in the new system, whose 'pirate' reproduction cannot easily be prevented (*IDLC* 421–4). Probably the two most plausibly *political* points of immanent systemic crisis potential Žižek lists, however, are:

1. *the ecological crisis*: 'what looms on the horizon today is the unprecedented possibility that a subjective intervention will intervene directly into the historical substance, catastrophically disturbing its course by triggering an ecological catastrophe, a fateful biogenetic mutation, a nuclear or similar military-social catastrophe' (*IDLC* 421);
2. *the growth of new underclasses, particularly in the Third World*: Lagos, Mexico city, the bustling, bursting cities of India, China and the Philippines; these sites contain millions of people, often 'outside of state control, in conditions half outside the law, in terrible need of the minimal form of organisation' (*IDLC* 424).

As Žižek writes, these new slums and *favellas* 'are the true "symptom" of slogans such as "development", "modernization" and the "world market": not an unfortunate accident, but a necessary product of the innermost logics of global capitalism' (*IDLC* 424).

MESSIANISM, UTOPIANISM, AND WISHFUL THINKING

Žižek has the political clear-sightedness to observe that many of the attempts to bring high theory to concrete politics over recent decades have produced forms of utopianism or libertarianism, which reflect the loss of any connection between theory and concrete political practice. These range from the revival of the ancient dream of a prelapsarian society without law evoked at the end of Agamben's hyper-pessimistic accounts of how the West is 'paradigmatically' defined by the concentration camp (*PV* 265–6); via the inevitable recourse to Melville's unlikely hero, the disaffected scrivener

Bartleby, who simply says 'I would prefer not to' when confronted with authority's call to act; to Yannis Stavrakakis's alleged recent celebration of (citing Žižek's dismissive gloss): 'Paleolithic communities practicing a Zen road to affluence' (*IDLC* 330).

Žižek's one exception to the theoretical rule of the disavowal of the economy, for instance, lies in Hardt and Negri, authors of the important works *Empire* (2000) and *Multitude* (2005). He notes that these books, unlike those of Žižek's other academic interlocutors, have the merit of actually engaging with the emerging global anti-capitalist movement (*PV* 261). Yet, among Žižek's many telling criticisms of Hardt and Negri, perhaps the clincher is that their work ends in an all-too-common, weak messianism. Messianism is the hope for a coming messiah who or which will redeem the present fallen world, without our own actions, but as if by divine grace. Historian Gerschom Scholem (1971) noted how messianism in the Jewish tradition always emerged at the moments of the gravest political crises and defeat (for instance, the expulsion of the Jewish community from Spain by the Inquisition), wherein no political solutions to present woes could be envisaged. Just so, Hardt and Negri end *Empire* by invoking the hope for new revolutionaries, and an absolute expressive democracy, which would somehow bring to politics the apolitical Christian spirit of St Francis of Assisi. As Žižek writes, in words that could, as we will see, very well read as a devastatingly ironic self-critique:

> That is to say, what we do and should expect is a description of the notional structure of this qualitative jump, from the multitudes resisting the One of sovereign power to the multitudes directly ruling themselves. Leaving the notional structure of this passage in a darkness elucidated only by vague analogies and examples from resistance movements cannot but arouse the suspicion that this self-transparent direct rule of everyone over everyone, this democracy tout court, will coincide with its opposite. (*PV* 262).

DISAVOWING THE STATE

Significantly, in *Parallax View* and *In Defence of Lost Causes*, Žižek has added a fourth dimension of political criticism of the other luminaries of contemporary Theory. This is that, as the utopian longing suggests, today's theorists want a politics without politics, or, more specifically, without the state. This is ironic, Žižek notes, in the very era where the predominant ruling ideology, neoliberalism, is also anti-'Big State' – perhaps another reinforcement of his claim that today's Theory is another inherent transgression sustaining the rule of global capitalism. It is also deeply symptomatic of what Žižek perceives as the deeply hysterical nature of Theory's *a priori* Theoretical radicalism: that it involves a set of reactive complaints about the present order bereft of any real desire to bring into being a new order. Again, the disavowal of the need for any new political movement actually to win the power of the state spans theorists ranging from ex-Maoist Alain Badiou to the ludic anarchist Simon Critchley. Critchley, for instance, evokes a politics that would, humorously or in a playful mode, 'occupy the interstices' between civil society and the state (*IDLC* 339–50). Badiou argues that what the failure of Mao's Cultural Revolution showed was that the era of the revolutionary desire to take control of the state has rightly come to an end (*IDLC* 399–404).

Žižek rightly asks how such theorists can hope to change the existing world if they eschew, in advance, any possibility of changing the state forms, those apparatuses that presently carry the monopoly on the legitimate use of force, together with all the deep, non-physical force of subjects' unconscious attachments to the national Thing:

> In other words, is Critchley's (and Badiou's) position not that of relying on the fact that someone else will assume the task of running the state machinery, enabling us to engage in taking the critical distance towards it? Furthermore, if the space of emancipitory politics is defined by a distance towards the state, are we not abandoning the field (of the state) all too easily to the enemy? (*IDLC* 402)

Žižek's Push towards the Act

Žižek is the most incisive critic, from within, of the shortcomings and nature of contemporary Francophile poststructuralist theory. His political criticisms of it are deeply important, especially the idea that this Theory turns our attention away from economics when economics has never been more politically important. Most contemporary 'radical' theory romantically (and falsely) assumes, alongside neoliberalism, that the state can only be a regressive force. This means that the multiple retreats into messianic utopianism – usually justified by recourse only to obtuse literary characters and esoteric or ludic textual exegeses – become increasingly unavoidable.

But does Žižek avoid the barbs of his own criticisms, and does he do so in ways we might want to defend? In particular, does the way he bases his own political prescriptions in a first philosophy of a unitary subject–object (the big Other) really allow him to avoid the malaises he so acutely diagnoses in others?

As we commented at the end of Chapter 2, Žižek's most insistent political prescription is that what is required today is what he calls a radical Act. Žižek's notion of the Act draws on Lacan's late theorisation of the end of the psychoanalytic cure. Applying this to the political realm, Žižek has in his recent texts advocated a suspension of the ordinary manner in which democratic politics is carried out. The polemical aim is to counteract the political Right's seeming monopoly on radical political action today (witness, for instance, the massive mobilisation of legislative, military and ideological arms after the 9/11 events; but also the continuing rise of neofascism around the globe). This suspension would take the form of a revolutionary Act that would not give *any* ground on our transformative political desire. If all socio-political systems, our own included, are ultimately bound by a set of undergirding ideological fantasies, Žižek reasons, what the Left needs are political acts that 'traverse' these fantasies. Such revolutionary Acts would hence be true, in action, to the theoretical insight that the Other never 'exists' as a wholly independent, authoritative and unchanging guarantee for our actions (*ES* 44-4-46; *PF* 223–4; *SO* 124–8; *TN* 251–7; *WDR* 152–4).

Searching around for political precedents for his recommendations, Žižek has increasingly valorised the Lenin of *What is to be Done?* and of the (for Žižek) radical decision in October 1917 to stage the Bolshevik insurrection (*OB* 3–4, 113–127; *RL*). Žižek has also brought several troubling literary precedents to the argumentative table: Antigone, whose heroic resistance to King Creon sees her brutally slain by the state; Medea, who 'pre-emptively' slays her own children to spite her unfaithful husband; and the main character who beats himself up in front of his boss in *Fight Club* (e.g. *ES* 46; *FA* 149–60).

What are the Criticisms of Žižek's Politics of the Act?

- Lacanians have argued that it misrepresents Lacan's notion of the psychoanalytic cure and Lacan's reading of Antigone (Grigg 2005).
- Philosophers have argued that it represents a departure from Žižek's earlier Kantian emphasis on human limitation, the ways

we are so deeply shaped by our historical and political situation – as if we could in one Act somehow recreate our entire way of life, or 'do the impossible', as Žižek sometimes says (Stavrakakis 2005).

- Others have worried about how Žižek's reference points are the same as the post-structuralists he criticises, up to and including advocating a politico-theological reading of Protestant theologian Søren Kierkegaard's emphasis on the 'madness' of religious decision (*OB* 147–8) (Resch 2005).

- Žižek's insistence that what is desirable is such a radical Act also seems to leave wide open the question of what, if anything, could follow this moment of joyous political 'suspension of the ethical' (we shall see about this in a moment) 'beyond the good' (*PF* 213) (see Devenney 2007: 58–9).

- Finally, Žižek is explicit that the type of revolutionary Act he wants cannot be justified with reference to any pre-existing standards of justice or vision of a better regime. Neither can it countenance any compromise with strategic reason. Rather, the Act will give birth to the constellation of beliefs that can then, retroactively, justify it. These propositions do seem to commit Žižek to a new form of the decisionistic political existentialism like that of Carl Schmitt. We are once again in the presence of a theory that opposes the need for a groundless authoritarian decision, suspending all our usual ways of doing things, to liberalism's interminable 'chattering' neutralisation of real political conflict.

Can we bring some order to this host of criticisms? It is remarkable that, for all the criticisms of Žižek's political Romanticism, no one has argued that the ultra-extremism of Žižek's political position might reflect his untenable attempt to shape his model for political action on the curative final moment in clinical psychoanalysis. The differences between these two realms, listed in Figure 5.1, are nearly too many and too great to restate – which has perhaps caused the theoretical oversight. The key thing is this. Lacan's notion of traversing the fantasy involves the radical transformation of people's subjective structure: a refounding of their most elementary beliefs about themselves, the world, and sexual difference. This is undertaken in the security of the clinic, on the basis of the analysands' voluntary desire to overcome their inhibitions, symptoms and anxieties.

As a clinical and existential process, it has its own independent importance and authenticity. The analysands, in transforming their subjective world, change the way they regard the objective, shared social reality outside the clinic. But they do not transform the world. The political relevance of the clinic can only be (*a*) as a supporting moment in ideology critique or (*b*) as a fully-fledged model of politics, provided that the political subject and its social object are ultimately identical. Option (*b*), Žižek's option, rests on the idea, not only of a subject who becomes who he is only through his (mis) recognition of the objective sociopolitical order, but whose 'traversal of the fantasy' is *immediately* identical with his transformation of the socio-political system or Other. Hence, according to Žižek, we can analyse the institutional embodiments of this Other using psychoanalytic categories. In Chapter 4, we saw Žižek's resulting elision of the distinction between the (subjective) Ego Ideal and the (objective) Symbolic Order. This leads him to analyse our entire culture as a single subject–object, whose perverse (or perhaps even psychotic) structure is expressed in every manifestation of contemporary life. Žižek's decisive political-theoretic errors, one substantive and the other methodological, are different (see Figure 5.1).

The *substantive problem* is to equate any political change worth the name with the total change of the subject–object that is, today, global capitalism. This is a type of change that can only mean equating politics with violent regime change, and ultimately embracing dictatorial government, as Žižek now frankly avows (*IDLC* 412–19). We have seen that the ultra-political form of Žižek's criticism of everyone else, the theoretical Left and the wider politics, is that no one is sufficiently radical for him – even, we will discover, Chairman Mao. We now see that this is because Žižek's model of politics proper is modelled on a pre-critical analogy with the total transformation of a subject's entire subjective structure, at the end of the talking cure. For what could the concrete consequences of this governing analogy be?

We have seen that Žižek equates the individual fantasy with the collective identity of an entire people. The social fantasy, he says, structures the regime's 'inherent transgressions': at once subjects' habitual ways of living the letter of the law, and the regime's myths of origin and of identity. If political action is modelled on the Lacanian cure, it must involve the complete 'traversal' – in Hegel's terms, the abstract versus the determinate negation – of all these lived myths, practices and habits. Politics must involve the periodic founding of

	Psychoanalysis	Emancipatory politics
Locale	Private Consensual, sought out by analysand	Public May involve constraint, compulsion between groups who may not consent to dialogue
Subject	Individual	Collective
Object	Individual unconscious symptoms, beliefs/fantasies and identifications	Institutions, norms, ideologies, social relations and groups with competing ideas of justice
Other	Analyst, empowered *Subjet suppose savoir*	Up for political grabs The only analogy for the analyst is vanguardist Leader/elite(s)
Means	Talking cure, free association Transference of love of *analysand* for *analyst*	Speech, organisation, violence
	Suspension of ordinary communicative norms (non-violent, non-physical), which presupposes constancy of wider social Other/order (Gadamer)	Not necessarily but may involve institutionalised 'political' spaces: e.g. parliament, right to strike or civil disobedience
Goal	Interpretation symptoms Traversal of fantasy Truth of individual desire Authenticity, 'cure'	A better or more just society More just distribution of goods and elimination of unnecessary suffering Recognition (privileges, sacrifices)
	Symptoms are quasi-other split-off parts of individual psyche only (as individually ucs)	'Symptoms' are suffering, privation and degrading of concrete individuals and groups
	Unconscious discourse signifiers undermine self-knowledge of agents (but not their control, in principle)	'Unconscious' are media-steered structures whose workings exceed self-knowledge or control by any one agent
	hence understanding symptoms Dissolves symptoms (because symptoms are only quasi-Other to subject/agent)	Thus understanding faults does NOT by itself 'dissolve' political problems (because politics involves a plurality of subjects and inherited material conditions)
So	Minimally, psychoanalysis's cure involves theoretical insight and clinical discursive action	Minimally, emancipatory politics requires theoretical insight, *plus* the work of forming or educating social movements, *plus* strategic, discursive and perhaps other actions

Figure 5.1 The differences between psychoanalysis and political action

entire new subject–objects. Providing the model for this set of ideas, the first Žižekian political subject was Schelling's divided God, who gave birth to the entire Symbolic Order before the beginning of time (*IDLC* 153; *OB* 144–8).

But can the political theorist reasonably hope or expect that subjects will simply give up on all their inherited ways, myths and beliefs, all in one world-creating moment? And can they be legitimately asked or expected to, on the basis of a set of ideals whose legitimacy they will only retrospectively see, after they have acceded to the Great Leap Forward? And if they do not – for Žižek laments that today subjects are politically disengaged in unprecedented ways – what means can the theorist and his allies use to move them to do so?

Žižek, as ever, does not shrink from drawing the only possible conclusion: the politics of the Act is a politics of voluntaristic, groundless or 'divine' violence (*IDLC* 162). Biting the pessimistic bullet, Žižek₂ indeed maintains that all political power (and even all speech itself) is tainted with 'obscene violence' (*IDLC* 378; *OV* 58–72; *PV* 307) This is an extrapolation of his claim that there is no Law and Symbolic Order without the superego, which we saw in Chapter 4. It is a repackaging of the (neo)conservative, later Freudian, position on civilisation's ineradicable discontents, whose bleakness invites us to wonder how any power could be legitimated as better than any other.

So it is understandable that Žižek has attracted the critical charge that he is a Schmittian 'ultra-politician': someone who militarises politics. Tellingly, his only response is to argue that, while the 'Right' externalises political conflict into war, the 'Left' accepts that conflict rives societies from within: this is class struggle. So Žižek does not give any ground, as we will see, on the equation of politics with potentially violent conflict between competing 'concrete universals'. It is as if he believes not in draining the Zuider Zee of irrational drives, but in learning to swim in it better than the antagonist can.

Žižek's move is to go from describing politics as based on traversing the fantasy to resting his model for revolutionary agency on the later Lacan's difficult notion that the end of the cure involves identifying with the *sinthome*. Notably, like Freud's later notion of the intractable death drive, this *sinthome* responds to the later Lacan's pessimism about the power of the talking cure. As per Žižek's critique of Stavrakakis above, it names an unmediatisable, unchanging 'knot' of *Jouissance*. It lies at the subject's most singular, idiosyncratic heart: an exceptional or 'extimate' mode of enjoyment that it can neither traverse nor publicly avow. When Žižek₂ applies this to

Žižek's Symptomatic Social-Theoretical Elisions

- So here is the force of the second, methodological component to Žižek's untenable erasure of the difference between politics and psychoanalysis. By looking at the contemporary world as a contemporary subject–object in need of the theorist's liberating 'psychoanalysis', Žižek is unable to make a series of key socio-theoretical distinctions long recognised in political and social-theoretical literature on complex societies.

- The key one of these, as we saw in 'Vanishing Mediations', is the distinction between the lifeworld of subjects (their lived world of meanings wherein a psychoanalytic ideology critique can be highly informative) and the media-steered subsystems – principally the economy--whose workings demand an objectifying social-scientific analysis, not a psychoanalytic account.

- The problem Žižek elides, in the words of his own teacher Althusser, is that modern post-traditional societies are a complex totality of 'relatively autonomous' instances – in Althusser's thinking, the economy, the ideological and the political instances.

- Then there is the question of which instance or level might be the predominant one in any particular historical regime. One practical consequence of this theoretical observation is that the peoples or potentials that might be either 'symptomatic' or particularly vital at one level (say, the ideological level) may be either well integrated or wholly disempowered at the other levels.

- Žižek's hero Lenin, for instance, was drawing on such a multidimensional theoretical account of modern society when he spoke of the need to strike at the 'weakest link' in a regime in order to achieve real change (*IDLC* 361–2).

the political subject–object, the *sinthome* turns out to be those whom Žižek calls 'proletarian': groups who represent the 'part of no-part' (*IDLC* 428; *PV* 268). Although they are parts of the existing order, they are absolutely unrecognised and excluded from the rest of the expressive totality. As we saw above, Žižek thinks our *sinthome* today are the slum-dwellers and other lumpenproletariat that mass at the gates of the global order's great cities (*IDLC* 424–6).

The concrete criticism of Žižek here then is that Žižek may well invoke the new dispossessed underclasses as the 'symptom' of the new global order, as some potential 'evental site' wherein a new revolutionary energy might be found. The problem is that the only thing the suffering millions in the *favellas* have in common with Marx's proletariat is that they have virtually nothing to lose within the existing regime. The key difference from the nineteenth-century proletariat is that the economic system precisely does not need these people's labour or support in order to reproduce itself – as Žižek typically confesses, as if this were not absolutely crucial (*IDLC* 420, 425; *PV* 269). Unlike the working class, they do not have any economic good or capacity – like collective labour – without which the existing order could not function, and which they could potently withdraw from the existing status quo. They are rather more like what Giorgio Agamben has called bleakly the *Homo Sacer*: human beings without rights, whose killing can have no sacrificial value to the system (*IDLC* 425; *PV* 269,). Nor, thinking politically, is there any reason to think that their abject impoverishment alone (rather than the education of working and operating the industrial means of production on which the system depends) can engender anything like a more technically and ethicopolitically enlightened form of political solidarity, to which the Left might appeal as a model for a new society.

In characteristic fashion, Žižek is too sophisticated not to note the weakness of romanticising the revolutionary potential of slum-dwellers, in his criticisms of Hardt and Negri (*IDLC* 359, 365; *PV* 264). The type of political movement that is actually flourishing in these semi-autonomous zones is Pentecostal Christianity, and other forms of religious fundamentalism (*IDLC* 424–5). In criticising Laclau's populist turn, Žižek makes the observation that cities' displaced lumpenproletarians, far from being the agents of progressive change, have most often in history been mobilised as the shock troopers of tyrannical regimes, like that of Louis Bonaparte (*IDLC* 280–1, 285–6). In this vein, Žižek recognises that the Third World lumpenproletariat lacks the most elementary political organisation, let alone constituting an imminent revolutionary movement 'at the gates' (*IDLC* 426). We can only infer that the sole way Žižek believes they could be so organised is from the outside, or from above, by a revolutionary vanguard (*IDLC* 427). It is little wonder in any case that the only 'revolutionary' potential Žižek sees in them is the 'divine' explosion of anomic violence he witnessed in Rio de Janeiro when the men and women of the favellas suddenly issued down into the city, 'blindly' smashing things like biblical locusts (*IDLC* 163), or Hugo Chaves's 'militarising' of the favellas (*IDLC* 427).

After the Act, or Repeating Sorel? No Thanks!

In the postmodern period where no viable progressive opposition to parliamentary liberalism exists, it is easy to forget that fascism and communism in the 1930s were *both* anti-capitalist movements hostile to liberal democracy. Anti-capitalism is not automatically left wing. Indeed, the complete and total rejection of liberal democracy is often the symptom, not of an anti-liberal democratic position, but of an anti-democratic authoritarianism. Thinkers throughout modernity, as Žižek notes in *In Defence of Lost Causes*, have been attracted to such positions like moths to a flame. It is only recently that the 'default' assumption has become that independent, anti-capitalist thinkers must be meaningfully progressive or on the Left.

Žižek has often said that he does not care if bleeding liberal hearts accuse him of left authoritarianism. The polemical implication is that anyone who does call him as much must be such a liberal bleeding heart. There are, however, Žižek's own later texts to consider, and how they fit into the range of political possibilities. Faced with the charge that his thought leads headlong into such authoritarianism, Žižek replies by amplifying the distinction we saw he made in Chapter 3. This is the distinction between fascism and forms of Leftist, 'totalitarian' regimes.

As we have seen, the key way Žižek tries to defend his form of extra-democratic radicalism against the charge of authoritarianism is by arguing that right-wing authoritarianism externalises the truly internal, immanent nature of political conflict within a society. The fascist worldview is one of 'clashes of civilisations', not clashes of classes within any one 'big Other'. In philosophical terms, that is, fascism is untrue to politics proper. This is Žižek's theoretical reason for rejecting it. Žižek does not dispute, by itself, fascism's licensing of terror, the real physical killing of large numbers of internal and external enemies (*IDLC* 280–5). For Žižek, this form of ultra-politics is a worthy enemy, authentically open to the unavoidability of political violence, unlike the liberals with their saccharine dreams of parliamentary pluralism.

This sort of glorification of political violence as a sign of political authenticity is of grave concern. One way to get at what is worrying here is to look at Žižek's recent recourse to Walter Benjamin's notion of 'divine violence' (*OV* 178–205). Benjamin's key source was the ultra-Leftist, anarcho-syndicalist thinker Sorel. Sorel also, without connection with any existing political party or progressive political cause, dreamed of a general strike that would pulverise capitalism all at once. Like Žižek, he shunned all compromises with the existing regime, because Sorel believed that reforms merely avoid this cataclysmic political confrontation. Now, as Herbert Marcuse argued in his 1936 *A Study of Authority*: 'Sorel's anarcho-syndicalism, his myth of the eschatological general strike, and of the proletarian violence which will "unalterably" destroy the bourgeois order, seem a long way from the theory of the authoritarian state' (Marcuse 2008: 103).

However, as Marcuse continues, in Hegelian mode: 'Sorel's work is a typical example of the transformation of an abstract anti-authoritarian attitude into reinforced authoritarianism'. The reason Marcuse gives as to why this is so anticipates uncannily the course Žižek has charted from *The Ticklish Subject* to *In Defence of Lost Causes*:

> Proletarian 'violence', which along with the myth of the general strike is engaged in the final struggle with the bourgeois order, is separated from its social and economic purpose; it becomes an authority in itself. If its criterion no longer lies in material rationality and greater happiness in the social life-process towards which this force is directed, then there is no rational explanation whatsoever as to why proletarian should be 'better' than bourgeois violence. (Marcuse 2008: 104)

But where then does authoritarianism creep into the formulations of the theorist, like Žižek or Sorel, who is committed only to the voluntaristic, abstract negation of what is? Marcuse's contention here again reads like an exact primer as to Žižek's argument in *In Defence of Lost Causes* (even the emphasis on the 'headless' party evokes one of Žižek's key metaphors for the new revolutionaries):

> The authority problem here appears under the heading of revolutionary 'discipline': Sorel establishes a basic distinction between the 'discipline which imposes a general stoppage of work on the workers, and the discipline which can lead them to handle machinery with greater skill' . . . The 'acephaly' of socialism is transformed into the theory of revolutionary 'elites': social revolution gives birth to 'new authorities' which . . . take over the disciplinary leadership of the production process . . . Freed from connection with a clear economic base and elevated into the 'moral' sphere, the conception of the elite tends towards formalistic authoritarianism. (Marcuse 2008, 105)

In Defence of Lost Causes takes up at last what Žižek thinks should happen when the divine violence of the Act has finished, and the revolutionary vanguards have finished storming the winter palaces of global capitalism. Žižek's solution – again constructed in his standard contrast to the detested liberals – is that the Left should have the courage unflinchingly to avow its own terrorist heritage: from the Jacobin Terror to Stalin's purges and Mao's cultural revolution (*IDLC* 6–7). To do anything less is inauthentically to pine for a 'revolution without revolution' (*IDLC* 163). This is Žižek$_2$'s political version of today's 'politically correct' coffee without caffeine, light beer without alcohol, and so on (*OV* 167).

The contrast with the radical-democratic Žižek$_1$ in some ways could not be greater. In Žižek's early texts, as we saw, Stalinism, for instance, was astutely analysed as a perverse distortion of the symbolic coordinates structuring social life. In the Stalinist universe, elementary political distinctions – between public and private, innocence and guilt – were collapsed as the revolution devoured many of its own children. In the show trials, individuals' protestations of factual innocence – that, in fact, they were not guilty of conspiracy against Stalin – could stand as proof of their 'objective guilt'. For by protesting their innocence they proved, at the level of their act of enunciation, that they put their own interests above that of the Party. In *In Defence of Lost Causes*, by contrast, the revolutionary-vanguardist Žižek$_2$ accepts the authenticity of exactly this political fanaticism in the mouth of Robespierre:

> What can be more 'totalitarian' than this closed loop of 'your very fear of being guilty makes you feel guilty' . . . One should nonetheless move beyond the facile dismissal of Robespierre's rhetorical strategy as the strategy of 'terrorist culpabilization' and discern its moment of truth: there are no innocent bystanders in the crucial moments of revolutionary decision, because in such moments innocence itself . . . is the highest treason . . . this fear [of being killed as guilty by the revolution], the fact that it emerged in me, demonstrates that my subjective position is external to the revolution, that I experience the 'revolution' as an external force threatening me. (*IDLC* 167).

It becomes difficult to see what differentiates the position Žižek now advocates from the Stalinist distortion he once denounced.

The issue is that Žižek wants us, authentically, to embrace whatever it takes to 'force' the type of total change he wishes for. However, in a due concession to political reality, Žižek recognises that this cannot reasonably occur all at once. But what is a revolution, Žižek asks, if it does not overthrow not simply the existing state or regime, but also all the existing cultural practices, ways of life and ideological fantasies? The answer is that terror will be required, and a highly disciplined cadre of elites willing to do whatever it takes. This is why, after 1999, Žižek does not shrink from arguing that Stalinism – particularly the Stalinism of 1928 to 1936, the period of the purges and the cult of personality – is the unavoidable truth of Leninism: what Leninism can and should embrace, if it wants to enact a new groundless mode or order. Horrible as it was, Žižek argues, Stalin's ultra-Left period involved the change of everything, down to the most minute practices in people's ways of living, courtship rituals, ways of working, making love, preparing food, and so on (*IDLC* 174–5; *PV* 287–8). This is what Žižek describes in *In Defence of Lost Causes* as the 'Stalinist carnival': a world in which indeed the Other, let alone a 'New Class', was never stabilised, since in the afternoon a condemned man could be freed as arbitrarily as he had been imprisoned or marked for extermination in the morning (*IDLC* 246–53).

The enemy of the type of ultra-Leftist total upheaval Žižek dreams of – and in whose light even Mao's Cultural Revolution, as we are surprised to learn, was not radical enough – is 'habit' (*IDLC* 171–4; *OV* 167–8). ('Habit' in fact corresponds in *On Violence* and *In Defence of Lost Causes* to the place formerly held by ideological fantasies and the material, inherent transgressions that sustain a regime.) To oppose habits, the party elite, meanwhile, need a remarkable list of 'virtues' that include the 'discipline of patience' (*IDLC* 391–2) required 'brutally [to] impose a new order' (*IDLC* 419), the 'Badiouian' courage (*IDLC* 152) ruthlessly to force through the total cultural upheaval despite people's lethargy and 'all-too-human' attachments, and the type of 'trembling' Heideggerian or Machiavellian 'terror' at the absence of any rational ground for the 'new beginning' (*IDLC* 431). The 'bitter truth to be fully endorsed', Žižek argues, is that to be fully human we must become inhuman, and 'assert the inhuman' (*IDLC* 160, 164–75). This is what it is to be an authentic subject of the drives: acephalous or mindless, like the dog Lassie in her pursuit of her duty (*AF* 81), the terminator in the classic sci-fi films, or Howard Roark, the hero of the Nietzschean-neoliberal author Ayn Rand's *Fountainhead* (*AF* 82–3). Stridently, Žižek cites Badiou's endorsement of Saint-Just's strict political Manicheism: 'For, as Saint-Just asked: "What do those who want neither virtue nor terror want?" His answer is well known: they want corruption – another name for the subject's defeat' (*IDLC* 160).

Žižek closes *In Defence of Lost Causes*, then, by listing the four components of his desired political new beginning. These are 'strict egalitarian justice', terror ('ruthless punishment of all who violate the imposed'), voluntarism and, 'last but not least', 'trust in the people' (*IDLC* 461). In classic philosophical style, Žižek tries to dress these prima facie terrifying axioms in examples that sound somewhat acceptable in today's world. When Žižek says 'strict egalitarian justice', what he means is just that all countries should be made to contribute equally in cutting carbon emissions! When he says 'terror', what he means is that we should not be afraid to punish people(s) or nations who do not play along with the new regime's laws. 'Voluntarism' does not mean the embrace of radical action for its own sake, bereft of any orienting normative ideal. It simply means that the world needs ('voluntarily') to decide collectively to do something about global warming and other pressing issues. And, when Žižek says that today we should 'reactivate' the figure of the informer (as 'a combination of terror and trust in the people'), all he means is that we should praise people like the insiders who lifted the lid on the Enron scandal! Here then, at the end of nearly 500 pages, Žižek seems to turn aside from his apparent advocacy of an authoritarian political community resulting from a total revolution carried out by a political vanguard who provide the citizens of the new Žižekian state with absolutely no guarantees that this will not be another totalitarian regime.

The problem is that the whole weight of Žižek's bold acceptance of the need for Stalinist–Jacobin terror makes these 'politically correct' closing examples ring false. Žižek has made clear that for him 'egalitarianism', the desire for 'strict egalitarian justice', expresses people's rancorous envy for the stronger or more fortunate, and their desire to bring them down (*HTR* 37–8; *IDLC* 333). What this implies is that 'strict egalitarian justice' is about getting even, not about new norms of fairness. If this is not contentious enough, Žižek seems to imply that, by 'trust in the people', he means the need to replace representative forms of democracy with regimes that would be more truly 'democratic', but no longer representative.

Žižek is not a right-wing authoritarian. But it is not sufficiently clear that his revolutionary vanguardist stance avoids left-wing authoritarianism, on the lines of Stalin or Mao. The uneasiness that Žižek's new positions generate spring from his examples, coupled with the political logic of total revolution on an arbitrary basis, and linked to his frank observation that the 'parts of no part' he looks to to prop up his Revolution lack any form of organisation of their own.

We wonder, then, whether the Leader could express the political will of the revolutionary vanguard in any other way than by messianically imposing it upon the *lumpenproletariat*, who would in turn impose it on society. The provocative rhetoric of 'reactivated' informers, the voluntaristic willingness to exercise 'brutal terror' in 'asserting the inhuman' supposedly inauthentically covered over by postmodern liberalism, and so forth, do not exactly set these concerns to rest.

Žižek concludes *In Defence of Lost Causes* by openly advocating that we completely ditch liberal democracy. It turns out that we should embrace the term 'dictatorship' – of course, a dictatorship of the proletariat, which would no doubt be claimed as a 'participatory democracy' even more democratic than the 'dictatorship of the bourgeoisie' that is representative government. But, when all this is combined with the apparent contradiction that Žižek first refuses the inclusive term 'the people' for the divisive term 'the proletariat', but ends up advocating 'trust in the people', we might well wonder how carefully thought out all this really is (*IDLC* 162, 414–15).

Žižek's analysis of contemporary 'post-politics' is acute and his criticisms of radical academia's alternatives are incisive. But Žižek himself sometimes seems uncertain as to what the alternative actually is. The logic of the position he has been developing since his turn to the Romantic philosophy of Schelling in the late 1990s, however, increasingly drives Žižek in the direction of a revolutionary vanguardism that smacks of left-wing authoritarianism. Although it is often difficult to disentangle the provocations from the positions, it seems that Žižek's frustration with the lack of political resistance to contemporary capitalism is leading him to adopt extreme positions that can easily (as they did with Sorel) prepare a political jump from Left to Right, across the bridge made by reactive hostility to liberal parliamentarianism and representative democracy.

Chapter 6

Religion and the Politics of Universal Truth

Why Political Theology?

One of the more curious events of the turbulent 1920s was the celebrated chess-playing automaton that toured Europe defeating various chess champions. The 'automaton' was eventually revealed as a fairground trick. A dwarf hidden in the apparatus secretly operated the controls of the chess-playing puppet. This intriguing fraud inspired German critical theorist Walter Benjamin to draw a famous analogy. Benjamin (1973: 255) claimed that theology was the wizened dwarf secretly operating the intellectual and political machinery of historical materialism, which, he said, 'guarantees that it will win every time'. What Benjamin was referring to was the way that Marxism drew upon a teleological philosophy of history, as culminating in the final goal (*telos*) of a communist world revolution. This understanding of history, Benjamin argued, was ultimately inspired by Judaeo-Christian ideas about the goal of history being God's redemption of humanity in the Last Judgment. The ideal of communism, in other words, was a secularised version of religious salvation. Benjamin was suggesting, amongst the many reflections his analogy opens up, that radical politics and dialectical materialism were the last refuge of religious faith in a secular epoch (*PD* 3).

Today, Žižek notes, things seem the other way around. The 'god that failed' is not the God of divine revelation and religious prophesy. It is Marxism as an intellectual doctrine and Communism as a political system. Historical materialism now seems to be the wizened dwarf that must secretly operate within the coordinates of theological doctrines, hoping to smuggle its agenda in behind more popular religious motifs. It is as if the return of religion is the last resort of political criticism in an age of the 'triumph of capitalism' and the 'victory of liberal democracy' (*FA* 1–2).

This diagnosis appears to motivate Žižek's engagements with the monotheistic faiths, and especially Christianity, from *The Fragile Absolute* (2000), through *The Puppet and the Dwarf* (2003), to *The*

Neighbor (2005). These texts seek to reclaim a radical interpretation of specifically Christian religious dogma as harbouring a revolutionary potential for today's Left. From a sceptical perspective, Žižek's theological turn seems a theoretical mysticism bordering on alchemical fantasia – from evocations of a 'materialist theory of grace', or of political militants as 'acephalous saints', to the theoretical transfiguration of St Paul into the Christian Lenin. But there is a serious political intervention in the current context at work in Žižek's 'Christian' texts (notably, Žižek insists that he remains an atheist), together with the exploration of a genuine intellectual problem.

> Today, more than ever [Žižek maintains], one has to insist that the only way open to the emergence of an Event is that of breaking the vicious cycle of globalisation-with-particularisation by (re)asserting the dimension of Universality *against* capitalist globalisation. . . . what we need today is the gesture that would undermine capitalist globalisation from the standpoint of universal Truth, just as Pauline Christianity did to the Roman global Empire (*TS* 211).

But reclaiming social criticism in a period characterised by the opposition between liberal democracy and fundamentalist terrorism is not the only stake in Žižek's engagement with religion. Alongside Lacan's dictum, which Žižek often cites, that 'the true formula of atheism is: God is unconscious' (Lacan 1998: 59), increasingly stands the idea that the biblical figure of the Neighbour provides the elementary matrix of human sociality. This figure of the Neighbour has become more and more prominent in Žižek's texts since the year 2000. How is it possible – the New Testament asks, on Žižek's reading – to turn from the Neighbour as a threatening figure who cannot pass the test of the *Shibboleth* (that is, cannot speak our language) and so can be killed with impunity, to the Neighbour of what Žižek calls 'universal Neighbour-love'?

For Žižek, these questions are profoundly linked: it is precisely because 'God is (the) unconscious' that the Christian solution to the problem of the Neighbour is so urgent and so compelling. This is because the encounter with the threatening Neighbour is the encounter with the elementary psychological ground of violence – the unconscious projection of one's own aggression onto the other, who then appears as the bearer of an obscene desire to achieve perverse satisfactions upon my body, together with a senseless 'death drive'. In the Žižek of this new millennium, the Judaeo-Christian figure of the Neighbour is at base what we might call the 'Other supposed to

Overdetermination: The Two Motives for Žižek's 'Theological' Turn

There are two reasons for Žižek's theological turn:

- First, religion is a resource for social criticism, in a supposedly post-political world that is actually characterised by frightening systematic or 'structural', as well as explicit, violence, and terrible injustice. Žižek will tie this to a progressive, 'participatory' reading of Christianity in The Fragile Absolute (2000) and The Puppet and the Dwarf (2003) and contemporary papers.
- Secondly, Žižek sees that religion has, since time immemorial, confronted the roots of the human propensity to violence. This irrational core of the human condition was rediscovered powerfully by psychoanalysis in terms of the death drive. Žižek believes, therefore, that psychoanalysis can propose a compelling solution to the question of social order in terms of the problem of the Neighbour.

These two reasons for the theological turn overlap, because, if religion is a resource for political criticism, and also provides a framework for social order, then this means an analysis of religion can do two things. Religion can be the blueprint for the Ego Ideal that Žižek believes society needs (Chapter 4). It can also be the model for the ideological conversion Žižek thinks is required for the political Act that is necessary to get this new order (Chapter 5).

rape and kill'. The other side of this new focus on the Neighbour is Žižek's wager that, because 'God is unconscious', religion outlines profound strategies for dealing with the frighteningly irrational kernel of aggression in the human being.

Žižek's idea is that capitalism itself, through the decline of symbolic authority that it engenders, also regenerates the biblical problem of the Neighbour in a particularly vivid way – the term 'the Neighbour', in other words, increasingly becomes the cipher for all the postmodern cultural discontents he diagnoses in pieces like 'Whither Oedipus?' The difficulty with this later-Žižekian conceptualisation of the world is the idea that society is at base a 'war of each against all' conducted by bestial, mutually hostile individuals.

Žižek constantly insists that the other person is one's neighbour, but that the Neighbour is a threatening figure who poses the question of anti-social aggression as the radical evil of the human condition (e.g. *IDLC* 16). The problem is that such a deeply cynical view has, in the history of political philosophy, rarely led to any conclusions except the need for authoritarian government legitimised in theological terms. For the neoconservatives, for instance, the recommendation is 'a blend of economic liberalism with a minimally 'authoritarian' spirit of community' (*IDLC* 2) – that is, the free market, the strong state and a return to religion.

We also saw in Chapter 4 how Žižek is committed to an account of political life according to which social order depends upon a unified framework of belief – that is, a form of the social bond in which all individuals are committed to a single Cause. When this is combined with an approach to the problem of social order that arises from the supposition that the basis of human sociality is the encounter between dangerous bearers of the death drive, the result is a solution that eerily resembles the neoconservative one. Unlike the neoconservatives, Žižek is hostile to market economics, but, like them, he thinks that a single unifying framework of beliefs modelled on religious faith solves the fundamental problem of human anti-sociality. Žižek makes a heroic attempt to differentiate his solution from that of orthodox religion, despite an evident attraction. He does this through his notion that a 'radical Christianity' would involve the emptying-out of particularistic religious belief into a pure formal universality. This would mean, ultimately, a sort of Christianity without God as Father, or a Christianity conceived as the only religion for which God as Transcendent Father is dead, having died in Christ on the cross.

Let us now examine how this is so.

Introducing Democratic Fundamentalism

The return of religion during the last twenty years was a surprise for many (*FA* 1–2; *PD* 3–10). It represents a real problem for the complacent narrative about the 'end of history' in liberal open societies. Yet we have seen repeatedly how, according to Žižek, religious fundamentalism and ethnic nationalism are the inverse of the 'rootless' or secular global cosmopolitanism denounced by today's Right. Žižek regards the fundamentalist's unyielding assertion of communal belonging and belief in a rationally unfathomable God as a fantasy compensation for the ruthless 'unplugging' from people's inherited traditions generated by global capitalism. As we saw in Chapter 1, according to Žižek the 9/11 terrorist attacks, for instance, represented the moment when America got its 'message returned in an inverted form'. If the American message is the 'triumph of capitalism' and the 'end of history', then the inverted form of the message, the Real of global capitalism, is the dislocation of traditional societies in 'systematic violence' (OV 9, 14).

But there is more to Žižek's position here than just the way that the violent message of fundamentalist terrorism actually brings out the darker underside of the 'end of history'. Žižek is also claiming that there is a structure of reciprocated, mutual projection at work in the contemporary world. This psychoanalytically informed insight is that each side – that is, religious fundamentalism and politically correct (PC) liberalism – enacts the fantasy of the other. Ultimately, Žižek maintains that the apparent opposites of 'liberal democracy or fundamentalist terrorism' are locked into a profound symbiosis, a 'speculative identity', which Žižek has this century named 'democratic fundamentalism'.

The War on Terror as 'Mutually Assured Projection'

- *Western projection (I): the other supposed to believe.* Western responses to Islamic fundamentalism are characterised by a sort of 'fundamentalism envy' – these are the people who *really believe in their moral Cause*, whereas we have operations named 'Just Cause' in which nobody really believes. Of course, if we *did* believe, then we would stop at nothing. For that very reason, the others are incredibly dangerous lunatics with whom it is impossible to have any form of dialogue ('we do not negotiate with terrorists'), whereas we are sane proponents of value pluralism and open debate.

- *Western projection (II): the other supposed to torture.* Because 'Islamo-fascism' rejects liberal democracy and human rights as absolutely binding moral frameworks, these people are capable of every atrocity, from the slaughter of innocents in terrorist attacks to videotaped beheadings, which combine contempt for the humanity of their victims with ritualised barbarism. By contrast, when we engage in cruel and degrading forms of interrogation in a global network of secret prisons, up to and including perverse tortures recorded digitally at Abu Ghraib prison in Iraq, or when we drop massively destructive bombs on weddings in the hope of taking out a single al-Queda operative, this is as a momentary and regrettable suspension of human rights in the interests of the greater good.

These Western projections are pitted against those of the fundamentalists:

- *Fundamentalist projection (I): the other supposed to fornicate.* For the Islamic fundamentalist, modern Western society is a cesspit of sexual depravity. Nothing signals this more clearly than the lewd and provocative attire and behaviour of Western women, like fresh meat at a butchers hung out as a satanic temptation for their men, whose lack of self-control, meanwhile, leads them into constant masturbation over pornography. The harsh penalties of Shari'a Law, by contrast, recognise that men and women need stern controls imposed on all forms of sexual display, for otherwise both genders would uncontrollably indulge in self-pollution and adultery.
- *Fundamentalist projection (II): the other supposed to crusade.* Islamic fundamentalism understands the secret truth of the spread of Western democracy to be a prolongation of the Crusades by new methods – that is, a combination of military conquest with religious conversion, in the name of a Holy War. For this very reason, the only appropriate response is the complete refashioning of *Jihad*, the struggle for purity in the Islamic community. *Jihadism* now represents the military struggle to destroy the unbelievers and expand an Islamic Caliphate through the Islamisation of Europe.

For Žižek, to accuse both sides of 'mutual hypocrisy' in the 'War on Terror', while true enough, is also to miss the roots of this celebrated 'clash of civilisations'. These roots lie for him specifically in the unconscious. Here, any appeals to the law of non-contradiction – that each side ought to be rationally consistent and self-aware – do not have force or effect. Most deeply, Žižek's proposition about the speculative identity of 'democratic fundamentalism' as a Hegelian 'unity of opposites' is claiming that there is a hidden common, libidinal ground of the social antagonists. What is this other common ground, a common ground or 'Other scene' wherein the enemies are united?

We can get at what this common ground might be if we consider the two possible meanings of Žižek's provocative description of where we are today as 'democratic fundamentalism':

1. *liberal democracy* is *another fundamentalist faith*, unquestioned and unquestionable by liberal subjects today – what Žižek identifies in terms of a 'prohibition on thinking' about a new politics that he suggests is meaningfully equivalent to an absolute, religious taboo;
2. on the other hand, *religious fundamentalism* is *basically modern* – more exactly, it is one part of a series of ideologies including populism and fascism that challenge pre-modern forms of tradition and hierarchy behind the guise of their 'return to fundamentals' (*IDLC* 332–3).

Surprisingly, then, Žižek's 'democratic-fundamentalism' thesis positions religious fundamentalism as part of that 'logic of egalitarian justice' that defines the modern overturning of traditional political hierarchies. Equally surprisingly, Žižek has increasingly tended towards an approach to this egalitarian logic that reflects most the reactionary critique of modernity in Friedrich Nietzsche's work.

The logic of egalitarian justice informing modern socialism and democracy is sustained by an ignoble affect, says Žižek (*HTR* 36–7; *OV* 88–90). The underlying common ground between the postmodern 'Last Men', incapable of dying for anything, and the religious fundamentalists, only too eager to die for the Cause, is that both religious fundamentalism and egalitarian justice are sustained by envy. On the one hand, the fundamentalist's obsession with the sexual goings-on and 'corruption' of Western liberals (*IDLC* 332; *OV* 85) has to do with resentment that the liberal is enjoying what is prohibited to the fundamentalist. On the other hand, the nihilistic 'Last Men' of consumerist societies, whose corrosive ideological cynicism prevents the defence of any belief whatsoever, more or less unconsciously passionately identify with the cause of egalitarian justice. Their resentful aim, if Žižek's Nietzschean remarks are to be taken seriously, can only be to relativise all beliefs (or impose 'value pluralism') in order to make sure that everybody is the same (*IDLC* 332–3). What is Žižek's logic here?

In psychoanalytic terms, resentment is a form of envy, driven by aggression towards the 'Other supposed to enjoy'. While we have had to sacrifice 'it', our enjoyment, the Others have somehow evaded the sacrifice. This is the deep reason why we hate them so, and must do everything – even potentially against our own interests (*IDLC* 45; *OV* 88–9) – to drag them down to our level. We must compel them to make the sacrifice that has so unjustly been visited upon us, at the same time as we project onto them the violent anger we feel towards them. The gaze that observes this sacrifice, then, for which both liberal democrats and religious fundamentalists are competing, is that of the big Other, although this big Other goes under two quite different names in the two camps – God and the Market.

Accordingly, 'democratic fundamentalism' is part of the constellation of 'generalised perversion' diagnosed in Chapter 4, on culture. The big question is: can we break out of the logic of the superego demand? Žižek's wager is that radical Christianity represents a new universality that dispenses with the logic of sacrifice through the 'sacrifice of sacrifice'. This represents an alternative to the global culture of 'generalised perversion' that he diagnoses. But, in order to make this plausible, Žižek must first differentiate his radical Christianity from conservative Christianity. Then he has to show how this solves the most fundamental problems of human sociality, which he calls the problem of the Neighbour.

Into the Heart of Darkness: Žižek's Romantic Dalliance with Orthodoxy

Žižek's proximity to a fundamentally dark or 'monstrous' (*FA* 69–81) theological vision is clearly evident in his enthusiasm for religious conservatives such as Søren Kierkegaard, G. K. Chesterton, T. S. Eliot, Alfred Hitchcock and C. S. Lewis. Žižek describes the way of thinking he discerns in their work as 'orthodoxy'. And Žižek is drawn to religious orthodoxy, despite himself, not least for the way that its expositors, like G. K. Chesterton, are often the most incisive critics of the liberal, cultural decadence Žižek also seeks to overcome. So what is this 'orthodoxy' central to Žižek's theological engagements, particularly in *The Puppet and the Dwarf*, arguably his most profound theological intervention? For 'orthodoxy' on this Žižekian understanding:

- 'God' is the universal, the master signifier that quilts the field of meanings for the believer and makes them experience the world as a rational universe with a providential shape and purpose. But, Žižek argues, this comforting religious fantasy can succeed only on condition that the arbitrary character of this master signifier is repressed, so that the 'irrational violence', the 'absolute crime' of the foundation of the Symbolic Law (or Ten Commandments), is concealed. In its place there appears a fantasy narrative of Paradise Lost, of the exile from Eden of a sinful humanity, a result of God's just punishment for wilful human transgressions. This fantasy retroactively makes the origin of the Law appear to be a sublime place denied to human access, a Tree of Knowledge of Good and Evil, which stands above the Law even as it is the site for the pronouncement of the Law. (In terms of Chapter 3, we recognise here the characteristic postulate of the Discourse of the Master.)

- It is possible for subjects to enter the universe of God's sacred design only through a leap of faith. Nothing about the material world speaks decisively to the Truth or Falsity of religious world views – arguments can go either way and thus do not settle anything. So entry into the believer's way of life depends on a pre- or irrational wager of the subject, with passage into orthodox faith the result of an existential decision. Once believers have taken the leap of faith, what they get is not a world of mystification, but rational dialogue. In other words, by believing staunchly in *something*, by having a firm moral foundation, believers can step confidently out into the world and engage with other perspectives. But this is on the condition that they do not look down at where they are standing. Ultimately they are standing in the void of the Master's founding Law-Making Act. There is nothing more under their feet than the 'abyss of freedom' of their own existential decision to believe. In other words, the standard coordinates of ideological interpellation with the empty master signifier we saw in Chapters 1–3 therefore apply to orthodoxy.

- There is considerable potential in orthodoxy, which Žižek recognises, for perverse self-instrumentalisation of the believer. This is because orthodoxy depends upon the superego as the policing mechanism that works through guilt for its enforcement. In particular, orthodox religion involves an appeal to sacrifice that is caught up in a logic of exchange. Humanity must die, in order to be resurrected. We must sin, in order to be redeemed. And, crowning this logic for orthodox Christians, Christ's sacrifice on the Cross is needed to 'repay the debt' incurred through humanity's 'original sin'. For Žižek, indeed, what he calls the hidden, 'perverse' core of Christianity concerns God's apparent 'strategy' to generate original sin in human beings in order then to redeem humanity through Christ's sacrifice, thereby proving His Infinite mercy. (*PD* 15).

Given then that orthodoxy thus defined seems so neatly to fit the coordinates of ideological interpellation Žižek has elsewhere decried, why does he feel such a confessed 'romance' for or in it? One thing about this form of orthodoxy that suggests itself is the way that it so frankly confronts and affirms this perverse logic at the heart of ideological interpellation: particularly in a wonderfully erudite and ironic observer of human affairs such as G. K. Chesterton. It is as if the orthodox theologian anticipates the psychoanalytic theory of the relation between the Ego Ideal and the superego and says, *per absurdum*, 'yes, please!', rather than feeling that this theory points to the inescapable falseness of the stance.

Indeed, the true orthodox believer fearlessly goes on to draw all the logical conclusions from her stance. This logical conclusion is a sort of 'sacrifice of the intellect': there are some things that must remain beyond question; there are some questions that it is better not to ask. The consequence is the standard anti-Enlightenment position of Christian conservatism – that the madness of the modern world begins with its crossing this line, interrogating the sacred, mysterious foundations of human society. From the Athenians of Socrates' day to now, rational enquiry into foundations is, for the reactionary conservative, the highest species of political irresponsibility, because it undermines the grounds of social Law itself:

> Chesterton's aim is thus to *save reason through sticking to its founding exception*: deprived of this, reason degenerates into blind self-destructive scepticism – in short: into total *irrationalism*. This was Chesterton's basic insight and conviction: that the irrationalism of the late nineteenth century was the necessary consequence of the Enlightenment attack on religion. (*PD* 47)

In other words, Žižek's ironic hero Chesterton – like Kierkegaard, Lewis, Eliot, Leo Strauss, Schmitt, De Maistre and a host of other reactionary cultural critics – maintains that the Enlightenment leads inevitably into today's world of nihilistic Last Men trapped in a condition of generalised value scepticism or relativism. The orthodox response is a fierce reassertion of the need for traditional values and a return to the hard distinction between the Ten Commandments and sinful transgressions. We certainly should not dilly-dally around with ineffective 'human rights', at best a secularised shadow of the former majesty of Divine Law (*FA* 109–11).

Whatever else we would have to say concerning Žižek's romantic dalliance with the radical theological Right, here, as elsewhere, it has to be said that he is also able to be its lucid analyst and critic. Strangely describing the Mosaic code as 'the Law' itself (namely, for Lacanians, a Universal condition for human sociability), Žižek nevertheless draws out the limitations of orthodoxy, and its latter-day, neoconservative calls to return to traditional religion:

> Is not the 'truth' of the opposition between Law and its particular transgressions that the Law itself is the highest transgression? That is not only the limit of Chesterton, but, more radically, the limit of the perverse solution that forms the core of 'really existing Christianity': with modernity proper, we can no longer rely on the pre-established Dogma to sustain our freedom, on the pre-established Law/Prohibition to sustain our transgression – this is one way of reading Lacan's thesis that the big Other no longer exists. Perversion is a double strategy to counteract this non-existence: an (ultimately deeply conservative, nostalgic) attempt to install the Law artificially, in the *desperate hope that it will then take this self-posited limitation 'seriously'*, and, in a complementary way, a no less desperate attempt to codify the very transgression of the Law. In the perverse reading of Christianity, God first threw humanity into Sin in order to create the opportunity for saving it through Christ's sacrifice . . . That is why today's desperate neoconservative attempts to reassert 'old values' are also ultimately a failed perverse strategy of imposing prohibitions that can no longer be taken seriously. (*PD* 53)

So the reader can see how Žižek's position on Chesterton and orthodoxy is highly ambivalent. He is strongly attracted to the writings of such men of faith because of his own opposition to the postmodern dispersion of ideological causes in cynical relativism, and the inability to live and die for a Cause that Žižek too wishes to counteract (*PD* 38). But he can see that an artificial return to religious orthodoxy, together with the paradoxes of the guilty conscience, can be no lasting answer, let alone for someone on the Left. Where then does Žižek's romance with Christianity finally lead him?

Love thy Neighbour? Yes Please! *Žižek's Participatory Christianity*

Žižek's alternative to orthodoxy is a radical, heterodox interpretation of Christianity. The key move this 'radical' Christianity involves is in Žižek asking whether it is possible to find an alternative reading to the idea of a sacrificial exchange at the heart of Christianity, and religious obligation *per se*. His proposition is that, understood correctly, the Christian crucifixion alone, of all the events and mysteries represented in the world's great religions, involves what he terms a 'sacrifice of (the logic of) sacrifice'. This is why, for him, a renewed, 'materialist' Christianity alone has the potential to liberate modern subjectivity and lead towards a renewed political order.

At the heart of this new Christianity is what Žižek calls a 'participatory', versus a 'sacrificial', reading of Christ's Crucifixion. According to Žižek's 'participatory reading' of the Crucifixion, true Christian believers symbolically participate in or live the Crucifixion just as they participate in the Holy Spirit through the rites of Holy Communion. This is because for Žižek – here following Hegel and others – what dies on the Cross is God-as-a-transcendent, punitive or vengeful, superegoic figure: God as transcendent or Other-Worldly Beyond (*SO* 206). The centrepiece of this reading of Christianity is hence Christ's 'cry of dereliction' on the Cross: 'Father, why hast Thou forsaken me?' (*PD* 14–15). Žižek proposes that, in this moment, when God is lost to Himself as Transcendent (as Žižek reads things), Christianity accomplishes a radically 'materialist' reversal *within* the history of religion. In his terms, this is the moment in the history of religion when an acknowledgement that 'the Other does not exist' (*PD* 88, 125–31) founds a new religious community of the Holy Spirit, imminent to that community and the subjectivity of the believers. What is born again as a result of this 'death of God' on the Cross is an imminent God-as-Ego-Ideal, the Holy Spirit of the spiritual community. The believer participates in a death of sin (and guilt) and is reborn in love (a form of idealisation untouched by superegoic aggression and envy of the Other). Here is how Žižek puts it:

> There are two main interpretations of how Christ's death deals with sin: sacrificial and participatory. . . . The first approach is legalistic: there is a guilt to be paid for, and, by paying our debt for us, Christ redeemed us (and, of course, thereby forever indebted us); from the participationist perspective, on the contrary, people are freed from sin not by Christ's death as such, but by sharing in Christ's death, by dying to sin, to the way of the flesh. (*PD* 102; cf. *FA* 157–8)

In psychoanalytic terms, this radical Žižekian Christianity – incidentally much closer to Catholic than Protestant theology – is supposed to liberate subjects from the pressure of the superego. That is because the 'way of the flesh' of which Žižek speaks is thematised by St Paul in terms that resonate unmistakably with the Freudian concept of the superego. Lacan reflected this by replacing 'the Thing' (the maternal Thing of *Jouissance*) for Paul's 'sin' in the famed passage from Romans 7: 7 in his own seventh *Seminar, The Ethics of Psychoanalysis*:

> What then should we say? That the Law is the Thing? By no means! Yet, if it had not been for the law, I would not have known the Thing, I would not have known what it is to covet had the law not said: 'Thou shalt not covet.' But the Thing, seizing an opportunity in the commandment, produces in me all kinds of covetousness. Apart from the law the Thing lies dead. I was once alive apart from the law, but when the commandment came, the Thing revived and I died, and the very commandment that promised life proved to be death to me. (Lacan 1997: 83)

In other words, for Pauline Christianity as for psychoanalysis, the Law itself provokes the desire in humans to transgress it, going towards *Jouissance* or sin. We may follow the Law, but, in doing so, we inevitably accumulate guilt. Guilt is the internal sign of our perverse desire to transgress, even as we behave so well, seen by the omniscient God – or in Freudian parlance, the superego. God as guarantor of the Law stands above or beyond the Law in the subjects' fantasy, on the side of the transcendent *Jouissance* that His paternal Word prohibits to us. By getting rid of the Other-Worldly God of the Transcendent Beyond, Žižek hence argues, the Pauline, participatory understanding of Christianity he wants dispenses with the superego, with its repetitive injunctions towards 'inherent transgression', the Thing/*Jouissance*: and the very stuff of ideological fantasies (Chapter 1). Those who have died to the Law, as St Paul put it, are born again in a new spirit. In this way, Žižek boldly argues, the conversion to Christianity – the dying to Law, and thereby the temptation to sin – anticipates what the Lacanian cure, traversing the fantasy, aims at:

> The fundamental lesson of the psychoanalytic notion of superego . . . is that there are few things more difficult than to enjoy, without guilt, the fruits of doing one's duty (in this case, the duty of telling the truth). While it is easy to enjoy acting in an egotistic way *against* one's duty, it is, perhaps, only as a result of psychoanalytic treatment that one can acquire the capacity to enjoy *doing* one's duty: perhaps this *is* [also] one of the definitions off the end of psychoanalysis. (FA 141–2)

But, if Christianity, on Žižek's interpretation, anticipates the psychoanalytic cure, what is the content of this Christian love that is said to be the result? For Žižek, it is a truly emancipated form of the social bond: a community that would not depend for its solidarity on scapegoating the Other(s). The problem Žižek faces as he frames any more concrete response to this political question, however, is that, having identified the agency of ethical and political Law in Pauline manner with guilt/the superego – what is to be transcended – he has little redemptive space to move in except promoting what he terms 'love *beyond the Law*'. Here, Žižek is in proximity with the work of Giorgio Agamben, and more widely with today's post-post-structuralist, messianic political dead ends.

One way to approach the specific nature of Žižek's final position, and its subtle distance from a thinker like Agamben, is to note the elective affinities, but at the same time the pointed opposition, of Žižek's premises here with Buddhism. Buddhism also seeks a form of religious conviction untouched by envy, guilt or resentment – and, in this sense, beyond Law – open to the strict 'non-existence' of the Other, indeed to the non-substantiality of material reality *per se*. Moreover, as Žižek observes in *The Fragile Absolute*:

> Christianity (and, in its own way, Buddhism) introduced into the [pagan] global balanced cosmic Order a principle that is totally foreign to it . . . according to which each individual has *immediate* access to universality (nirvana, the Holy Spirit) . . . [so that] Buddha's followers form a community [that] has broken with the hierarchy of the social order. (*FA* 120)

Why then does Žižek not rush to embrace Buddhism? Why Christianity, with its ambiguous political and institutional history, and its divisive claim to exclusive Truth? In fact, Žižek's comments on Buddhism tend to be of two types. First, Žižek notes how Buddhism can and has been seamlessly integrated into the rush of neoliberal life as a means for subjects to stay sane and content in an increasingly uncertain, dynamic, capitalist world (*OB* 12–15). If Max Weber were still alive, Žižek taunts those who believe Buddhism is 'alternative', Weber would write today a book entitled *Taoism and the Spirit of Late Capitalism* (*OB* 13). Secondly, and more revealingly, Žižek is at pains to show how Buddhism's 'more "gentle", balanced, holistic, ecological approach' (*PD* 26) is compatible not only with a pacifistic comportment to the world, but also with the dispassionate commitment of violent, warlike actions. Buddhism, in fact, amounts to 'a kind of universalized indifference', Žižek wants to stress. As such is equally suited to the unthinking proto-fascistic militarism of the Samurai as to the types of pacific living that Western yuppies dream of as they take their after-work meditation classes (*IDLC* 364; *PD* 26–33).

What then does Žižek see as lacking in Buddhism, which he finds in Christianity alone, as a religion of love? Significantly, from 1999, the radical Protestant thinker Søren Kierkegaard – the self-proclaimed anti-Hegel *par excellence* – has emerged as a key reference point for Žižek's theologico-political reflections. In precise theological terms, Žižek argues in *The Puppet and the Dwarf* that Buddhism's assertion of the nothingness (*anatman*) of all worldly attachments, and the withdrawal into a prior innocence or Peace, somehow refuses a preferred alternative, the dialectical possibility of elevating a particular thing to 'a Something which would give body to the Nothing' (*PD* 23). What this means, in terms of ethics, is that Christianity from the start engages – through the person of Christ – in a 'stubborn' attachment to a particular object elevated to the dignity of the Thing, which Žižek tells us is the marker of love *per se*:

> To put it in mystical terms, the Lacanian act is, rather, the exact opposite of this 'return to innocence': Original Sin itself, the abyssal disturbance of the Primordial Peace, the primordial 'pathological' Choice of an unconditional attachment to some specific object (like falling in love with a specific person who, thereafter, matters to us more than anything else). (*PD* 22)

This valorisation of an Act of love that, in its unconditional attachment to a particular Thing would repeat the diabolical evil of the fall (*PD* 81–3), is what brings Žižek to Kierkegaard. Kierkegaard famously introduced the motif of a 'teleological suspension of the ethical' as lying at the heart of properly religious faith. This suspension involves a supra-rational commitment or 'leap' into belief, which potentially transcends the moral rules governing ordinary political life. His model is the *Ashedah*, or sacrifice of Isaac, carried out by the Patriarch Abraham in the name of the father, despite all moral law and familial affection. But what can a truly Revolutionary Act today involve, Žižek began to wonder around the millennium, if not such a political suspension of ordinary ethical and moral constraints, in the 'loving' attachment to a particular Cause that would take upon itself the responsibility of founding a new mode or order? Indeed, when we look back at the pages of history, do we not see that what Vladimir Lenin represents is nothing if not such a 'revolutionary version of what Kierkegaard referred to as the religious suspension of the ethical' (*OB* 149)? There may well be no rational ground for the 'Christian' political decision Žižek asks his readers to take. Indeed, Žižek flirts romantically at every moment with the position that asking for such reasons is a sign of existential failure to commit or decide: the inability to achieve the type of religious–political devotion he wants is readers to embrace. What is certain is that what Žižek wants from Kierkegaard is a legitimating emphasis on standing by one's decision, no matter what the consequences. 'Liberal leftists reject the Social Democratic "compromise",' Žižek prophesies:

> they want a true revolution, yet they shirk the actual price to be paid for it and thus prefer to adopt the attitude of a Beautiful Soul and to keep their hands clean. In contrast to this false radical Leftists' position (who wants true democracy for the people, but without the secret police to fight counter-revolution, without their academic privileges being threatened), a Leninist, like a Conservative, is *authentic* in the sense of *fully assuming the consequences of his choice,* i.e., of being fully aware of what it actually means to take power and to exert it. (*OB* 4)

This is why *On Belief* opens, with typical Žižekian aplomb, by commenting on an episode of *Larry King Live* wherein a rabbi and several priests discussed their hopes for a better world:

> Only the Baptist – a young, well-tanned, slightly overweight and repulsively slick Southern yuppie – insisted that, according to the letter of the Gospel, only those who 'live in Christ' by explicitly recognizing themselves in his address will be redeemed, which is why, as he concluded with a barely discernible contemptuous smile, 'a lot of good and honest people will burn in hell'. In short, goodness (applying common moral norms) which is not directly grounded in the Gospel is ultimately just a perfidious semblance of itself, its own travesty. . . . The basic premise of this book is that, cruel as this position may sound, if one is to break the liberal-democratic hegemony and resuscitate an authentic radical position, one has to endorse its materialist version. IS there such a version? (*OB* 1)

It has to be said that such far-reaching sympathy with religious fundamentalism would seem severely to qualify Žižek's claims to 'radical universality', or indeed to any progressive form of politics. Žižek comes dangerously close to licensing a position that inverts religious love (*agape*) into political hate. Žižek talks significantly in *On Violence* concerning divine violence – a deeply ambiguous concept taken from Walter Benjamin, and meaning at the very least a species of revolutionary violence that is not supported by rational, discursive (read 'human') justification (*OV* 178–205). Unsurprisingly, it is Carl Schmitt (the ultra-conservative Catholic 'political theologian' we have met often in this book) who supplies Žižek with his 'Pauline' formula for revolution today: far from a pastoral forbearance and turning the other cheek, Christian love is 'the emergency political suspension of the law in the name of an ethical teleology' (*PD* 112). Certainly, we now have travelled the strangely short distance from Žižek's emphasis on Pauline love to the type of authoritarian vanguardism we saw him endorse in Chapter 5.

Nasty, Brutish and Short: Meet the Neighbours

Žižek has what he considers a decisive reply to these disquieting questions, however, because he maintains that his is the only position that truly confronts the anti-social nature of the human being. According to Žižek, his anti-humanist universalism can avoid the fetishistic disavowal of the monstrosity inherent in human being that lies at the heart of every other ethical system. Aside from the neo-Lacanian ethics of Badiou and Žižek, all other ethical systems affirm the screen of humanity and civility that merely masks 'the traumatic Thing that our Judeo-Christian tradition calls the "Neighbour"' (*IDLC* 16). To clarify, Žižek adds: 'the Neighbour is the (Evil) Thing which potentially lurks beneath every homely human face' (*IDLC* 16).

The Neighbour is the 'Other supposed to enjoy' who appeared in the early work as the ideological specter *par excellence*, the fantasy that we should seek to traverse. In the period of democratic fundamentalism, the decline of paternal authority and traditional boundaries between cultures, we have seen how this might best be recast as the 'Other supposed to rape and kill'. It is the threat posed by this 'Other supposed to rape and kill' that Žižek deals with in his recent, theological discussions of the 'problem of the Neighbour'.

For Žižek, all the postmodern injunctions of 'political correctness' – from those mandating certain ways of speaking to and about others to growing regulations on personal conduct (for instance, smoking in public places) – are so many efforts to maintain a minimal distance between such Neighbours in today's world. The deep problem for Žižek is that they do not in any way deal with the problem of the Neighbour in its Real dimension. Žižek mercilessly lampoons the 'decaffeinated' society of contemporary liberal capitalism, with its non-alcoholic beer, non-caffeinated coffee, smoking only outside and not in public places, protected or cyber sex, and so on. The postmodern liberal, Žižek proposes, does not confront the logic of envy that underlies social antagonism. Instead, he embraces the 'difference' and proclaims himself beyond resentment of otherness. But the moment the other asserts himself in the name of any political or religious Cause, the repressed truth – that the liberal actually does resent the other furiously – returns. The 'decaffeinated liberal' senses the spectre of the fearful 'Other supposed to rape and kill'. Then, says Žižek, the liberal suddenly becomes a coercive authoritarian and brings the powers of the state to bear on the other.

That is why Žižek is highly critical of liberal tolerance and, if push comes to shove, actually prefers fundamentalist intolerance. Žižek, for instance, has provocatively saluted the Taliban's destruction of ancient Buddhist statues as an authentic response to the intolerable 'Neighbour supposed to enjoy' (*PD* 7). Here at least are people willing to *believe* strongly in the superiority of their own Cause. Like Badiou, Žižek is especially critical of the Levinasian ethics of alterity, which he regards as a translation of liberal tolerance into high theory, closed to the possibility of any genuine Act (*DSST* 152; *IDLC* 16–17; *PV* 111–13). According to Žižek, Levinas only obfuscated the monstrosity of the Neighbour, the monstrosity on account of which Lacan applied to the Neighbour the term Thing (*das Ding*) (*DSST* 187; *IDLC* 16, 345). For Žižek, then, Levinas merely restates in the language of phenomenological philosophy the standard liberal injunction, as if by saying:

> I know very well that the Other is obscene and dangerous, but all the same, I must behave as if they were infinitely important – and although I personally shall have nothing to do with their disgusting way of life, which I shall keep at a distance through legislation on sexual harassment, racial vilification, religious diversity and multicultural tolerance.

In other words, the Other may keep the formal shell of its way of life, but only with the decaffeinated substance of exotic rituals, clothing and interesting cuisine. How then does Žižek propose to break out of this contemporary *malaise* of false projections and fetishisations of the Other? Žižek since 2000 has sought to return us to what he now evidently regards as the elementary matrix of human sociality:

> When Freud and Lacan insist on the problematic nature of the basic Judeo-Christian injunction to 'love thy neighbour', they are thus not just making the standard critico-ideological point about how every notion of universality is coloured by our particular values and thus implies secret exclusions. They are making a much stronger point about the incompatibility of the Neighbour with the very dimension of universality. What resists universality is the properly inhuman dimension of the Neighbour.

This brings us back to the key question: does every universal ethics have to rely on such a gesture of fetishistic disavowal? The answer is: every ethics that remains 'humanist' (in the sense of avoiding the inhuman core of being-human), that disavows the abyssal dimension of the Neighbour. 'Man', 'human person', is a mask that conceals the pure subjectivity of the Neighbour. (*IDLC* 16)

So we have to note that Žižek here is suggesting that the encounter with the Neighbour is not merely something that comes with today's decline of symbolic authority (although this is true). It is something fundamental to human existence, and recalcitrant to all symbolic 'universality'. The 'pure subjectivity of the Neighbour' is the encounter with the Other as bearer of the Real *qua* 'kernel of human existence': 'at its most fundamental, the proximity of the Neighbour, with all the Judaeo-Christian–Freudian weight of this term, [is] the proximity of the thing which, no matter how far away it is physically, is always by definition too close"' (*OV* 45).

The present decline of symbolic authority in this light has the merit of confronting us with this usually repressed Truth most openly, and provoking us to make a decision. What is needed, Žižek boldly asserts in *In Defence of Lost Causes*, is an ethics of 'practical anti-humanism', rather than the postmodernists' theoretical attacks on modern humanistic politics and ideas, coupled with their increasingly fraught, repetitive invocations of messianic Otherness (*IDLC* 164–6).

But what on earth can a 'practical anti-humanism' amount to, especially since Žižek is quite open in saying that it alone would confront the abyssal or diabolical evil at the death drive's heart of subjectivity? The reply of the revolutionary-vanguardist Žižek is: theology. For, like Lacanian psychoanalysis as he reads it, theological discourse is nothing if not 'anti-humanist'. From the theological perspective, humanity is not the standard of value but subordinate to God.

The biblical solution to the problem of the Neighbour is the external imposition of a religiously grounded legal code: the Ten Commandments of Mosaic Law, in *Exodus*. This Law is internalised as the voice of conscience, or Ego Ideal, of the orthodox subject. But for him, this Law represents God's revealed Will for human beings, mediated by His prophets. The Ten Commandments, for instance, were experienced by the ancient Hebrews as a traumatic external injunction originating from their transcendent Ego Ideal, YHWH. Interestingly, following Lacan in a way that brings him close to this orthodox stance, Žižek has long seen the imposition of Mosaic Law as paradigmatic of the operation of the universal Symbolic Law on human subjectivity *per se*. The idea is that the Decalogue interposes a minimal distance between hostile Neighbours, within the community of believers. In more exact psychoanalytic terms, the 'Thou Shalt Nots' of the Commandments represent a series of prohibitions against enacting projected aggression and sexual desire. In this way, they encounter, head on, the problem of the Neighbour – indeed, again like Lacan before him, Žižek discerns in Jewish scripture the force of an invisible, abyssal God whose Will itself – even as it lies at the basis of pacifying social Law – is, like the Neighbour as Neighbour, far beyond the human ability to fathom, or any concern for human well-being (*TS* 313–22).

Repeating Hobbes: The Vanishing Other and the Authoritarian Solution

The problem is that confronting the supposedly anti-social nature of the human being, instead of allaying concerns about the authoritarian direction Žižek's ideas are taking, seems to confirm them. Regarding the human being as a selfish atom driven by projected aggression and sexual drives, whose rapacious attitude towards her fellow human beings can be controlled only by a moral code that seems to derive from on high, does not yield a new liberation. It seems to deliver us up to a repetition of the authoritarian politics of Thomas Hobbes.

We have argued in this culminating chapter that there are, then, two distinct strata in Žižek's analysis of religion in general, and Christianity in particular:

- Often, particularly in his earlier interventions into theology, Žižek is concerned to demonstrate, via his Lacanian dialectics, that there is a progressive, 'participatory' alternative to the dominant interpretation of revealed religion. Against the orthodox understanding of religion, for whom the believer is the instrument of God's will, Žižek intends to show that there is an emancipatory reading of Christianity at least, according to which the community of believers participates in the godhead because God as Transcendent Other is dead.
- In Žižek's works after 2003, however, a different argument is increasingly played out. Žižek assumes that the paradigm for human society is the religious community *because* religion deals with the elementary matrix of human sociality: 'the problem

213

of the Neighbour'. His question here is still whether a religious community is compatible with the Lacanian dictum on the 'non-existence of the Other'. But, in this more recent work, this means: can we form new political collectives composed of 'practical anti-humanists', fully open to the dimension of the Neighbour, death drive and diabolical evil. Because the Good News of the Gospels as Žižek reads them is that this is possible, the solution to the elementary matrix of human sociality can be formally religious: a closed, atheistic community based on a single Ego Ideal modelled on a kind of Christianity. This will be founded on a willingness to suspend ordinary political rules in a 'loving', unconditional attachment to the Cause of the Great Leap Forward to the new society.

The intertwining of these two registers in Žižek's heterodox Christianity is one of the many difficulties of comprehending his recent work. Why, in particular, despite Žižek's early advocacy of Hegel, does his most recent work point in exactly the opposite direction – towards a position that embraces a form of 'Neighbour Love' that licenses a Kierkegaardian suspension of the ordinary norms of political life, more or less as a goal in itself? In fact, we believe the key to this transition lies largely within Žižek's treatment of the Neighbour in his more recent works, which is literally 'the Other' of his changed conception of the subject as bearer of the infinite death drive (see 'Žižek's Vanishing Mediation'). For Žižek, as we have said, the problem of the Neighbour is the elementary matrix of both the question of religion and the problem of social order, because the figure of the Neighbour confronts us with the zero-degree of human sociability – its condition of possibility and impossibility.

We have repeatedly commented that one of the most troubling signs of our postmodern condition is the lack of cultural memory. This can make theorists like Žižek, but also Badiou, Agamben and others, seem to students the radical novelties that these theorists claim to be. Yet, if we take a moment to reflect on Žižek's type of recent position concerning the Neighbour in the history of political ideas, we see something telling. This is that Žižek's psychoanalytically framed concern with the Neighbour is not as novel as it might have seemed, when it emerged as central to Žižek's work early in the new millennium. In *Civilization and its Discontents* – after all one of the key texts in which Freud introduced the later notion of the death drive central to Žižek's recent work – Freud also raises the political theorist Thomas Hobbes. In particular, Freud notes the proximity of psychoanalysis to the Hobbesian notion of *homo homini lupus* (man is wolf to man), when it posits an irremovable seed of aggression in human nature that makes any too progressive, too 'idealistic' approaches to politics so many species of whistling in the wind (Freud 1985: 302).

We can say, therefore, that Žižek's Neighbour is just a recent version of the type of argument Hobbes made when he contended that humans in the prepolitical 'state of nature' were prone to mutual violence, which is itself a secular echo of grimmer Augustinian and Lutheran views about the unredeemable Evil of the cities of men. Žižek$_2$'s twist on this argument consists of his in fact far bleaker Freudo-Lacanian pendant to the Hobbesian way of framing the problem of social order – that is, of how to bring peace to violent, self-interested human beings. If Žižek's view of the Neighbour is right, individuals confront one another not just as proud and self-interested but rational calculators, as in Hobbes. The Žižekian Truth is that we are each to the Other irrational projectors, imaginary rivals who are also bearers of the death drive, drawn to obscene *Jouissance*. In the later Žižek's view, that is, the fragile rationality of individuals is undermined by this mechanism of projection (for which the Other confronts the ego as the bearer of perverse satisfactions) and our instinct for self-preservation itself is undermined by the death drive – for Žižek rightly notes that psychoanalysis teaches that, once the question of perverse satisfactions has been raised, subjects can and very often will go beyond the pleasure principle in their drive to annihilate the 'Other supposed to enjoy'. In terms of political realism, if the human being is a Žižekian Neighbour to the other, then human societies are permanently threatened by the possible outbreak of fighting in a libidinally supercharged war of each against all.

We cannot help but remark that what has vanished in this Freudo-Hobbesian framing of the question of social order is what *was* present in the early Žižek's Hegelian work – namely, the notion of the Symbolic Order as both the peaceful medium of human sociability, and the minimal condition for subjects to take on any kind of political identity at all (Chapter 1). As we pass from the early Hegelian works, beyond Schelling, into the later theological works, that is, we pass between two completely distinct conceptions of the political subject:

- Žižek₁ stresses that socialisation goes right to the root of the human being and that the idea of an isolated, self-creating individual is a misrecognition of the human condition – paradigmatically, the human being confronts the other as a potential social/ sexual partner within the constraints of symbolic gender codes that make possible each other's individual identity;
- Žižek₂ maintains that socialisation is a veneer covering asocial drives and, accordingly, that the individual as bearer of the death drive is fundamentally self-sufficient, capable of acting to traverse all his inherited symbolic commitments, if she has revolutionary Virtue enough. Although Žižek's Lacanianism should prohibit this, we are close indeed to the type of position that can see subjects' motives for entering into the social contract only as more or less instrumental: a position wherein, paradigmatically, the human being confronts the other as a potential object of satisfaction or as an intruder portending perverse fulfilments. It is troubling in this light that Žižek has repeatedly argued in this vein that all sexuality is essentially masturbatory (*OB* 24), a position that he elsewhere rightly recognises is deeply problematic.

We wonder, in relation to the later revolutionary-vanguardist Žižek: once we are working with such a bleak conception of pre-political subjectivity, what political options are available to us to conceive of a new political order, or to decide between the competing goods posed by different regimes? Could political order even be conceivable, short of very harsh restrictions to keep the Neighbours at bay?

Here again, Thomas Hobbes points our way towards some understanding. For Hobbes, the problem of the exit of subjects from the 'war of each against all' in the 'state of nature' was only ever incompletely solved by the famous 'social contract' struck between rationally calculating, self-preserving individuals, which issues in the establishment of an authoritarian, policing state. Hobbes's anxiety was that, despite the benefits to self-interest of the rule of law, human beings were highly unreliable when it came to keeping their promises. In particular, Hobbes accepted that it is unreasonable to expect allegedly wholly self-interested beings who had 'covenanted' with an authoritarian state to swap their rights for protection, to continue to support that state when it no longer provided reasonable guarantees of protection. But that means, of course, that, at the first hint of danger – in war or civil strife, for instance – the good citizens desert.

Or, rationally, they take the law into their own hands. The only way to prevent a constant relapse into the state of nature, then, is to make certain that 'individuals keep their covenants'. And Hobbes, with consummate materialistic cynicism, proposes that religion is just the ticket. Where people do not sufficiently understand how the rule of law benefits their self-interest, or fear the State, the dread of God and infinite punishment for transgressions should be deployed by Leviathan to keep them in line.

An onus falls on defenders of Žižek's recent turn to political theology to show that this type of cynical solution does not beckon at the gates of his recent thought, especially in the light of the sharp authoritarian turn we documented in Chapter 5. If liberalism is to be overcome, new Žižekian subjects committed unconditionally to the Cause will be required. These subjects must accept the need teleologically to suspend the ethical in the revolutionary moment, and then purge outsiders and counter-revolutionaries after the revolutionary Act has succeeded. Yet Žižek has no concrete vision of a better world that might inspire the New Men, nor does he present any compelling vision of human flourishing, beyond the rather grim, Romanticist appeal to us authentically to accept the death drive at our hearts. Subjects' rational, debated commitment to the New Cause cannot be asked by him – at the threat of our regressing back into the idle chatter of liberal postmodernism. Certainly also, we know that Žižek refuses to oppose Christian love to 'divine violence', with the distinct implication that the liberated community of believers may be freed to suspend the ordinary rules of human sociability. On the other hand, the only solution to the encounter between Neighbours Žižek proposes is their both accepting the same, neo-Christian master signifier – a conversion, in other words, to a new faith based on a 'love' without determinate ethical or political content, more a 'belonging to belonging' or 'stubborn attachment' to a Cause, rather than an ennobling political vision. In this way, incidentally, it is tempting to say in the language of recent political debate that there is a 'communitarian' core to Žižek's dialectical psychoanalysis, most potently displayed in his hostility to liberal multiculturalism and his advocacy of religious communities as the paradigm for a new form of political solidarity.

Building on what we argued in Chapter 4, we think that Žižek's preference for Christianity and his hostility to multiculturalism suggest his inescapable belief that only a monocultural order can survive. This is consistent with the notion that every society is bound by a ruling ideology, and that every ideological field must turn upon allegiance to a communal Ego Ideal – a proposition that rules out value pluralism as a possible solution to the problem of social order. Specifically, the new public Ego Ideal Žižek wants us to embrace – the common Leftist, 'Christian' Cause or unifying Belief – is the result of a leap of faith whose coordinates are counter-modern anti-Enlightenment theology and existential religion. The art of politics, as Žižek understands it, is the art of violently enacting a theologically grounded political contract that captures the faith of the masses while binding together a unitary community – hence Žižek's advocacy of 'psychoanalytic collectives and revolutionary communes' as anticipations of his 'emancipated' society. The medieval church would seem to be a prime example of such a community – a fact that might explain how, in Žižek's more unusual prescriptive moments, he can valorise 'the acephalous saint', and encourage subjects to identify themselves as Christian 'excremental remainders' on the face of the political world.

Of course, with all the whirl of textual and dialectical fireworks, together with Žižek's incredible wit and evident enjoyment at playing the jester, it is hard to believe that even Žižek can quite believe in the theologico-political prescriptions his most recent books continue to promote. Most readers probably consider Žižek as a provocateur only. What is certain is that, beneath the ceaseless novelty of book upon book and article upon article, Žižek has found his way slowly but surely to a neighbourly love for a long line of deeply politically problematic figures – Sorel, Heidegger, Nietzsche, Kiekegaard, Schmitt, Chesterton – whose abstract anti-liberalism combined with political Romanticism led them to flirt with wholesale irrationalist reactions against modernity. We hope that, in response to the liberal blackmail about the triumph of capitalism and the supremacy of political liberalism, Žižek is not reacting by rejecting political rationalism altogether.

Conclusion

Quilting Points

The reader will by now see in full the extent to which *Žižek and Politics* is the *critical* introduction its subtitle promised. We have introduced the reader to the three undoubted contributions Žižek has made to today's political theory:

1. *Žižek's Lacanian theory of ideology.* The idea of an ideological fantasy focuses uniquely on the importance of subjects' fantasmatic beliefs and the transgressive enjoyment that accompanies ideological practices. Beneath subjects' conscious attitudes, and the explicit ideals promised by regimes' 'master signifiers' ('democracy', 'freedom', 'equality' and so forth), ideological fantasy binds them to regimes that may be completely unjust;
2. *Žižek's Lacanian rereading of the Cartesian subject and his rehabilitation of German Idealism.* Žižek rehabilitates modern philosophy from the dustbin of theoretical fashion. He does this by asserting that the subject is not a substantial Thing, hell-bent on reducing all difference, or Otherness, to identity, or sameness. The subject, beneath the layers of its symbolic mandates (social roles) and fantasmatic misrecognitions (as the victim of a 'theft of enjoyment' by others), is a negativity that underlies all our perceptions and speech acts ('enunciations') without ever being objectifiable in any one of them. Žižek's subject is first of all a gap in the social or linguistic 'substance' (to use a Hegelian term) or 'Other' (to use the Lacanian), capable in principle of withdrawing from or 'traversing' the deepest commitments that sustain this Other, our political regimes.
3. *Žižek's use of Lacan's later theory of the four discourses to generate a new understanding of the different modern regimes (capitalist, Stalinist, fascist).* Žižek's approach yields some important insights into the ideological fantasies underlying modern regimes. His typology also opposes the liberal tendency to equate

all non-liberal regimes as 'totalitarian'. For Žižek, fascism is the reactionary attempt to reinstate the 'Discourse of the Master' that characterised the absolute monarchies, and the semblance of an organic closed community, while preserving capitalist economic relations. Stalinism is the Enlightenment gone mad: an instance of the 'Discourse of the University', which wholly objectifies and terrorises the populace in the name of the 'laws of history'. But the consumerism of later capitalism is not as distant from this as liberals might hope. It too institutes a form of the 'Discourse of the University,' wherein subjects are invited to objectify themselves in the pursuit of the endless supply of consumer goods, upon whose consumption the global economy depends.

But *Žižek and Politics* has not just recounted these notions. Written on the twentieth anniversary of the first appearance of *The Sublime Object of Ideology*, the book aims also to 'quilt' the voluminous body of criticism that has emerged since the late 1990s on Žižek's work. This criticism has focused largely on Žižek's politics, although it has ranged more widely than that, down to criticisms of Žižek's fame and style. Certain themes have become well established. In particular, these are:

- *The criticism of Žižek's prescriptive notion of a radical political Act.* This has been arraigned as unrealistic, untrue to Lacan, and potentially meaninglessly violent. This is because the revolutionary Act in question is grounded in nothing more normatively robust than the call 'courageously' to take a decisionistic leap, in the political night where all extant regimes are morally black.
- *The sense that Žižek's works are, beyond their characteristic stylistic pastiche, intellectually inconsistent.* Žižek's texts are accused of inconsistency, if not at the level of his unwavering 'dogmatic' commitments to Lacan and Hegel, then as soon as Žižek tries to 'apply' his 'Lacanian dialectics' to politics. The criticisms have targeted both Žižek's descriptive political work (his attempts to give an account of the way the world is) and his prescriptive sallies (aiming to recommend possible or desirable ways to change the world).

So our deeper aim in *Žižek and Politics* has lain beyond providing new readers a way into Žižek and the important political and theoretical issues he raises. It has been to provide an interpretative framework that might also account for the strangely divided reception Žižek has received, in this way making a new intervention in the debates. These divided responses, we think, are 'reflective determinations' – as Žižek would say in Hegelian terms – of internal divisions in Žižek's work. From the start, Žižek's new account of the way ideology grips subjects, shaping their deepest fantasies, left him with two theoretical options:

- *On the one hand, such an insight could lead to a sophisticated, Enlightenment appeal to reshape societies in the direction of self-determination or autonomy.* Žižek could have called for a psychoanalytic Enlightenment beyond Enlightenment rationalism and based a democratic politics on the resulting robust conception of human subjectivity and moral philosophy. The psychoanalytic model here would be the earlier Freud, optimistically convinced that the talking cure (in Lacanese, the work of symbolisation) could cure the neurotic maladies of modern women and men's souls. It would do this in politics by revealing to subjects the deepest ways in which they continue to be duped into attachment to avoidably unjust regimes. This would then point towards the possibility of new political modes and orders not founded on ideological fantasies concerning the way external Others have thieved 'our' enjoyment from us.

- *On the other hand, the revelation that political commitment is much more irrational than more naïve enlighteners had supposed is fully consistent with more conservative, even reactionary conclusions.* The reasoning goes like this. Given how deep and unconscious subjects' irrational attachments to power are, it is folly even to consider new regimes not founded on the irrational appeal to subjects' passions, fears and fantasies. This is irremovable, so injustice ceases to be the result of political arrangements that might be changed by conscious, collective action and new institutions. In such a pessimistic world view, one can only reasonably countenance creating new regimes that reorganise subjects' unconscious fantasies differently, on the bases of new identifications and new enemies.

Looking at the range of Žižek's texts since 1989, our argument has been that Žižek oscillates between these two possible inferences from his Lacanian–Hegelian premises. Yet, we have argued, the dominant direction – the 'structure in dominance', to use an idea from the structuralists' analyses of texts – in Žižek's work has changed discernibly. It has changed from the earlier, pro-Enlightenment direction towards the later, at base conservative or reactionary, direction.

Of course, on top of this change in reasoning or emphasis, Žižek's political conclusions have radicalised, and seemingly gone far to the Left. But psychoanalysis and Hegelianism both have explanations for why things can at first appear in a disguised or distorted form. People do not always consciously know the significance of what they do. Žižek, for his part, continues to use the language of universality, for instance, and of the Cartesian subject. But we hoped to show in Part Two that the meanings he gives to these terms in more recent works are very different from what they are in the early work. The subject for the recent Žižek is bearer of the death drive, a Neighbour to his fellows that they would do well to approach with caution. They are also supposedly capable of acting to 'touch the Real' and engender a new ideological order, just as God created the Symbolic Order of natural causality. And Žižek's 'universality', if it has any determinate content at all, becomes the work of Christian 'Neighbour love' open to the possibility of extra-rational 'divine violence' to overthrow all global capitalism, and *any* particular order you care to name (hence its optative 'universalism'). We have made clear our deep reservations about the disquieting questions that this raises, and the prospects it affords, in Chapters 5 and 6, and invite readers to draw their own conclusions. We doubt whether Žižek's later work can connect with any really existing classes or social movements, or generate any positive ideals of a distinctly Leftist or progressive nature – let alone justify Žižek's call for the Left to return to the moments of terror in its heritage that are arguably its most retrograde and inhumane legacy.

The other novel exegetical argument we make is to date the change in Žižek's orientation around 1996–7, and to give it a theoretical basis. We find this basis in Žižek's encounter with Schelling's theology, documented in *The Indivisible Remainder* of 1996, *The Abyss of Freedom* of 1997 and *The Fragile Absolute* of 2000. We do not, and need not, deny that political factors and events of course influenced Žižek's changing political assessment of democratic politics. But we think that it is significant that, from the time of his encounter with Schelling's theogony, the weight of his theoretical account of subjectivity – the centre of his political ontology – also changes. The changed politics reflects the changed theory. From this time onwards, Žižek's subject is no longer the finite, empty or non-substantial subject of Kant and Hegel; it is the subject as bearer of an infinite death drive of the later Lacan, Freud and Schelling, influenced also by Žižek's growing debt to the ultra-Leftist positions of Alain Badiou.

Whatever the force or weight of Žižek's political shifts, we believe that this theoretical change also demands a theoretical explanation.

In fact, we have suggested (and see below) that we think that Schelling's heterodox account of the way God gave birth to the causally determined world from out of his abyssal freedom gives an unusually direct statement of what we think is the deepest limitation in Žižek's attempt to use psychoanalysis to provide a totalising political theory. This is Žižek's tendentious positing of society or political regimes, under the rubric of the 'big Other', as what we have variously called a 'subject–object', a 'metasubject' or an 'expressive totality', all of whose features can be analytically deciphered by one methodology – Žižek's own Lacanian dialectics.

To Anticipate

It is worth saying that we are under absolutely no illusions as to how Žižek, in his revolutionary vanguardist mode (and many readers who identify strongly with him), will respond to our claims. Žižek's response to critics so far has only seen him further radicalising his arguments and provocations, rather than reconsidering his theoretical premises or their political applications. Two rhetorical strategies predominate in Žižek's texts, ostensibly devoted to responding to critics:

1. Žižek asks, with outrage, 'Where did I say what X [insert name of critic] has alleged? Did I not also say [at another point in his work] exactly the opposite of what X asserts? And does not critic Y, to prove my point, say exactly the opposite of what X asserts?' Often Žižek expresses frustration that he has been even asked to respond to the 'standard boring reproaches' that people astonishingly insist on making against his work (CND; WDLT). What Žižek rarely does, however, is account for the things that he *did* say, as documented by critic X, or respond to the substantive claims raised against these passages;
2. Žižek uses what are called technically *ad hominem* arguments. This type of response has the form of saying: 'X is of course an orthodox (for example) Marxist, so of course she would say . . .' or 'Y is a conservative Lacanian/deconstructionist, so of course he would assert that . . .'.The force of *ad hominems* is to deflect attention from assessing the substance of the charges (which may of course be true, *even if* they happen to be made from a partisan

perspective!). The most important of Žižek's characteristic *ad hominem* replies is to assign everything that has been said in criticism of his work to the 'contemporary political deadlock' – the problem, in other words, is not that Žižek's text is problematic, but that everyone else supposedly lacks radical commitment.

In this vein, it is not difficult for us to anticipate what those interpellated by the recent, revolutionary vanguardist Žižek writings might say concerning the critical side of *Žižek and Politics*. On the one hand, they will be delighted that we acknowledge Žižek to be probably the most important theoretical writer working today. But, on the other hand, they will assert that, although the things that we cite in the text were indeed said, their status as problems disappears when we set them in the context of other passages in his work that contradict the citations. In particular, the following arguments will probably be made.

1. The 'Žižek$_1$' and 'Žižek$_2$' distinction is a typical example of the way academia operates to gentrify, cut up and disembowel original thought, repackaging it into neat periods ('the early versus late Wittgenstein/Heidegger/Derrida/Habermas'), in order to avoid confronting its radical transformative force. Moreover, the date of 1996–7 for Žižek's alleged change from 'Žižek$_1$' to 'Žižek$_2$' is more or less arbitrary. The types of claims that our 'Žižek$_2$' is cited as making are already present in the 'Žižek$_1$' works.

2. Sharpe and Boucher belong to the brigade of politically correct academics whose 'Leftism' is merely social democratic. In this light, is there any *surprise* that Sharpe and Boucher seek out a 'Žižek$_1$' who seems to agree with their 'radical-democratic' position? Does not this mean that they have failed fully to confront the reality of global injustice and the politics of universal truth necessary to end this once and for all?

We have given our textual and argumentative reasons for the positions we take in Part Two of *Žižek and Politics*. We take it that the process of intellectual debate is about rational arguments as well as political commitments, and we have supplied the textual sources and logical claims to support our positions. So we can again only invite the reader to assess things by their own lights. Nevertheless, let us close by trying to rebut some of these anticipated charges by making our deepest theoretical arguments clear again to close the book.

Repeating Lenin, an Infantile Disorder?

Perhaps our deepest criticism of Žižek's work is that, from the true premise that what is needed is a set of alternatives to the present neoliberal order and its accelerating crises, Žižek infers that what is needed is an absolute break with everything that exists. For Žižek, and despite his professed Marxism, there are no dialectical contradictions at the very heart of capitalism, as Marx thought. Instead, there are marginalised groups who belong only liminally to the world order, as the alleged *sinthomes* of global capital: the disenfranchised peoples of the favellas, the long-term unemployed and so on.

Any other analysis, any strategy that looks to groups within the system, fails to disturb the fundamental fantasy. For Žižek, this 'compromise' is not a sign of virtue in analysis, a necessary intellectual response to the way that modern societies are multi-dimensional, containing may potentially contradictory dynamics and sites of potentially efficacious struggles. On the contrary, we must learn, in the language of Žižek loyalists Rex Butler and Scott Stephens, to 'play it *** loud' (Butler and Stephens 2006) – angrily to reject everything that presently exists. In truth, Žižek announces, the question is simple: are readers ready for a total social transformation, or are they insipidly complicit with our perverse capitalist society (*IDLC* 1)?

At its worst, it seems to us that this type of strident position is deeply anti-Hegelian, even irrationalist. It is certainly not Marxist in any robust sense. For what is Marx's *Capital*, for instance, if not an attempt, massive in its scale and research, to understand the way complex modern capitalist economies work, so that its central dynamic and potential for crisis can be mapped onto the largest group in the system with an interest in social change?

Better still, to make our political point here concerning the limitations of the revolutionary vanguardist Žižek's increasing hostility to complex social-theoretical analysis and its connection with strategic political considerations, let us consider the case of Vladimir Lenin. Žižek in *Repeating Lenin* has nominated the Bolshevik Leader as the modern precedent (in the shadow of St Paul) that the Left needs to 'repeat', in order to reanimate radical politics today. But Lenin – the actual historical Lenin, rather than Žižek's fantasmatic figure – repudiates two major ideas that Žižek now holds about politics. These are:

1. The idea that the political Act happens in a normative and descriptive void, as a radical break with the existing Symbolic Order or big Other. Žižek's Lenin, the Lenin of April–October 1917, is presented as the purest historical example of an evental subject who has had the courage to Act without the sanction of the big Other of any pre-existing 'situation' or normative frame.

2. The idea that politics is the art of the *impossible* – an art based on the death drive, in the style of the surrealist slogans of the Parisian students in May 1968 – and that everyone who says that politics is the art of the possible is guilty of 'compromise' with the system. From this position follows the desire to short-cut political struggles and go directly to the political Act, hand-in-hand not with the masses who are at the heart of the dynamics of capitalism, but with the most marginalised groups on its fringes.

Žižek can get away with this type of caricature today because nobody reads Marx and Lenin any more, so a generation of students has no idea that they are the butt of a sort of (im)practical joke.

Until April 1917, Lenin had held that the backwards capitalism in Tsarist Russia meant that only a democratic revolution (that is, bourgeois society with a parliamentary government) was possible. The Marxists should hasten this process, the Russian version of the French Revolution, forward, in order then to prepare the forces for a socialist revolution. But Lenin's theoretical study of imperialism, catalysed by the First World War, convinced him that Russian capitalism was part of a world capitalist system whose parts could not be analysed in isolation from one another. Lenin's *April Theses* argue that it followed from the world character of imperialism and the political opportunity presented by the hostility of the masses to the war that socialist revolution in Russia was possible, provided that it was followed by socialist revolutions in Germany and France. So, rather than calling for a socialist uprising in a moral and historical void, Lenin's *April Theses* announced that, all along, Lenin had radically misread the historical situation (Žižek's Symbolic Order, or big Other).

But this radical alteration in Lenin's understanding of the historical process did not mean that he also scrapped twenty years of intense hostility towards those who wanted to substitute terrorist actions and the marginalised fringes for the self-organisation and self-emancipation of the masses. Published in 1920, only three years after His Revolutionary Act, Lenin's *Left Wing Communism: An*

Infantile Disorder tells a different tale from Žižek's one, concerning how Lenin understood politics. In it, Lenin berates those he terms 'left-wing communists': the ultra-Leftist thinkers who would, like Žižek, shun the possibility of alliances with existing forces – such as trade unions and social-democratic parliamentary parties. How can we explain the anomaly that Lenin calls strident oppositional positions an 'infantile disorder', rather than boldly praising their revolutionary virtue?

Lenin's culminating chapter in *Left Wing Communism: An Infantile Disorder* is entitled: 'No compromises?' And, of course, Lenin is no more a bleeding heart than he is a good liberal. Lenin is, however, a politician, who adjures his readers again and again that 'it is extremely "dangerous", incomprehensible and wrong not to permit compromises' (Lenin 1921: VIII. 1). Why? Well, on the one hand, 'it is surprising . . . that these [European] Leftists do not condemn Bolshevism' if they are serious about rejecting 'all maneuvering and compromise within the existing world':

> After all, the German Leftists cannot but know that the entire history of Bolshevism, both before and after the October revolution, is full of instances of changes of tack, conciliatory tactics and compromises with other parties, including bourgeois parties! (Lenin 1921: VIII. 3)

This is a difficult passage for Žižek to assimilate into his position at all. For Lenin, though, the political realm, unlike that which opens up before the philosopher's *a priori* gaze, is empirically complex. What follows is Lenin teaching 'the necessity, the absolute necessity, for the Communist party' *not* to 'renounce in advance any change of tack . . . [the] utilisation of conflicts of interests (even if temporary) among one's enemies, or any conciliation or compromise with possible allies . . .' (Lenin 1921: VIII. 3) All of this, moreover, is useless unless the revolutionary vanguard, the 'semi-conscious part of the proletariat', cannot appeal to real grievances among the majority of ordinary people: 'at the same time you must soberly follow the actual state of class-consciousness and preparedness of the entire class (not only its communist vanguard), and of all the working people (not only their advanced elements)' (Lenin 1921: VII. 3). To trade such strategic considerations, and engagement with the existing commitments of real subjects and social movements, for uncompromising declamations is 'ridiculous' and 'immature', says Lenin.

This is why Lenin suggests that the genuine Left 'must wage an unremitting struggle' against ultra-Leftists, if it is to look forward to political success (Lenin 1921: VIII. 2–3). In the light of this testimony, the reader has to wonder whether Žižek, again closer to Sorel than to the Bolshevik leader he praises, is using Lenin for his own purposes, in order to try to create a new Sorelian revolutionary mythology, a story of betrayed origins that – despite our very different political situation (see Kellogg 2008: 15–17) – could animate a new vanguard?

For Multi-Dimensional Political Theory

Our argument in this book is that the revolutionary vanguardist Žižek's 'left-wing Communist' rejection of any compromises with the existing order rests on theoretical, even philosophical premises. The deepest or most far-reaching theoretical aim of this book has been to uncover these premises, and show the descriptive and political short-comings they produce. Žižek's reading of Schelling's theogony is so revealing for us because it presents a direct account of how God – a 'subject' – produces the Symbolic Order or Other (which is an object) from out of itself. He does so as a means to resolve his own internal crisis, 'the rotary motion of the drives'.

Such an account, when applied, as Žižek does apply it, to an account of individual human subjects, is first of all profoundly anti-Lacanian. No Lacanian could suggest that, for all the chaos of the infantile drives in infants, that entry into the Symbolic Order, which stabilises this libidinal discord, involves the subject's 'self-externalisation'. A Lacanian would rather suggest that the infant's identification is with an Other that pre-exists it, and whose external bearers introduce the child to it through the imposition of the imper-sonal, trans-generational prohibitions against incest and parricide.

Our key point is that his reading of Schelling commits Žižek directly to positing that the object of his analysis is an 'identical subject–object', with the Symbolic Order as the expression–objecti-fication of the subject. What Žižek finds in Schelling is actually his own deepest assumptions confirmed. Or rather, Žižek 'posits his own presuppositions' when he reads Schelling, to use another Hegelian phrase. As we examined in Chapter 3, Žižek talks in his earlier work of the 'structural homologies' he finds between a philosophy of the subject, an account of modern, Kantian ethics, and the modern dem-ocratic political system. Such structural homologies license Žižek to pass so seamlessly between analyses at these levels, in the paratactic way Žižek is now famous for, which fascinates many readers and horrifies many critics. There are other areas of 'structural homology' that Žižek can and does adduce in his work: the analysis of cultural products, books, poems, films, and so on, and since 1996 increasingly (although already in the final chapter of *The Sublime Object of Ideology*) theological considerations.

To emphasise, we do not dispute the power, even the genius, of many of Žižek's analyses, particular at the levels of theology, and the exegeses of philosophical and cultural artefacts. We do, however, think that one method alone is not adequate to address the particularities of all these different realms as readily as Žižek supposes. This is our basic or deepest explanation for what we take Žižek's theoretical and political shortcomings to be, those that the existing critical literature on his work have identified and turned around.

Our particular claim is twofold:

1. First: Žižek's theoretical object, what he rediscovers in every field to which he turns his eye, is 'the big Other', which shapes the coordinates of subjects' identifications and understandings of the world. This category in Žižek's work at different points can and does describe:

   - the natural, causally determined world;
   - the ideology of any political system;
   - the psychoanalyst in the clinic;
   - the parent(s), especially the father, and any other authority figure;
   - the (Kantian) moral Law;
   - the material political institutions of any political regime;
   - the written laws of any society;
   - the unwritten conventions of any society;
   - the Symbolic Law prohibiting incest and parricide at the bases of all human sociability or any society whatsoever;
   - the particular syntactical and other rules of any natural language;
   - the differential ordering of any language system, as such a system or structure.

   In Žižek's defence, it has to be said that Lacan before him did use 'the Other' in different contexts as a condensation of many of these different object domains.

2. Second: in Žižek's work, the tendency to posit the big Other as what needs to be analysed, albeit in order to show how it 'does not exist', leads to two telling theoretical conflations:

i. Žižek conflates the objective Symbolic Order of any society with its ideological representations: in psychoanalytic terms, with the Ego Ideal or I(O): namely, the way subjects (mis) recognise the Other as a single reified totality. Hence, he can claim that contemporary capitalism, like a particular subject, is perverse or psychotic – as a metasubject afflicted with a clinical condition that also afflicts specific individuals whom psychoanalysts treat. The fact that Žižek oscillates between these two, too total diagnoses, however, attests that he is too subtle an observer of cultural and political life not to notice that there are many different manifestations of contemporary culture. Yet some of these are more distinctly perverse in terms of the way that they invite subjects to shape their conduct, while others more closely model the real, symbolic and imaginary (de)formations in play in individual psychosis. What Žižek does not infer from this is the limitations of trying to describe the entire contemporary cultural constellation as one reified big Other, whether perverse or psychotic. This monolithic vision of the social totality, we argue, also jaundices Žižek's political prescriptions, pushing them towards a monocultural, (post-) Christian political theology. Žižek, to say the least, is theoretically ill-disposed towards any multicultural society. His tendency to conflate the Ego Ideal with the Symbolic Order means that he is again and again drawn to seeing the pluralisation of Ego Ideals in complex societies as the collapse of the Symbolic Order itself, confronting us with the fearsome problematic of the Neighbour supposed to enjoy, rape or kill. If contemporary society is breaking down into perverse depravity or worse, what is needed is a new unifying Ego Ideal, a single New Cause that would cut through the multiplicitous tangle of people's inherited particularistic 'habits'. If this Ego Ideal is to resolve the problem of the Neighbour, too, it can be readily seen why Žižek has told us that what the Left needs to do is reconsider the importance of widespread political violence or Terror, just as Hobbes opted for the symbol of the biblical Leviathan to 'subdue the children of the proud'.

ii. As (i) implies, Žižek equates society with a single metasubject or expressive totality. Each of the apparently analytically distinct elements of the contemporary order – culture or ideology, politics or administration, economy or civil society – are for him so many expressions of the single expressive principle. This is why Žižek can tell us that the key to everything, from why the USA invaded Iraq to how politics relates to the economy in today's world, can, for instance, be found in *The Interpretation of Dreams* – a proposition that we presume would be as much news to Freud as it is to today's political theorists, scientists, economists, international relations experts (IDLC 285–93).[1]

If the USA under the neocons fell in for imperial overstretch, we claim, Žižek in the era of the neocons fell in for theoretical overstretch. One of his key references is Louis Althusser, but it is notable that it is only one part of Althusser's work that shapes his own. This is Althusser's famous work on ideology examined in Chapter 1 – which points us exactly to the political scope and limits of Žižek's psychoanalytic analyses of the Other and the subject – namely, the field of ideology. To take it that 'the Other' that subjects misrecognise is the sufficient object of political theory is to join these subjects in their misrecognition. In other words, if we grant the force of Žižek's analyses that 'the Other does not exist', and the enlightening function such an insight can play, political theory needs to begin trying to work empirically and conceptually at describing the symbolic and material-political orders that people actually *do* live in, despite their misrecognitions of it as a 'single reified' Other. This is not merely an academic point either. For in doing this descriptive and conceptual work, we will be able to move towards a set of strategic political programmes with more purchase and hope than grand calls to overthrow everything all at once, in some kind of Žižekian equivalent of the Sorelian myth of the general strike.

We realise that this argument, which we propose as a new 'quilting' framework to explain Žižek's theoretical oscillations and political prescriptions, raises some large issues of its own. While this is not the place to further that discussion, we think its analytic force leads into a much wider critique of 'Theory' in parts of the later-twentieth-century academy, which emerged following the 'cultural turn' of the 1960s and 1970s in the wake of the collapse of Marxism. Žižek's paradigm to try to generate all his theory of culture, subjectivity, ideology, politics and religion is psychoanalysis. But a similar

---

[1] See also Slavoj Zizek, 'Iraq's False Promises', www.lacan.com/zizek-iraq2.htm (accessed May 2009).

criticism would apply, for instance, to theorists who feel that the method Jacques Derrida developed for criticising philosophical texts can meaningfully supplant the methodologies of political science, philosophy, economics, sociology and so forth, when it comes to thinking about 'the political'. Or, differently, thinkers who opt for Deleuze (or Deleuze's and Guattari's) Nietzschean Spinozism as a new metaphysics to explain ethics, politics, aesthetics, ontology and so forth, seem to us candidates for the same type of criticism, as a reductive passing over the empirical and analytic distinctness of the different object fields in complex societies.

In truth, we feel that Theory, and the continuing line of 'master thinkers' who regularly appear particularly in the English-speaking world, is the last gasp of what used to be called First Philosophy. The philosopher ascends out of the city, Plato tells us, from whence she can espie the Higher Truth, which she must then bring back down to political earth. From outside the city, we can well imagine that she can see much more widely than her benighted political contemporaries. But from these philosophical heights, we can equally suspect that the 'master thinker' is also always in danger of passing over the salient differences and features of political life – differences only too evident to people 'on the ground'. Political life, after all, is always a more complex affair than a bunch of ideologically duped fools staring at and enacting a wall (or 'politically correct screen') of ideologically produced illusions, from Plato's timeless cave allegory to Žižek's theory of ideology.

We know that Theory largely understands itself as avowedly 'post-metaphysical'. It aims to erect its new claims on the gravestone of First Philosophy as the West has known it. But it also tells us that people very often do not know what they do. And so it seems to us that too many of its proponents and their followers are mourners who remain in the graveyard, propping up the gravestone of Western philosophy under the sign of some totalising account of absolutely everything – enjoyment, *différance*, biopower . . . Perhaps the time has come, we would argue, less for one more would-be global, all-purpose existential and political Theory than for a multi-dimensional and interdisciplinary critical theory that would challenge the chaotic specialisation neoliberalism speeds up in academe, which mirrors and accelerates the splintering of the Left over the last four decades. This would mean that we would have to shun the hope that one method, one perspective, or one master thinker could single-handedly decipher all the complexity of socio-political life, the concerns of really existing social movements – which specifically does not mean mindlessly celebrating difference, marginalisation and multiplicity as if they could be sufficient ends for a new politics. It would be to reopen critical theory and non-analytic philosophy to the other intellectual disciplines, most of whom today pointedly reject Theory's legitimacy, neither reading it nor taking it seriously.

For Žižek is right: global capitalism 'does not exist', at least, not as a monlithic expressive totality. As we write this (early 2009), capitalism's contradictions and limitations are becoming more and more evident by the hour. So now more than ever the Left needs to confront those who would argue 'there is no alternative'. But shrill denunciations of today's lack of Virtue, coupled with too sweeping, too pessimistic and too one-dimensional forms of analysis are in truth one more obstacle on the road. A renewed Western Left will have to involve engaged, concrete proposals for how to change the world to institute a more just, post-neoliberal global order. A brilliant theory of ideology and the subject, such as are present in Žižek's work, is a necessary part of this task. But it is not sufficient, even in the realm of theory, and certainly not for a new praxis.

References

Adorno, Theodor, and Max Horkheimer (1986). *Dialectic of Enlightenment*. London: Verso.

Agamben, Giorgio (1998). *Homo Sacer: Sovereign Power and Bare Life.* Stanford: Stanford University Press.

Agamben, Giorgio (1999). *Remnants of Auschwitz: The Witness and the Archive.* New York: Zone.

Agamben, Giorgio (2001) *The State of Exception.* Stanford: Stanford University Press.

Althusser, Louis (1971). *Lenin and Philosophy and Other Essays.* London: New Left Books.

Althusser, Louis (1994). 'Ideology and Ideological State Apparatuses (Notes towards an Investigation)', in Slavoj Žižek (ed.), *Mapping Ideology.* London: Verso, pp. 100–40.

Althusser, Louis, and Étienne Balibar (1970). *Reading Capital*, trans. Ben Brewster. London: New Left Books.

Arato, Andrew, and Paul Brienes (1979). *The Young Lukács and the Origins of Western Marxism.* London: Pluto Press.

Arendt, Hannah (1966). *The Origins of Totalitarianism.* New York: Harcourt-Brace.

Badiou, Alain (2001). *Ethics: An Essay on the Understanding of Evil.* London and New York: Verso.

Beck, Ulrich, Anthony Giddens and Scott Lash (1994). *Reflexive Modernization: Politics, Tradition and Aesthetics in the Modern Social Order.* Cambridge: Cambridge University Press.

Bellamy, Elizabeth (1993). 'Discourses of Impossibility: Can Psychoanalysis be Political?' *Diacritics*, 23/1: 24–38.

Benjamin, Walter (1973). 'Theses on the Philosophy of History', in *Illuminations*, ed. with an introduction by Hannah Arendt, trans. Harry Zohn. New York: Schocken Books.

Berger, Claudia (2001). 'The Leader's Two Bodies: Slavoj Žižek's Postmodern Political Theology', *Diacritics* (Spring).

Bloom, Peter (2008). 'Capitalism's Cynical Leviathan: Cynicism, Totalitarianism, and Hobbes in Modern Capitalist Regulation', *International Journal of Žižek Studies*, 2/1, online.

Bosteels, Bruno (2001). 'Alain Badiou's Theory of the Subject: Part I. The

Recommencement of Dialectical Materialism?' *Pli: The Warwick Journal of Philosophy*, 12: 200–29.

Boucher, Geoff (2005). 'The Law as a Thing: Žižek and the Graph of Desire', in Matthew Sharpe, Geoff Boucher, and Jason Glynos (eds), *Traversing the Fantasy: Critical Responses to Slavoj Žižek*. London: Ashgate, pp. 23–44.

Bowie, Andrew (1993). *Schelling and Modern European Philosophy*. London: Routledge.

Bowman, Paul (2007). 'The Tao of Žižek', in Paul Bowman and Richard Stamp (eds), *The Truth of Žižek*. London: Continuum, pp. 27–44.

Bowman, Paul, and Richard Stamp (2007) (eds). *The Truth of Žižek*. London: Continuum.

Boyle, Kirk (2008). 'The Four Fundamental Concepts of Slavoj Žižek's Psychoanalytic Marxism', *International Journal of Žižek Studies*, 2/1, online.

Boynton, Robert (1998). 'Enjoy Your Žižek!: An Excitable Slovenian Philosopher Examines the Obscene Practices of Everyday Life – Including his Own', *Lingua Franca*, 8/7, www.lacan.com/Zizek-enjoy.htm (accessed 22 Oct 2009).

Breger, Claudia (2001). 'The Leader's Two Bodies: Slavoj Zizek's Postmodern Political Theology', *Diacritics*, 31/1: 73–90.

Briggs, Kate (2008). 'An Obsessional Act of Erasure: Žižek on L'Origine du Monde', *International Journal of Žižek Studies*, 2/4, online.

Brooks, Jeffrey (2006). 'Totalitarianism Revisited', *Review of Politics*, 68: 318–28.

Bryant, Levi R. (2007). 'Symptomal Knots and Evental Ruptures: Žižek, Badiou and Discerning the Indiscernible', *International Journal of Žižek Studies*, 1/2, online.

Bryant, Levi R. (2008). 'Žižek's New Universe of Discourse: Politics and the Discourse of the Capitalist', *International Journal of Žižek Studies*, 2/4, online.

Buchanon, Ian (2005). 'Žižek and Deleuze', in Matthew Sharpe, Geoff Boucher and Jason Glynos (eds), *Traversing the Fantasy: Critical Responses to Slavoj Žižek*. London: Ashgate, pp. 69–85.

Butler, Judith (1993). *Bodies that Matter: On the Discursive Limits of 'Sex'*. London and New York: Routledge.

Butler, Judith (1997). *The Psychic Life of Power: Theories in Subjection*. Stanford: Stanford University Press.

Butler, Judith (2000a). 'Competing Universalities', in Judith Butler, Ernesto Laclau and Slavoj Žižek, *Contingency, Hegemony, Universality*. London: Verso, pp. 136–81.

Butler, Judith (2000b). *Antigone's Claim: Kinship between Life & Death*. New York: Columbia University Press.

Butler, Judith, Ernesto Laclau and Slavoj Žižek (2000). *Contingency,*

Hegemony, Universality: Contemporary Dialogues on the Left. London and New York: Verso.

Butler, Rex, and Scott Stephens (2005). 'The Inhuman', in Rex Butler and Scott Stephens (eds), *Interrogating the Real*. London: Continuum, pp. 9–10.

Butler, Rex, and Scott Stephens (2006). 'Play It Fuckin' Loud!', in *Symptom*, 7; www.lacan.com/symptom7_articles/butler.html (accessed Apr. 2009).

Chiesa, Lorenzo (2007). 'Forthcoming – Phantoms of Inconsistency: Badiou, Žižek and Lacan on Repetition', *International Journal of Žižek Studies*, 1/2, online.

Clemens, Justin (2005). 'The Politics of Style in the World of Slavoj Žižek', in Matthew Sharpe, Geoff Boucher and Jason Glynos (eds), *Traversing the Fantasy: Critical Responses to Slavoj Žižek*. London: Ashgate.

Conley, Verena (1999). 'Whither the Virtual? Slavoj Žižek and Cyber-Feminism', *Angelaki*, 4/2: 129–36.

Coombs, Nathan (2008). 'Rejecting both Mao and Deng: Slavoj Žižek and Waiting for the Leftist Critique to Come', *International Journal of Žižek Studies*, 2/2, online.

Coombs, Nathan (2009). 'Christian Communists, Islamic Anarchists?', *International Journal of Žižek Studies*, 3/1, online.

Copjec, Joan (1996). 'Introduction: Evil in the Time of the Finite World', in Joan Copjec (ed.), *Radical Evil*. London: Verso, pp. vii – xxvii.

Critchley, Simon (2000). 'Demanding Approval: On the Ethics of Alain Badiou', *Radical Philosophy*, 100: 16–27.

Critchley, Simon (2007). 'Foreword: Why Žižek Must Be Defended', in Paul Bowman and Richard Stamp (eds), *The Truth of Žižek* .London: Continuum, pp. xi–xvi.

Daly, Glyn (2007). 'Sympathy for the Human', *International Journal of Žižek Studies*, 1/1, online.

Daly, Glyn (2007). 'The Materialism of Spirit – Žižek and the Logics of the Political', *International Journal of Žižek Studies*, 1/4, online.

Davis, Walter A. (2007). 'A Postmodernist Response to 9–11: Slavoj Žižek, or the Jouissance of an Abstract Hegelian', *International Journal of Žižek Studies*, 1/0, online.

De Beistegui, Miguel (2007). 'Another Step, Another Direction: A Response to Žižek's "Why Heidegger Made the Right Step in 1933" ', *International Journal of Žižek Studies*, 1/4, online.

De Kesel, Marc (2007). 'Truth as Formal Catholicism - On Alain Badiou, Saint Paul', *International Journal of Žižek Studies*, 1/2, online.

Dean, Jodi (2006). *Žižek's Politics*. London: Routledge.

Dean, Jodi (2007). 'Why Žižek for Political Theory?', *International Journal of Žižek Studies*, 1/1, online.

Deleuze, Gilles, and Felix Guattari (1983). *Anti-Oedipus: Capitalism and Schizophrenia*. Minneapolis: University of Minnesota Press.

Deleuze, Gilles, and Felix Guattari (1987). *A Thousand Plateaus: Capitalism and Schizophrenia*. Minneapolis: University of Minnesota Press.

Derrida, Jacques (1976). *Of Grammatology*, trans. Gayatri Spivak. Baltimore: Johns Hopkins University Press.

Derrida, Jacques (1982). *Margins of Philosophy*, trans. Alan Bass. Brighton: Harvester.

Devenney, Mark (2007). 'Žižek's Passion for the Real: The Real of Terror, the Terror of the Real', in Paul Bowman and Richard Stamp (eds), *The Truth of Žižek*. London: Continuum, 45–60.

Dews, Peter (1995). 'The Tremor of Reflection: Slavoj Žižek's Lacanian Dialectics', in Peter Dews (ed.), *The Limits of Disenchantment: Essays on Contemporary European Philosophy*. London and New York: Verso, 236–57.

Dews, Peter (1999). 'The Eclipse of Coincidence: Lacan, Merleau-Ponty and Schelling', *Angelaki*, 4/3: 121–42.

Dews, Peter (2005). 'The Eclipse of Coincidence', in Matthew Sharpe, Geoff Boucher and Jason Glynos (eds), *Traversing the Fantasy: Critical Responses to Slavoj Žižek*. London: Ashgate, 197–215.

Dolar, Mladen (1998). 'Cogito as the Subject of the Unconscious', in Slavoj Žižek (ed.), *Cogito and the Unconscious*. Durham, NC, and London: Duke University Press, 11–40.

Donahue, Brian (2002). 'Marxism, Postmodernism, Žižek', in *Postmodern Culture*, 12/2 (Jan.), online.

Dudley, Will (2007). *Understanding German Idealism*. London: Acumen.

Eagleton, Terry (2001). 'Enjoy!', *Paragraph: A Journal of Modern Critical Theory*, 24/2 (Special Issue on Slavoj Žižek), 40–52.

Eagleton, Terry (2006). 'On the Contrary', *Artforum International*, 44/10 (June), 61–2.

Edelman, Gerald (1989). *The Remembered Present: A Biological Theory of Consciousness*. New York: Basic Books.

Elliott, Anthony, and Charles Lemert (2006). *The New Individualism*. New York: Routledge.

Farran, Roque (2008). 'The concept of citizenship in postmarxist political theory. The return of the political and the problem of madness.' *International Journal of Žižek Studies 2(3)*.

Finlay, Christopher (2006). 'Violence and Revolutionary Subjectivity: Marx to Žižek', *European Journal of Political Theory*, 5: 4: 373–397.

Flemming, Gregory C. (2008). 'From Marx to the Act', *International Journal of Žižek Studies*, 2/1, online.

Flisfeder, Matthew Joshua (2008). 'Reading Emancipation Backwards: Laclau, Žižek and the Critique of Ideology in Emancipatory Politics', *International Journal of Žižek Studies*, 2/1, online.

Foucault, Michel (1979). *Discipline and Punish*. Harmondsworth: Penguin.

Foucault, Michel (1990). *The History of Sexuality, Volume One: The Will to Knowledge*. London: Penguin.

Freud, Sigmund (1984). *The Ego and the Id*, in *Penguin Freud Library Volume 11: On Metapyschology*, trans. James Strachey. London: Penguin.

Freud, Sigmund (1985). *Civilization and its Discontents*, in *Penguin Freud Library Volume 12: Civilization, Society and Religion*, trans. James Strachey. London: Penguin.

Fried, Gregory (2007). 'Where's the Point? Slavoj Žižek and the Broken Sword', *International Journal of Žižek Studies*, 1/4, online.

Friedrich, Karl, and Z. Brzezinski (1956). *Totalitarian Dictatorship and Autocracy*. New York: Praeger.

Fukuyama, Francis (1992). *The End of History and the Last Man*. London: Penguin.

García, George, and Carlos Sánchez (2008). 'Psychoanalysis and Politics: The Theory and Ideology of Slavoj Žižek', *International Journal of Žižek Studies*, 2/3, online.

Gigante, D. (1998). 'Towards the Vortex of Self-Creation: Slavoj Žižek and the "Vortex of Madness" ', *New Literary History*, 29/1: 153–68.

Gilbert, Jeremy (2007). 'All the Right Questions, All the Wrong Answers', in Paul Bowman and Richard Stamp (eds), *The Truth of Žižek*. London: Continuum, pp. 61–81.

Grigg, Russell (2005). 'Absolute Freedom and Major Structural Change' in Matthew Sharpe, Geoff Boucher and Jason Glynos (eds), *Traversing the Fantasy: Critical Responses to Slavoj Žižek*. London: Ashgate, pp. 183–94.

Gunkel, David J. (2008). 'Žižek and the Real Hegel', *International Journal of Žižek Studies*, 2/2, online.

Habermas, Jürgen (1984). *Theory of Communicative Action: Critique of Functionalist Reason*. Boston: Beacon.

Habermas, Jürgen (1987a). *Theory of Communicative Action: System and Lifeworld*. Boston: Beacon.

Habermas, Jürgen (1987b). *The Philosophical Discourse of Modernity: Twelve Lectures*. Cambridge: Polity Press.

Hamilton-Grant, Iain (2007). 'The Insufficiency of Ground: On Žižek's Schellingerianism', in Paul Bowman and Richard Stamp (eds), *The Truth of Žižek*. London: Continuum, pp. 82–98.

Hamilton-Wells, Charles (2008). 'Acts of Freedom: Revolution and Responsibility', *International Journal of Žižek Studies*, 2/1, online.

Han, Zhenjiang (2009). 'Slavoj Žižek in Post-Marxism', *International Journal of Žižek Studies*, 3/1, online.

Hardt, Michael, and Antonio Negri (2000). *Empire*. Cambridge, MA: Harvard University Press, 2000.

Hardt, Michael, and Antonio Negri (2005). *Multitude*. London: Penguin, 2005.

Harpham, Geoffrey Galt (2003). 'Doing the Impossible: Žižek and the End of Knowledge', *Critical Inquiry*, 29/3: 453–85.

Hegel, G. W. F. (1977). *The Phenomenology of Spirit*, trans. A. V. Miller. Oxford: Oxford University Press.

Heidegger, Martin (1990). *Kant and the Problem of Metaphysics*, trans. Richard Taft. Bloomington: Indiana University Press.

Herbold, Sarah (2005). ' "Well-Placed Reflections": On Woman as Symptom of Man', in Matthew Sharpe, Geoff Boucher and Jason Glynos (eds), *Traversing the Fantasy: Critical Responses to Slavoj Žižek*. London: Ashgate, pp. 125–46.

Holbo, John (2004). 'On Žižek and Trilling', *Philosophy and Literature*, 28/2: 430–40.

Homer, Sean (1996). 'Psychoanalysis, Representation, Politics: On the (Im) possibility of a Psychoanalytic Theory of Ideology', *The Letter: Lacanian Perspectives on Psychoanalysis*, 7: 97–108.

Homer, Sean (2001). 'It's the Political Economy, Stupid! On Žižek's Marxism', *Radical Philosophy*, 108: 7–16.

Honneth, Axel (1995). *The Struggle for Recognition*. Cambridge: Polity Press.

Jackson, Ken (2007). 'Žižek's Struggle with 'the Usual Gang of Suspects', *International Journal of Žižek Studies*, 1/2, online.

Jameson, Fredric (1991). *Postmodernism, Or, The Cultural Logic of Late Capitalism*. Durham, NC: Duke University Press.

Jameson, Fredric (1994). *The Seeds of Time*. New York: Columbia University Press.

Johnston, Adrian (2007aa). 'From the Spectacular Act to the Vanishing Act: Badiou, Žižek, and the Politics of Lacanian Theory', *International Journal of Žižek Studies*, 1/0, online.

Johnston, Adrian (2007b). 'Revulsion is not without its Subject: Kant, Lacan, Žižek and the Symptom of Subjectivity', *International Journal of Žižek Studies*, 1/0, online.

Johnston, Adrian (2007c). 'The Cynic's Fetish: Slavoj Žižek and the Dynamics of Belief', *International Journal of Žižek Studies*, 1/0, online.

Johnston, Adrian (2007d). 'The Quick and the Dead: Alain Badiou and the Split Speeds of Transformation', *International Journal of Žižek Studies*, 1/2, online.

Johnston, Adrian (2007e). 'There is Truth, and then there are Truths – or, Slavoj Žižek as a Reader of Alain Badiou', *International Journal of Žižek Studies*, 1/0, online.

Johnston, Adrian (2008). *Žižek's Ontology: A Transcendental Materialist Theory of Subjectivity*. Evanston, IL: Northwestern University Press.

Kant, Immanuel (1960). *Religion within the Limits of Reason Alone*. New York: Harper Torchbooks.

Kant, Immanuel (1993). *Critique of Pure Reason.* London: Everyman.

Kay, Sarah (2003). *Žižek: A Critical Introduction.* Cambridge and Malden, MA: Polity.

Kellogg, Paul (2008). 'The Only Hope of the Revolution is the Crowd: The Limits of Žižek's Leninism', *International Journal of Žižek Studies*, 2/2, online.

Kisner, Wendell (2008). 'The Concrete Universal in Žižek and Hegel', *International Journal of Žižek Studies*, 2/2, online.

Kovac, M. (1988). 'The Slovak Spring', *New Left Review*, 171: 115–28.

Krips, Henry (2007). 'A Mass Media Cure for Auschwitz: Adorno, Kafka and Žižek', *International Journal of Žižek Studies*, 1/4, online.

Kunkle, Sheila (2007). 'Žižek's Choice', *International Journal of Žižek Studies*, 1/3, online.

Kunkle, Sheila (2008). 'Embracing the Paradox: Žižek's Illogical Logic', *International Journal of Žižek Studies*, 2/4, online.

La Berge, Leigh Claire (2007). 'The Writing Cure? Slavoj Žižek, Analysand of Modernity', in Paul Bowman and Richard Stamp (eds), *The Truth of Žižek*. London: Continuum, pp. 9–26.

Lacan, Jacques (1971). *The Seminar of Jacques Lacan: The Knowledge of the Analyst*, trans. Cormac Gallagher. London: Karnac.

Lacan, Jacques (1986). *The Seminar of Jacques Lacan, Book VII: The Ethics of Psychoanalysis.* New York and London: Norton.

Lacan, Jacques (1997). *The Seminar of Jacques Lacan, Book VII: The Ethics of Psychoanalysis*, trans. with notes Dennis Porter: New York and London: Norton.

Lacan, Jacques (1998). *The Seminar of Jacques Lacan, Book XI: The Four Fundamental Concepts of Psychoanalysis.* London and New York: Norton.

Lacan, Jacques (2006). *Seminar XVII: The Other Side of Psychoanalysis*, trans. Russell Grigg. London: Norton.

Lacan, Jacques (2007). *Écrits. The First Complete English Edition*, trans. Bruce Fink. London: Norton.

Laclau, Ernesto (1989). 'Preface', in Slavoj Žižek, *The Sublime Object of Ideology*. London and New York: Verso, pp. ix–xv.

Laclau, Ernesto (2000a). 'Constructing Universality', in Judith Butler, Ernesto Laclau and Slavoj Žižek, *Contingency, Hegemony, Universality: Contemporary Dialogues on the Left*. London and New York: Verso, pp. 281–307.

Laclau, Ernesto (2000b). 'Structure, History and the Political', in Judith Butler, Ernesto Laclau and Slavoj Žižek, *Contingency, Hegemony, Universality: Contemporary Dialogues on the Left*. London and New York: Verso, pp. 182–212.

Laclau, Ernesto, and Chantal Mouffe (1985). *Hegemony and Socialist Strategy: Toward a Radical Democratic Politics*. London: Verso.

Laplanche, Jean (1976). *Life and Death in Psychoanalysis*. Baltimore: Johns Hopkins University Press.

Lasch, Christopher (1979). *The Culture of Narcissism*. London: Abacus.

Lefort, Claude (1986). *The Political Forms of Modern Society*. Cambridge: Polity Press.

Lefort, Claude (1988). *Democracy and Political Theory*. Cambridge: Polity Press.

Lenin, Vladimiir (1921). *Left-Wing Communism: An Infantile Disorder*, www.marxists.org/archive/lenin/works/1920/lwc/index.htm (accessed December 2008).

Lukács, Georg (1971). *History and Class Consciousness*. London: Merlin.

McLaren, P. (2002). 'Slavoj Žižek's Naked Politics: Opting for the Impossible, a Secondary Elaboration', *Journal of Advanced Composition Quarterly*, 21/2: 614–37.

McMillan, Chris (2008). 'Symptomatic Readings: Žižekian Theory as a Discursive Strategy', *International Journal of Žižek Studies*, 2/1, online.

MacPherson, C. B. (1962). *The Political Theory of Possessive Individualism: From Hobbes to Locke*. London: Oxford University Press.

MacPherson, C. B. (1972). *The Real World of Democracy*. New York: Oxford University Press.

MacPherson, C. B. (1973). 'Post-Liberal Democracy', in C. B. MacPherson (ed.), *Democratic Theory: Essays in Retrieval*. Oxford: Clarendon Press.

MacPherson, C. B. (1977). *The Life and Times of Liberal Democracy*. New York: Oxford University Press.

Malone, Kareen Ror (2008). 'Female Rivals: Feminism, Lacan & Žižek Try to Think of Something New to Say', *International Journal of Žižek Studies*, 2/4, online.

Marchart, Oliver (2007). 'Acting and the Act: On Slavoj Žižek's Political Ontology', in Paul Bowman and Richard Stamp (eds), *The Truth of Žižek*. London: Continuum, pp. 99–116.

Marcuse, Herbert (1969). 'Repressive Tolerance', in Robert Paul Wolff, Barrington Moore, Jr, and Herbert Marcuse (eds), *A Critique of Pure Tolerance*. Boston: Beacon Press, pp. 95–137.

Marcuse, Herbert (2008). *A Study on Authority*. London: Routledge.

Marx, Karl (1962a). *Capital, Vol. 2*. Moscow: Progress Publishers.

Marx, Karl (1962b). *Capital, Vol. 3*. Moscow: Progress Publishers.

Marx, Karl (1963). *Capital, Vol. 1*. Moscow: Progress Publishers.

Marx, Karl (1986). 'Preface to *A Contribution to the Critique of Political Economy*', in Karl Mark and Frederick Engels, *Marx-Engels Selected Works in One Volume*. Moscow: Progress Publishers, pp. 311–31.

Mastnak, Tomaz (1994). 'From Social Movements to National Sovereignty', in Jill Benderly and Evan Kraft (eds), *Independent Slovenia: Origins, Movements, Prospects*. New York: St. Martin's Press, 92–112.

Mead, Rebecca (2003). 'The Marx Brother: How a Philosopher from Slovenia Became an International Star', *New Yorker*, 79: 10 (5 May).

Miklitsch, Robert (1998). ' "Going Through the Fantasy": Screening Slavoj Žižek', *South Atlantic Quarterly*, 97/2: 475–507.

Miklitsch, Robert (2005). 'Flesh for Fantasy: Aesthetics, the Fantasmatic, and Film Noir', in Matthew Sharpe, Geoff Boucher and Jason Glynos (eds), *Traversing the Fantasy: Critical Responses to Slavoj Žižek*. London: Ashgate, pp. 47–68.

Mouffe, Chantal (1999). 'Carl Schmitt and the Paradox of Liberal Democracy', in Chantal Mouffe (ed.), *The Challenge of Carl Schmitt*. London and New York: Verso, pp. 39–55.

Mowitt, John (2007). 'Trauma Envy', in Paul Bowman and Richard Stamp (eds), *The Truth of Žižek*. London: Continuum, pp. 17–143.

Myers, Tony (2003). *Slavoj Žižek*. London and New York: Routledge.

Osborne, Peter (1996) (ed.). *A Critical Sense: Interviews with Intellectuals*. New York: Routledge.

Osborne, Peter (2003). 'Interpreting the World – September 11, Cultural Criticism and the Intellectual Left', *Radical Philosophy*, 117 (Jan.–Feb.), 2–12.

Packman, Carl Robert (2009). 'Towards a Violent Absolute: Some Reflections on Žižekian Theology and Violence', *International Journal of Žižek Studies*, 3/1, online.

Parker, Ian (2004). *Slavoj Žižek: A Critical Introduction*. London: Pluto.

Parker, Ian (2006). 'Žižek: Ambivalence and Oscillation'. www.nskstate.com (accessed May 2009).

Parker, Ian (2007). 'The Truth of Over-Identification', in Paul Bowman and Richard Stamp (eds), *The Truth of Žižek*. London: Continuum, pp. 144–60.

Parker, Ian (2008). 'Conversation with Slavoj Žižek about *Slavoj Žižek: A Critical Introduction*', *International Journal of Žižek Studies*, 2/3, online.

Pfaller, Robert (1998). 'Negation and its Reliabilities: An Empty Subject for Ideology?', in Slavoj Žižek (ed.), *Cogito and the Unconscious*. London and Durham, NC: Duke University Press, pp. 225–46.

Pfaller, Robert (2005). 'Where is Your Hamster? The Concept of Ideology in Žižek's Cultural Theory', in Matthew Sharpe, Geoff Boucher and Jason Glynos (eds), *Traversing the Fantasy: Critical Responses to Slavoj Žižek*. London: Ashgate, pp. 105–22.

Pfaller, Robert (2007). 'Why Žižek? – Interpassivity and Misdemeanours', *International Journal of Žižek Studies*, 1/1, online.

Pluth, Ed (2007). 'Against Spontaneity: The Act as Over-Censorship in Badiou, Lacan, and Žižek', *International Journal of Žižek Studies*, 1/2, online.

Polt, Richard (2007). 'The Burning Cup: Or, Am Anfang war die Tat', *International Journal of Žižek Studies*, 1/4, online.

Pound, Marcus (2008). *Žižek a (Very) Critical Introduction*. Amsterdam: Eerdmanns.

Radloff, Bernhard (2007). 'The Life of the Universal: Response to Slavoj Žižek', *International Journal of Žižek Studies*, 1/0.

Rancière, Jacques (1999). *Disagreement: Politics and Philosophy*. Minneapolis: University of Minnesota Press.

Resch, Robert (1992). *Althusser and the Renewal of Marxist Social Theory*. Berkeley and Oxford: University of California Press.

Resch, Robert (1999). 'Running on Empty: Žižek's Concept of the Subject', *JPCS: Journal for the Psychoanalysis of Culture & Society*, 4/1: 92–9.

Resch, Robert (2001). 'The Sound of Sci(l)ence: Žižek's Concept of Ideology-Critique', *JPCS: Journal for the Psychoanalysis of Culture & Society*, 6/1: 6–19.

Resch, Robert (2005). 'What if God Was One of Us: Žižek's Ontology', in Matthew Sharpe, Geoff Boucher and Jason Glynos (eds), *Traversing the Fantasy: Critical Responses to Slavoj Žižek*. London: Ashgate, 89–104.

Robinson, Andrew, and Simon Tormey (2005). 'A Ticklish Subject: Žižek and the Future of Left Radicalism', *Thesis Eleven*, 80: 94–107.

Sagiv, Asaf (2005). 'The Magician of Ljubljana: The Totalitarian Dreams of Slavoj Žižek', *Azure* (Autumn). www.azure.org.il/download/magazine/1443az22_sagiv.pdf (accessed June 2008).

Samuels, Robert (2008). 'Lacan after Žižek: Self-Reflexivity in the Automodern Enjoyment of Psychoanalysis', *International Journal of Žižek Studies*, 2/4, online.

Santner, Eric (1996). *My Own Private Germany. Daniel Paul Schreber's Secret History of Modernity*. Princeton: Princeton University Press.

Schelling, F. W. J. von (1997). 'The Ages of the World', in Slavoj Žižek (ed.), *The Abyss of Freedom*, Ann Arbor: University of Michigan Press.

Schmitt, Carl (1976). *The Concept of the Political*, trans. Georg Schwab. New Brunswick, NJ: Rutgers University Press.

Schmitt, Carl (1988). *The Crisis of Parliamentary Democracy*, trans. Ellen Kennedy. Cambridge, MA: MIT Press.

Schmitt, Carl (1985). *Political Theology: Four Chapters on the Concept of Sovereignty*. Translated by Guy Oakes. Cambridge, MA: MIT Press.

Schmitt, Carl (1996). *The Concept of the Politcal*, trans. George Schwab. Chicago: University of Chicago Press.

Schmitt, Carl (1998). 'The Age of Neutralizations and Depoliticizations', trans. Matthias Konzett and John McCormick, *Telos*, 96: 120–45.

Scholem, Gershom (1971). *The Messianic Idea in Judaism, and Other Essays on Jewish Spirituality*. London: Allen and Unwin.

Sharpe, Matthew (2001a). '*Che Vuoi?* What Do You Want? The Question of the Subject, the Question of Žižek', *Arena Journal*, 16: 101–20.

Sharpe, Matthew (2004). *Slavoj Žižek: A Little Piece of the Real*. London: Ashgate.

Sharpe, Matthew (2005). 'What's *Left* in Žižek? The Antinomies of Žižek's Sociopolitical Reason', in Matthew Sharpe, Geoff Boucher and Jason Glynos (eds), *Traversing the Fantasy: Critical Responses to Slavoj Žižek*. London: Ashgate, pp. 147–68.

Sharpe, Matthew (2007). 'De Maistre avec De Sade, Žižek contra De Maistre', *International Journal of Žižek Studies*, 1/4, online.

Sharpe, Matthew (2008). 'Kant, or The Crack in the Universal: Slavoj Žižek's Politicising of the Transcendental Turn', *International Journal of Žižek Studies*, 2/2, online.

Sharpe, Matthew, Geoff Boucher and Jason Glynos (2005) (eds). *Traversing the Fantasy: Critical Responses to Slavoj Žižek*. London: Ashgate.

Sinnerbrink, Robert (2008). 'The Hegelian "Night of the World": Žižek on Subjectivity, Negativity, and Universality', *International Journal of Žižek Studies*, 2/2, online.

Smith, Daniel (2004). 'The Inverse Side of the Structure: Žižek on Deleuze on Lacan', *Criticism*, 46/4: 635–50.

Sohn-Rethel, Alfred (1978). *Intellectual and Manual Labour: A Critique of Epistemology*. London: Macmillan.

Sophocles (1984). *Antigone*. London: Penguin.

Stamp, Richard (2007). ' "Another Exemplary Case": Žižek's Logic of Examples', in Paul Bowman and Richard Stamp (eds), *The Truth of Žižek*. London: Continuum, pp. 161–76.

Stavrakakis, Yannis (1999). *Lacan and the Political*. London: Routledge.

Stavrakakis, Yannis (2005). 'The Lure of Antigone: *Aporias* of an Ethics of the Political', in Matthew Sharpe, Geoff Boucher and Jason Glynos (eds), *Traversing the Fantasy: Critical Responses to Slavoj Žižek*. London: Ashgate, pp. 171–82.

Stavrakakis, Yannis (2007). *The Lacanian Left: Psychoanalysis in Contemporary Political Theory*. Edinburgh: Edinburgh University Press.

Stephens, Scott (2007). 'ŽIŽEK, MY NEIGHBOUR– regarding Jodi Dean's Žižek's Politics', *International Journal of Žižek Studies*, 1/1, online.

Strauss, Leo (2000). *On Tyranny: Edited with Correspondence by Alexandre Kojeve*. Chicago: University of Chicago Press.

Taylor, Paul A. (2007). 'The Importance of Žižek's Thought', *International Journal of Žižek Studies*, 1/0, online.

Vaden, Tere (2008). 'Žižek's Phenomenology of the Subject', *International Journal of Žižek Studies*, 2/2, online.

Valenci, Tonci (2007). 'Socialism Reconsidered: Remarks on Žižek's Repeating Lenin', *International Journal of Žižek Studies*, 3/1, online.

Valentic, Tonci (2008). 'Symbolic Violence and Global Capitalism', *International Journal of Žižek Studies*, 2/2, online.

Valentine, Jeremy (2007). 'Denial, Anger, and Resentment', in Paul Bowman and Richard Stamp (eds), *The Truth of Žižek*. London: Continuum, pp. 177–96.

Vogt, Erik, and Hugh Silverman (2004) (eds). *Über Žižek: Perspektiven und Kritiken.* Vienna: Turia + Kant.

Weatherill, Rob (2008). 'Žižek: Silence and the Real Desert', *International Journal of Žižek Studies*, 2/4, online.

Williamson, Roland (2009). 'Hegel among the Quantum Physicists', *International Journal of Žižek Studies*. 3/1, online.

Wright, Elizabeth, and Edmond Wright (1999) (eds). *The Žižek Reader.* Oxford and Malden, MA: Blackwell.

Zerilli, Linda (1998). 'This Universalism Which Is Not One', *diacritics*, 28/2: 3–20.

Žižek, Slavoj (1989). *The Sublime Object of Ideology.* London and New York: Verso.

Žižek, Slavoj (1990a). 'Beyond Discourse Analysis', in Ernesto Laclau (ed.), *New Reflections on the Revolution of Our Time.* London and New York: Verso, pp. 249–60.

Žižek, Slavoj (1990b). 'Rossellini: Woman as Symptom of Man', *October*, 54: 19–44.

Žižek, Slavoj (1991a). *For They Know Not What They Do: Enjoyment as a Political Factor.* London and New York: Verso. 2nd edn. 2002.

Žižek, Slavoj (1991b). *Looking Awry: An Introduction to Jacques Lacan through Popular Culture.* Cambridge, MA, and London: MIT Press.

Žižek, Slavoj (1991c). 'The "Missing Link" of Ideology', *Mesotes: Zeitschrift für philosophischen Ost-West-Dialog*, 1: 50–65.

Žižek, Slavoj (1992) (ed.). *Everything You Always Wanted to Know About Lacan (But Were Afraid to Ask Hitchcock).* London and New York: Verso.

Žižek, Slavoj (1993). *Tarrying with the Negative: Kant, Hegel and the Critique of Ideology.* London and New York: Verso.

Žižek, Slavoj (1993–4). 'Eastern European Liberalism and its Discontents', *New Left Review*, pp. 25 ff.

Žižek, Slavoj (1994a). *The Metastases of Enjoyment: Six Essays on Woman and Causality.* London and New York: Verso.

Žižek, Slavoj (1994b). 'The Spectre of Ideology', in Slavoj Žižek (ed.), *Mapping Ideology.* London: Verso, pp. 1–33.

Žižek, Slavoj (1995a). 'Caught in Another's Dream in Bosnia', in R. Ali and L. Lifschultz (eds), *Why Bosnia?* Connecticut: Pamphleteers Press.

Žižek, Slavoj (1995b). 'The Fetish of the Party', in Richard Feldstein and Willy Apollon (eds), *Lacan, Politics, Aesthetics.* Albany, NY: SUNY Press, pp. 3–29.

Žižek, Slavoj (1995c). 'Ideologie zwischen Fiktion und Phantasma'. *Zeitschrift für Psychoanalyse*, 10/29–30): 131–49.

Žižek, Slavoj (1996a). 'I Hear You with my Eyes', in S. Žižek and R. Salecl (eds), *Gaze and Voice as Love Objects.* Durham, NC: Duke University Press.

245

Žižek, Slavoj (1996b). *The Indivisible Remainder: An Essay on Schelling and Related Matters.* London and New York: Verso.

Žižek, Slavoj (1997a). 'From Joyce-the-Symptom . . .', *Lacanian Ink*, 11: 12–25.

Žižek, Slavoj (1997b). *Die Pest der Phantasmen. Die Effizienz des Phantasmatischen in den neuen Medien.* Vienna: Passagen.

Žižek, Slavoj (1997c). *The Plague of Fantasies.* London and New York: Verso.

Žižek, Slavoj (1997d). 'Multiculturalism, or the Cultural Logic of Multinational Capitalism', *New Left Review*, 225 (Sept.–Oct.), 28 ff.

Žižek, Slavoj (1998a). 'The Cartesian Subject versus the Cartesian Theatre', in Slavoj Žižek (ed.), *Cogito and the Unconscious.* Durham, NC, and London: Duke University Press, 247–74.

Žižek, Slavoj (1998b). *Ein Plaedoyer für die Intoleranz.* Vienna: Passagen.

Žižek, Slavoj (1998c). 'From "Passionate Attachments" to Dis-Identification', *Umbr(a)*, 1: 3–17.

Žižek, Slavoj (1998d). 'The Seven Veils of Fantasy', in Danny Nobus (ed.), *Key Concepts of Lacanian Psychoanalysis.* London: Rebus Press, pp. 190–218.

Žižek, Slavoj (1999a). 'Carl Schmitt in the Age of Post-Politics', in Chantal Mouffe (ed.), *The Challenge of Carl Schmitt.* London: Verso, pp. 18–37.

Žižek, Slavoj (1999b). 'Preface: Burning the Bridges', in Elizabeth Wright and Edmond Wright (eds), *The Žižek Reader.* Oxford and Malden, MA: Blackwell, pp. i–xi.

Žižek, Slavoj (1999c). *The Ticklish Subject: The Absent Centre of Political Ontology.* London and New York: Verso.

Žižek, Slavoj (1999d). 'The Undergrowth of Enjoyment', in Elizabeth Wright and Edmond Wright (eds), *The Žižek Reader.* Oxford and Malden, MA: Blackwell.

Žižek, Slavoj (2000a). *The Art of the Ridiculous Sublime: On David Lynch's Lost Highway.* Seattle: Walter Chapin Simpson Centre for the Humanities.

Žižek, Slavoj (2000b). 'Class Struggle or Postmodernism? Yes, Please!', in Judith Butler, Ernesto Laclau and Slavoj Žižek, *Contingency, Hegemony, Universality: Contemporary Dialogues on the Left.* London and New York: Verso, pp. 90–135.

Žižek, Slavoj (2000c). '*Da Capo senza Fine*', in Judith Butler, Ernesto Laclau and Slavoj Žižek, *Contingency, Hegemony, Universality: Contemporary Dialogues on the Left.* London and New York: Verso, pp. 213–62.

Žižek, Slavoj (2000d). 'Die Substitution zwischen Interaktivitaet und Interpassivitaet', in Robert Pfaller (ed.), *Interpassivitaet. Studien über delegiertes Genießen.* Vienna and New York: Springer, pp. 13–32.

Žižek, Slavoj (2000e). *The Fragile Absolute – Or, Why Is the Christian Legacy Worth Fighting For?* London and New York: Verso.

Žižek, Slavoj (2000f). 'From *History and Class Consciousness* to *The Dialectic of Enlightenment* and Back Again', *New German Critique*, 81: 107–24.

Žižek, Slavoj (2000g). 'From Proto-Reality to the Act: A Reply to Peter Dews', *Angelaki: A Journal of the Theoretical Humanities*, 5/2: 141–7.

Žižek, Slavoj (2000h). 'Holding the Place', in Judith Butler, Ernesto Laclau and Slavoj Žižek, *Contingency, Hegemony, Universality: Contemporary Dialogues on the Left*. London and New York: Verso, pp. 308–29.

Žižek, Slavoj (2000i). 'Postface: Georg Lukács as the Philosopher of Leninism', in Georg Lukács, *A Defence of* History and Class Consciousness. London: Verso.

Žižek, Slavoj (2000j). 'Why is Kant Worth Fighting For?', in Alenka Zupančič (ed.), *The Ethics of the Real: Kant, Lacan*. London and New York: Verso.

Žižek, Slavoj (2001a). *Did Somebody Say Totalitarianism? On the Abuses of a Term*. London and New York: Verso.

Žižek, Slavoj (2001b). *Enjoy Your Symptom! Jacques Lacan in Hollywood and Out*. 2nd edn. London and New York: Routledge. First published 1992.

Žižek, Slavoj (2001c). *The Fright of Real Tears: Krzysztof Kieślowski between Theory and Post-Theory*. London: British Film Institute Publishing.

Žižek, Slavoj (2001d). *On Belief*. London and New York: Routledge.

Žižek, Slavoj (2001e). 'Repeating Lenin'. http://lacan.com/replenin.htm (accessed 1 Oct. 2004).

Žižek, Slavoj (2002a). 'I am a Fighting Atheist: Interview with Slavoj Žižek', *Bad Subjects*, 59. http://bad.eserver.org/issues/2002/59/zizek.html (accessed 22 Oct. 2009).

Žižek, Slavoj (2002b). 'The Real of Sexual Difference', in Suzanne Barnard and Bruce Fink (eds), *Reading Seminar XX: Lacan's Major Work on Love, Knowledge, and Feminine Sexuality*. Albany, NY: SUNY Press.

Žižek, Slavoj (2002c). *Welcome to the Desert of the Real: Five Essays*. London and New York: Verso.

Žižek, Slavoj (2003a). 'Happiness as an Ideological Category', in *Madam, I'm Adam: The Organization of Private Life*. Kunstuniversitaet Linz Piet Zwart Institute/Hogeschool Rotterdam/Experimentelle Gestaltung, Brugge: de Keure, pp. 114–30.

Žižek, Slavoj (2003b). *Organs without Bodies: On Deleuze and Consequences*. New York and London: Routledge.

Žižek, Slavoj (2003c). *The Puppet and the Dwarf: The Perverse Core of Christianity*. Cambridge, MA, and London: MIT Press.

Žižek, Slavoj (2004a). 'Herschaftsstruktur Heute', in Hugh Silverman and

M. Vögt (eds), *Über Žižek: Perspektiven und Kritiken.* Vienna: Turia, pp. 210–30.

Žižek, Slavoj (2004b). *Iraq: The Borrowed Kettle.* London: Verso.

Žižek, Slovoj (2005). 'Against Human Rights', *New Left Review,* 34 (July–Aug.), 15–31.

Žižek, Slovoj (2006). *The Parallax View.* Cambridge, MA: MIT Press.

Žižek, Slovoj (2007). *How to Read Lacan.* New York: Norton.

Žižek, Slovoj (2008a). *In Defence of Lost Causes.* London: Verso.

Žižek, Slovoj (2008b). *On Violence.* London: Picador.

Žižek, Slavoj, and F. W. J. Schelling (1997). *The Abyss of Freedom.* Ann Arbor: University of Michigan Press.

Žižek, Slovoj, with Kenneth Reinhard and Eric Santner (2005). *The Neighbor.* Chicago: University of Chicago Press.

Zupančič, Alenka (2000). *The Ethics of the Real: Kant, Lacan.* London and New York: Verso.

Index

act, the, 83–4, 118, 127–9, 170, 181–2, 188–93
Adorno, Theodor, 42, 89
Agamben, Giorgio, 85, 95, 178, 187, 207, 214
al-Qaeda, 36–7, 40
Althusser, Louis, 44–7, 129, 148, 186, 231
anti-humanism, 212
anti-Semitism, 20
anxiety, 8, 52, 99, 102, 109, 143–7, 154, 216
Arendt, Hannah, 88, 96
Aristotle, 86, 91
atonal worlds, 162
authenticity, 26, 116, 182, 184, 188, 190
autonomy, 26, 63, 87, 114–16, 123, 221

Badiou, Alain, 4, 16, 82, 84, 173–4, 177, 180, 191, 210–11, 214, 222
Balibar, Étienne, 4, 5, 16, 173, 174
Bartelby, 85, 178
Beck, Ulrich, 34, 37, 141–2
belief, 31, 35, 44, 46–51, 53–9, 62, 67, 72, 73–5, 93, 113–14, 135, 146, 150, 155–7, 176, 182, 184–5, 197, 200, 208–9, 217–19
Bell, Daniel, 147
Benjamin, Walter, 188, 194, 209
big Other, 49, 51, 54, 67, 106, 136–7, 158, 201, 228, 229
biopolitics, 131
Bolshevik, 181, 225, 228
Bourdieu, Pierre, 129
Bush, George W., 6, 32, 35, 37
Butler, Judith, 4, 5, 16, 32, 131, 174

capitalism, 5–6, 26, 32–6, 39–40, 43, 57, 81, 88, 94, 100, 109–10, 114, 129–35, 139–44, 145–6, 148, 152, 154, 157–9, 160, 162, 164–5, 170, 173, 177–8, 180, 183, 189–90, 193–4, 196–8, 207, 210, 218, 222, 225–6, 230, 233
cause *see* sublime object
Chesterton, G. K., 201, 203–4
Christ, 52, 197, 202–6, 208
commodity fetishism, 131–6, 140–1, 149, 151, 158–62, 177–8
communism, 6, 31, 43, 55, 88, 113, 142, 188, 194, 226–7
concrete universal, 147–8, 176, 185
consumption, 65, 93–4, 98–100, 139, 141, 150–1, 154, 162, 220
contingency, 81
contradiction, 31, 35, 38–40, 75, 156, 193, 199, 225, 233
Critchley, Simon, 16, 174, 180
cultural revolution, 180, 190–1

Dean, Jodi, 7, 15, 17
death drive, 8–9, 13, 18, 19–20, 26–7, 51, 82–4, 115–16, 120–2, 124–7, 153, 175, 185, 195–7, 212, 214–17, 222, 226
decisionism, 84
Deleuze, Gilles, 1, 4, 16, 61, 85, 99, 100, 232
Derrida, Jacques, 1, 4, 16, 34, 61, 65, 68–9, 70–4, 85, 224, 232
Descartes, René, 60–4, 65, 68, 69–70, 72–5, 79, 82, 93, 103, 105, 161, 219, 222
desire, as 'discourse of the Other', 44, 50

249